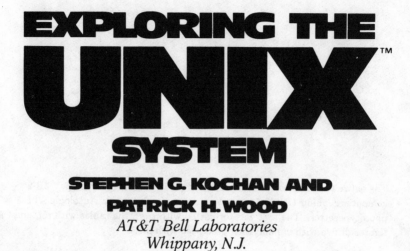

EXPLORING THE UNIX™ SYSTEM

STEPHEN G. KOCHAN AND
PATRICK H. WOOD

AT&T Bell Laboratories
Whippany, N.J.

HAYDEN BOOKS

A Division of Howard W. Sams & Company
4300 West 62nd Street
Indianapolis, Indiana 46268 USA

The entire text was edited and processed on an AT&T Technologies' 3B-20S computer running UNIX System V and was typeset on an Autologic APS-5 phototypesetter. The text was formatted with *troff*, the tables with *tbl*, and the figures drawn with *cip* and then processed with *pic*.

FIRST EDITION
EIGHTH PRINTING—1988

International Standard Book Number: *0-8104-6268-0*

Acquisitions Editor: *Douglas McCormick and Prijono Hardjowirogo*
Production Editor: *Maureen Connelly*
Copy Editor: *Juliann Colvin*
Cover Design: *Jeannette Jacobs*

Printed in the United States of America

To my wife, Leela
S. G. K.

To my mother
P. H. W.

HOWARD W. SAMS & COMPANY
HAYDEN BOOKS

Kochan & Wood's
Hayden Books UNIX® System Library

Topics in C Programming
Stephen G. Kochan and Patrick H. Wood

UNIX® Shell Programming
Stephen G. Kochan and Patrick H. Wood

UNIX® System Security
Patrick H. Wood and Stephen G. Kochan

UNIX® Text Processing
Dale Dougherty and Tim O'Reilly

UNIX® System Administration
David Fielder and Bruce H. Hunter

Related Titles

The Waite Group's UNIX® Communications
*Bart Anderson, Bryan Costales,
Harry Henderson*

The Waite Group's UNIX® Primer Plus
*Mitchell Waite, Donald Martin,
Stephen Prata*

The Waite Group's UNIX® Shell Programming Language
Rod Manis and Marc H. Meyer

The Waite Group's UNIX® System V Primer, Revised Edition
*Mitchell Waite, Donald Martin,
Stephen Prata*

The Waite Group's Tricks of the UNIX® Masters
Russell G. Sage

The Waite Group's UNIX® Papers
The Waite Group

The Waite Group's UNIX® System V Bible
Stephen Prata and Donald Martin

The Waite Group's Advanced UNIX®—A Programmer's Guide
Stephen Prata

The Waite Group's Inside XENIX®
Christopher L. Morgan

---

*For the retailer nearest you, or to order directly from the publisher,
call 800-428-SAMS. In Indiana, Alaska, and Hawaii call 317-298-5699.*

We would like to thank the following people for their help and suggestions: Sallie Johnson, Barbara Swingle, Irene Peterson, Anthony Iannino, Jo Anne Brown, John Kolb, Ed Lipinski, Charles Leiwant, John Musa, Dick Duane, Dick Fritz, and Mikie Wood. We would also like to thank the following people from Hayden Book Company: Douglas McCormick, Juliann Colvin, Maureen Connelly, and Jono Hardjo.

C O N T E N T S

1

INTRODUCTION

So you want to learn about the UNIX[†] system? Well, you've come to the right place. This book will introduce you to the operating system that is rapidly becoming the *de facto* standard in the computer industry. And not without reason.

The UNIX operating system was pioneered by Ken Thompson and Dennis Ritchie at Bell Laboratories (now more precisely identified as AT&T Bell Laboratories) in the late 1960s. One of the primary goals in the design of this operating system was to create an environment that promoted efficient program development. Also important was that the operating system be small and memory efficient, and that it be easy to maintain.

Historically, operating systems were developed with a specific computer model in mind. For example, IBM's VM and CMS operating systems were designed for IBM's 360 and 370 computer line, Digital Research's CP/M for the Zilog Z80, MS-DOS for the Intel 8086, and so on. Because each computer system has its own operating system, using a different computer entails undergoing an extensive relearning process. Simple procedures such as getting onto the system, copying a file, editing a file, or even finding out the time are different across operating systems. Application programs that you are accustomed to using may not even be available on the other system. Even your own programs may not run under another operating system without a significant amount of rework—or they may not run at all if they were developed in a programming language that's not supported under the new operating system.

And then along came the UNIX system. While the first UNIX system *was* developed with a particular computer system in mind (the DEC PDP-7), it was shortly thereafter that a version was developed that could be easily transferred ("ported") to different computer systems. This was accomplished by designing the operating system without making many assumptions about the particular architecture of the computer and also

---

† UNIX is a trademark of AT&T Bell Laboratories.

by writing most of the operating system in the higher-level programming language C.

Today the UNIX system can be found running on a multitude of computer systems, ranging from small personal computers to large mainframe systems. These include AT&T Technologies' 3B series of computers, IBM's PC and 370 computers, DEC's PDP-11 and VAX-11 family, Interdata's 8/32, Motorola's 68000, and Zilog's Z8000 system. All told, the number of different computers that support the UNIX system is impressive! This large diversity makes it easier on programmers and users: a programmer can expect the same programming tools and environment on any system that runs UNIX and can write programs to run *without modification* on any computer running UNIX; a user can learn one set of procedures and commands that can be used on any UNIX system.

This book proposes to teach you how to use the UNIX system— from typing in basic commands to administrating a small system.

The first thing you have to learn is just what an operating system is. After all, it doesn't do much good to learn about the UNIX "operating system" without knowing the meaning of these words. Chapter 2 serves this purpose by introducing you to operating systems and the types of functions they provide.

Since one of the most important features of the UNIX system is its *file system*, we decided to devote a separate chapter to it early on. Chapter 3 teaches the organization of the UNIX file system and the method that is used to identify files.

Chapter 4 is titled "Getting Started," and, as its names implies, teaches you how to get onto the computer, perform some simple functions, and then get off. You'll learn how to create, copy, rename, and remove files, and how to create your own file *directories* and work with them. This chapter also provides a short tutorial introduction to the text editor ed.

In Chapter 5, you are shown how to start putting the UNIX system to work for you. New commands are introduced, and two of the key concepts of the UNIX system, *I/O redirection* and *pipes*, are taught. By the end of this chapter you will have a good working knowledge of the UNIX system and an appreciation of its power.

Chapter 6 introduces the program that interprets everything you type in at the terminal: the *shell*. The shell also has its own built-in programming language. The primary purpose of this chapter is to introduce you to this language. You'll learn how you can effectively customize UNIX commands to your own liking, as well as develop your own.

Chapter 7 provides a tutorial introduction to the vi screen editor. This editor makes it easy to edit files on video terminals by allowing you to work with your file a "screenful" at a time.

Chapter 8 shows the usefulness of the UNIX system in an office environment. Among the topics covered are the *electronic mail* facilities and how to use the word processing packages to format and analyze documents.

Chapter 9 gives an overview of how to use the UNIX system for program development. The various tools and languages that are available for the programmer are described.

One of the most important aspects of any computer system is how secure it is. Until recently, however, this topic was not given much attention. Chapter 10 explains how you, the user, can ensure that no one tampers with your files or gains access to your account. This is done by giving you an overview of the security designed into the system and the commands you can use to make things more secure. As you will see, the UNIX system is by design a very secure system, but it needs your cooperation to guarantee this security.

In Chapter 11 the topic of communication is covered. This includes intra as well as intersystem communications. As you'll see, the UNIX system provides many commands that make it simple to send data over a network.

The last chapter, Chapter 12, was written for new UNIX system owners and administrators. It explains how to start up a system, how to ensure security at the system level, how to add new users to the system, and so on. If you have just purchased a small UNIX system or are about to, then you should find this chapter particularly helpful.

We have included a complete command summary in Appendix C. Also included in the appendices are a list of references and some tables that you may find useful.

Since every reader will probably have different intended uses of the UNIX system, we have included Table 1-1. If you find a description of your interest in the first column, then in the second column you'll find a list of chapters you should read to satisfy this interest, and in the third column you'll find a list of chapters you may want to read. Chapters not listed in either column should be skimmed at the very least to get a good overview of the features and capabilities of the system. Of course, there's no harm to be served by thoroughly reading all chapters.

TABLE 1-1. How to read this book

If you're interested in	Then read these chapters	And optionally read chapters
Turning your system on	2, 12 (first half)	
Word processing	3-5, 7, 8	6
Office automation	3-5, 7, 8	6
Program development	2-7, 9	8, 10,11
System administration	2-6, 10-12	7-9
Running application programs	3, 4	5, 7, 8
Don't know	2-5	Whatever interests you

If you have access to a UNIX system, then as you read through the text you should try the examples at your terminal. And don't be afraid to experiment! The best way to learn about the UNIX system is by actually using it.

This book describes UNIX System V. The release of newer versions of this operating system is inevitable. However, System V has been targeted by AT&T as *the* system for standardization and compatibility, meaning that future releases of the operating system will be compatible. System V Release 2 is the most recent version of the UNIX system as of the time this book went to press. In many instances throughout the text we have noted differences between this release and System V.

One last point about the philosophy of this book. It would be impossible to teach you every command and every option available in the UNIX system; such a treatment would fill several volumes. Our main goals here are to get you started, to give you a good overview of what's available, and primarily to teach the UNIX philosophy. This philosophy preaches the doctrine that "small is beautiful." The UNIX user is provided with a vast assortment of commands that perform small, well-defined functions and the tools necessary to combine these commands to perform more sophisticated functions. If you are a programmer, then you will realize that this same principle forms the foundation of the structured programming discipline.

And now, welcome to the UNIX world!

2

WHAT IS AN OPERATING SYSTEM?

An *operating system* is a collection of programs that coordinates the operation of computer hardware and software. It usually provides the functions depicted in Fig. 2-1.

Fig. 2-1. Operating system functions

Input/output

Input and output (or I/O) is essential to the operation of any computer. I/O allows the computer to store and retrieve data on disks or tapes, to interact with the users' terminals, and to print output on paper. Every operating system must provide some form of I/O.

Command interpreter

The command interpreter reads the commands a user types in at a terminal and changes, or *interprets*, them into instructions the computer can understand. Command interpreters vary widely from one operating system to another, but again, it's something that almost every one provides.

Data management

Data management allows the users to organize their data into logical groupings called *files*. Although not all operating systems provide data management, the few that don't are severely limited in their flexibility and usefulness.

Program development tools

Program development tools assist users in writing and maintaining programs. Compilers, assemblers, debuggers, and software maintenance systems fall into this category.

Time-sharing

Time-sharing is a way of allowing several people to run programs on different terminals at the same time. This feature is usually found only on larger operating systems.

Security

Security protects one user from another and the operating system from all users. Its main function is to make sure only authorized users access the computer and its data and that users do only things they are authorized to do. Most operating systems that don't have time-sharing have little or no security, since only one user is involved. Most large operating systems provide some measure of security, but the degree varies from one to another.

Communication

Communication refers to the ability of one computer to communicate with other computers and terminals to transfer programs and/or data.

Accounting
Accounting keeps track of what each person has done on a computer in order to bill each one for the resources used. This is necessary on computers that have many users who must be charged for their use of the machine.

The UNIX operating system provides all of these functions.

• The UNIX Operating System •

The UNIX operating system can be broken down into three basic components: the *scheduler*, the *file system*, and the *shell*. In this chapter, we will discuss the scheduler in detail and touch lightly on the shell. Chapter 3 will cover the file system, and Chapters 4–6 will cover the shell more fully.

The UNIX Scheduler

The UNIX scheduler is a program that allows more than one person to all use the computer at the same time. The scheduler shares computer resources among these users, allowing each a small *slice* of the computer's processor. As mentioned before, this concept is known as *time-sharing*.

For example, suppose three people want to run different programs, *a*, *b*, and *c*. The scheduler copies these three programs from the disk that stores programs into the computer's memory. In the UNIX system, these copies in memory are referred to as *processes*; in this way we make the distinction between a *program* that is kept in a file on the disk and a *process* that is in memory doing things.

The scheduler allows process *a* to run for a few hundredths (or less) of a second and do a little of the work it was designed to do. After this *time slice* is over, process *a* is temporarily stopped, or *suspended*, and process *b* is allowed to run. Later, when process *b*'s time slice is over, process *c* gets its chance to run (see Fig. 2-2).

When each has had a chance to run a while, the scheduler comes back to process *a*. It doesn't start *a* over at the beginning; instead, it starts *a* where it left off when it was suspended at the end of its time slice. In this way, the scheduler allows each process to work its way to completion, a little bit at a time.

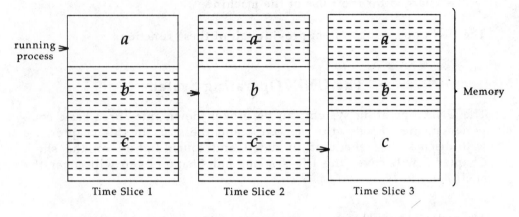

Fig. 2-2. Time slices

Most time-sharing systems allow many more than three processes to run at the same time; in fact, the UNIX scheduler can keep track of several hundred processes. It also allows each user to effectively run more than one process at a time.

Due to the high speed of computers, the overall effect of time-sharing is to give the users the impression they are all being served simultaneously, even though the scheduler serves them one at a time.

Swapping

This simple model of scheduling works fine at first, but sooner or later, all of the computer's memory gets filled with running processes. At this point, if a user wants to run a process, the scheduler must find a way to fit it in.

This brings up the concept of *swapping*. When memory is full and a new program needs to be run, the scheduler takes a process in memory and copies it to a disk. The scheduler then places the new program in memory (creating a new process) and allows it to run. Later, the process copied to disk is swapped with one of the processes in memory That is, the process in memory is copied to disk, and the process on the disk is copied back into memory.

For example, let's say there are three processes, *a*, *b*, and *c*. Now a request is made by a user to run program *d*:

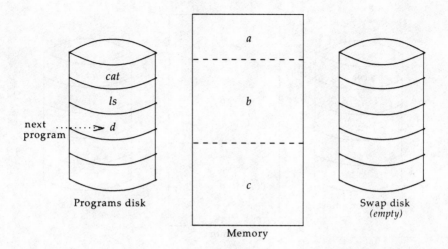

Fig. 2-3. New program *d*

Since there is no room left in memory for process *d*, process *a* is copied to the disk.

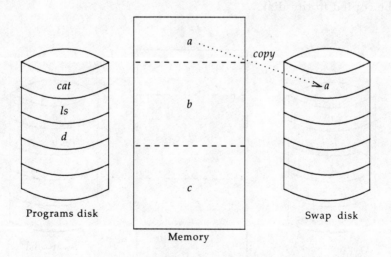

Fig. 2-4. Copy *a* to swap disk

After *a* is copied to the disk, a copy of *d* is then put in memory where *a* was.

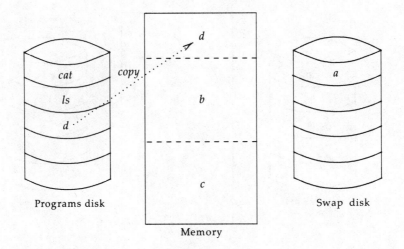

Fig. 2-5. Copy *d* to memory

After a few time slices, the scheduler will swap process *a* back into memory, usually exchanging it with the process that has been in memory the longest. Let's assume that *a* will be swapped with *b*. First, *b* must be copied to the disk.

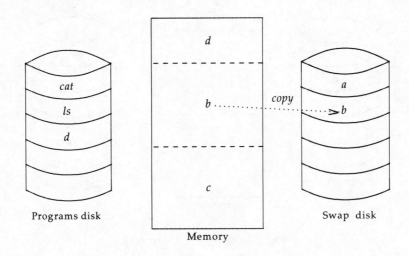

Fig. 2-6. Copy *b* to swap disk

Then *a* is copied back into memory.

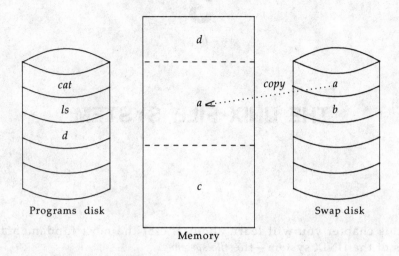

Fig. 2-7. Copy *a* to memory

This method of copying processes to and from disk and memory continues as long as there is not enough room for all of the processes to fit in memory. Of course, this example is very simple compared to the actual operation of the UNIX scheduler. It must handle hundreds of processes of all different sizes, of which only thirty or forty might fit into memory at one time.

The UNIX Shell

The shell is the UNIX system's command interpreter. It is a program that reads the lines you type in at a terminal and performs various operations depending on what you type in. The shell is the part of the UNIX system that sits between you and the "guts" of the system, forming a shell around the computer that is relatively consistent in its outward appearance. It attempts to convert your rantings and ravings into instructions that the computer can understand and act on.

Everyone on a UNIX system has his own copy of the shell program. So a user can do things without bothering or being bothered by other users. We'll talk more about the shell and the shell's environment in the next several chapters.

3

THE UNIX FILE SYSTEM

In this chapter you will learn about one of the most fundamental elements of the UNIX system—the *file system*.

· Files ·

In its simplest form, a file system is a collection of *files* stored on a storage device, usually a *disk*.   There are many different types of disks—floppy disks, hard disks, Winchester disks, and so on—and the most distinguishing qualities among them is the amount of information they can contain (their *storage capacity*) and the average amount of time it takes to retrieve information from them (their *access speed*).

As you can see from Fig. 3-1, there are two main types of storage on a computer system called *primary* and *secondary* storage.

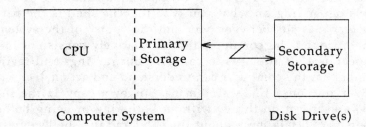

| CPU | Primary Storage | Secondary Storage |

Computer System   Disk Drive(s)

Fig. 3-1. Primary and secondary storage

Primary storage is the computer's memory. Secondary storage is the computer's disk. The computer can only execute programs or manipulate data that are in primary storage. Since the amount of secondary storage usually far exceeds the amount of primary storage on a particular system, programs and data are stored on the secondary storage device and are transferred to the computer's primary storage only as necessary. As mentioned in the previous chapter, this function is handled automatically by the operating system.

Whenever data is to be stored onto the disk from the primary storage, it is recorded onto a particular section of the disk, just as a song is recorded onto a particular section of a record. (But unlike a record, the information on the disk can later be recorded over if desired.) And just as a song has a title, so does a file. This title, called the *file name*, uniquely identifies particular information stored on the disk. You can have many files on the disk, just so long as they each have different names. You need be concerned only with the file's name. The operating system keeps track of all sorts of other information, such as who the file's owner is, when the file was last modified, precisely where on the disk it is located, and how large it is. This last piece of information is expressed in terms of the number of *bytes* (or characters) of data contained in the file.

• File Directories •

File directories enable you to organize files in a logical and structured fashion. This type of organization has many analogies to everyday life; a recipe file is one of them. Recipe files are usually divided into categories such as "Appetizers," "Entrees," and "Desserts." Under each category are stored all of the recipes of the particular type. So your recipe file might be organized as depicted in Fig. 3-2. Whenever you wanted to make a particular dessert, for example, you would simply turn to the recipe file and scan through the recipes filed under "Desserts." Or if you didn't know which dessert to make, you could simply thumb through all of the dessert recipes without having to sift through the appetizer and entree recipes. Obviously, a system of this type saves time since recipes are easier to find as well as to add. And if your recipe file were very large, you might even consider creating subcategories. For example, you might subcategorize "Entrees" into "Meat," "Poultry," and "Fish" recipes.

To make the analogy between the recipe file described above and the UNIX file system, think of the box that contains the recipes as the disk, the various categories and subcategories as file directories, and the recipes themselves as data files.

Suppose you had a set of files consisting of various memos, proposals, and letters. Further suppose that you had a set of files that were computer programs. It would seem logical to group this first set of files into a directory called `documents`, for example, and the latter set of files into a directory called `programs`. Such a directory organization is illustrated in Fig. 3-3.

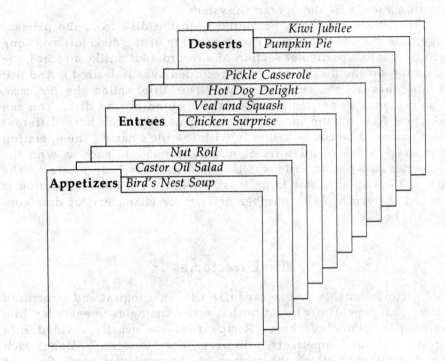

Fig. 3-2. Organization of a recipe file

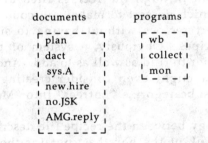

Fig. 3-3. Example directory structure

Here the files are divided into two categories: documents and programs. As mentioned, these categories are known as file directories under the UNIX system. So the file directory documents *contains* the files plan, dact, sys.A, new.hire, no.JSK, and AMG.reply. The directory programs contains the files wb, collect, and mon.

At some point you may decide to further categorize the files in a directory. This can be done by creating subdirectories and then placing each file into the appropriate subdirectory. For example, you might wish to create subdirectories called `memos`, `proposals`, and `letters` inside your `documents` directory. This is depicted in Fig. 3-4.

documents

```
┌ ─ ─ ─ ─ ─ ─ ─ ─ ─ ─ ─ ─ ─ ─ ─ ─ ─ ─ ─ ─ ─ ─ ┐
│  memos        proposals      letters         │
│  ┌ ─ ─ ─ ┐    ┌ ─ ─ ─ ─ ┐    ┌ ─ ─ ─ ─ ─ ┐   │
│  │ plan  │    │ sys.A   │    │ no.JSK    │   │
│  │ dact  │    │ new.hire│    │ AMG.reply │   │
│  └ ─ ─ ─ ┘    └ ─ ─ ─ ─ ┘    └ ─ ─ ─ ─ ─ ┘   │
└ ─ ─ ─ ─ ─ ─ ─ ─ ─ ─ ─ ─ ─ ─ ─ ─ ─ ─ ─ ─ ─ ─ ┘
```

Fig. 3-4. Directories containing subdirectories

Here, the file directory named `documents` contains the subdirectories `memos`, `proposals`, and `letters`. These directories in turn presumably contain files of the particular document type.

The file directory structure depicted in Fig. 3-4 is more precisely known as a *hierarchical* directory structure (since it is organized in levels) and is one of the most distinguishing qualities of the UNIX system. Perhaps the structure of the `documents` directory is clearer if conceptualized as in Fig. 3-5.

Fig. 3-5. Hierarchical directory structure

`documents` is at the top of this directory hierarchy. It contains the subdirectories `memos`, `proposals`, and `letters`. Each of these directories in turn contains two files: `memos` contains `plan` and `dact`; `proposals` contains `sys.A` and `new.hire`; and `letters` contains `no.JSK` and `AMG.reply`.

Let's now take a look at the directory structure with the `programs` directory included. As you will recall, the files `wb`, `collect` and `mon` were placed in that directory. Figure 3-6 shows the overall directory structure.

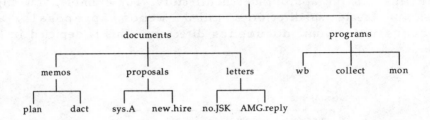

Fig. 3-6. Hierarchical directory structure

(We have illustrated the documents and programs directories as if they themselves belong to a higher-level directory. As you shall see shortly, this is indeed most likely the case.) While each file in a given directory must have a unique name, files contained in different directories do not. So, for example, you could have a file in your programs directory called dact, even though there also exists a file by that name in the memos subdirectory.

The HOME Directory and Path Names

The UNIX system always associates each user of the system with a particular directory. When you log into the system, you are placed automatically into a directory called your HOME directory. This directory was assigned to you by the system administrator when your account was created on the system.

On my system, my HOME directory is called steve. In fact, this directory is actually a subdirectory of a directory called a1. Therefore, if I had the directories documents and programs as illustrated in Fig. 3-6, my directory structure would actually look something like this:

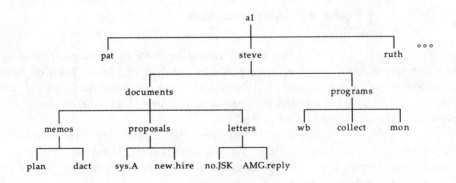

Fig. 3-7. File system a1

Since a1 is at the top of the directory structure, it is known as the *root*.
The root directory and all associated subdirectories are collectively
called a file system. By convention, the name of the root is also the
name of the file system. Therefore, the file system depicted in Fig. 3-7
would be called a1.

Whenever you are "inside" a particular directory (called your
current working directory), the files contained within that directory are
immediately accessible. If you wish to access a file from another directory, then you can either first issue a command to "change" to the
appropriate directory and then access the particular file, or you can
specify the particular file by its *path name*.

A path name enables you to uniquely identify a particular file to
the UNIX system. In the specification of a path name, successive directories along the path are separated by the slash character /. A path
name that *begins* with a slash character is known as a *full* path name,
since it specifies a complete path from the root. So, for example, the
path name /a1/steve identifies the directory steve contained in
the a1 file system. Similarly, the path name /a1/steve/
documents references the directory documents as contained in the
directory steve under the a1 file system. As a final example, the
path name /a1/steve/documents/letters/AMG.reply identifies the file AMG.reply contained along the appropriate directory
path.

In order to help reduce some of the typing that would otherwise
be required, UNIX provides certain notational conveniences and also
does not require that a full path name be specified. Path names that do
not begin with a slash character are known as *relative* path names. The
path is relative to your current working directory. For example, if I just
logged into the system and was placed into my HOME directory
/a1/steve, then I could directly reference the directory documents
simply by typing documents. Similarly, the relative path name
programs/mon could be typed to access the file mon contained inside
my programs directory.

By convention, the directory name .. always references the
directory that is one level higher. For example, after logging in and
being placed into my HOME directory /a1/steve, the path name ..
would reference the directory a1. And if I had issued the appropriate
command to change my working directory to documents/letters,
then the path name .. would reference the documents directory,
../.. would reference the directory steve, and
../proposals/new.hire would reference the file new.hire contained in the proposals directory. Note that in this case, as in most
cases, there is usually more than one way to specify a path to a particular file. Usually, you'll want to use the one that requires the least
amount of typing. The following table shows some examples of ways to
reference the directory memos depending on your current directory.

TABLE 3-1. Path names to memos

Current directory	Path to memos
/a1	steve/documents/memos
/a1/steve	documents/memos
/a1/steve/documents	memos
/a1/steve/documents/letters	../memos
/a1/steve/programs	../documents/memos

Another notational convention is the single period ., which always refers to the current directory. You will see in later chapters of this book how this notation is used.

• File Types •

Since files can be used to contain all sorts of information, most operating systems usually associate a *type* with a file. For example, on many systems a file that contains human readable information (e.g. text information) is usually distinguished from a file that contains machine executable instructions. The UNIX system makes no such distinction on file types. In fact, under UNIX there are only three different types of files: *directory* files, *ordinary* files, and *special* files. You have already seen the directory file. An ordinary file is just that: any file on the system that contains data, text, program instructions, or just about anything else. As its name implies, a special file has a special meaning to the UNIX system, and typically is associated with some form of I/O. For the most part, you need not be concerned with these special files—at least not now. These files will be discussed in more detail in later sections of this book.

This concludes the brief introduction to the UNIX file system. In the next chapter you will put this new knowledge to work and you will see the many commands for working efficiently with files that the UNIX system provides.

4

GETTING STARTED

· Logging In ·

The first thing you must learn in order to use a UNIX system is how to *log in*. This is the process by which you identify yourself to the system. When the UNIX system is ready for you to log in, it prints:

    login:

    You respond to this *prompt* (request for information) by typing in your *user-id* and then pressing the RETURN key. Your user id uniquely identifies you to the system and usually is supplied by a person who administrates the system (known as a *system administrator*).
    For this example, the user id pat will be used:

    login: **pat**

Note that **pat** is in **boldface type**; throughout the book boldface represents what you type in and regular type represents what the UNIX system types back. Also note that, unlike other systems you may have used, the UNIX system distinguishes upper and lowercase letters. Therefore, the user id **pat** is not the same as the user id **Pat** or the user id **pAT**. (In fact, if you type in your user id in all capital letters then the UNIX system will assume you are using a terminal that does not support lowercase letters. From that point on, all messages will be displayed by the system in uppercase. If this happens to you, simultaneously press the keys labeled CTRL and d and start over again.)
    After typing in your user id to the login: prompt, the UNIX system responds with:

```
Password:
```

This means that you are now to enter your *password*. Your password is a sequence of letters and digits that is used to verify to the UNIX system that you are allowed to use this user id. Your particular password may be selected by the system administrator, or you may have the option to select your own password when you request a computer account on the system. In either case, since the password is the *only* way the system knows that you are authorized to use your user id, you should not reveal it to anyone.

When you type in your password, it won't get printed on the screen. This is to protect your password from others who may be around while you are logging in.

```
login: pat
Password: wizard2
```

The password *wizard2* is shown in italics and in a smaller typeface to emphasize that it will *not* be typed back at the terminal. After typing in your password followed by RETURN, the UNIX system may print various messages. Often the date is printed, along with a "message of the day" that contains information that is of interest (sometimes) to the users.

Once you have successfully logged in, you can begin your work. The UNIX system will indicate that it is ready to accept your commands by displaying a dollar sign ($) as the first character on the line. This character is your *prompt character*. It will *always* be displayed when the system is waiting for you to enter a command.

```
login: pat
Password: wizard2

Sat Oct 29 15:40:52 EDT 1983

*** The system will be shutdown at 19:00 for PM ***

$
```

If you misspell your password when typing it in the UNIX system will not log you in but instead will respond with Login incorrect and will print out login: again.

```
login: pat
Password: wizrd2
Login incorrect
login:
```

If this should happen to you, don't worry; just type in your user id and password again. Chances are you'll get it right the second time around.

Some Simple Commands

Now you are ready to type in a *command*. A command tells the UNIX system to do something. For example, the command `date` tells the system to print the date and time:

```
$ date
Sat Oct 29 15:40:52 EDT 1983
$
```

As you can see, the `date` command prints the day of the week, month, day, time (24 hour clock, eastern daylight time), and year.

Try typing in `date` followed by a RETURN at your terminal. A similar response should be displayed.

Note now that *every* UNIX command must be ended with a RETURN. RETURN informs the system that you are finished typing things in and are ready for the UNIX system to do its thing. Unless it is stated otherwise, you can assume that every line typed in is ended with a RETURN.

The `who` command can be used to get information about all users who are currently logged into the system:

```
$ who
pat        tty29    Oct 29 14:40
ruth       tty37    Oct 29 10:54
steve      tty25    Oct 29 15:52
$
```

Here there are three users logged in, `pat`, `ruth`, and `steve`. Along with each user id, is listed the *tty* number of that user and the day and time that user logged in. The tty number is just a unique identification number the UNIX system gives to each terminal.

The `who` command also can be used to get information about yourself:

```
$ who am i
pat        tty29    Oct 29 14:40
$
```

Instead of printing information about all users, `who am i` prints only information about you. `who` and `who am i` are actually the same command: `who`. In the latter case, the `am` and `i` are *arguments* to the `who` command. Arguments tell a command to do something different from what it normally does. The am i arguments to who are *optional*. If they are supplied, then the who command performs the special function described above.

You will see later that most UNIX commands will do slightly different things depending on what arguments are supplied.

Let's now take a look at another command called echo. The echo command is a very simple and straightforward command; it prints (or *echoes*) at the terminal whatever else you happen to type on the line:

```
$ echo hello, world
hello, world
$
```

Try experimenting with the echo command on your terminal. Here are a few examples to show how it works.

```
$ echo this is a test
this is a test
$ echo why not print out a longer line with echo?
why not print out a longer line with echo?
$ echo
```
A blank line is displayed
```
$ echo one          two      three            four    five
one two three four five
$
```

You will notice from the last example that echo squeezes out extra blanks between words. That's because on a UNIX system, it's the words that are important; the blanks are merely there to separate the words. Generally, the UNIX system ignores extra blanks.

Correcting Typos

Sometimes when typing something in at the terminal you will make a mistake. If you type in whom instead of who, you'll get something that looks like this:

```
$ whom
whom: not found
$
```

The message whom: not found means that the UNIX system couldn't find the command whom. There is a way to counteract "finger-failure" or typos. The UNIX system allows you to back up over typing errors: each time you type in a *number sign* '#', also known as the *pound* or *sharp* sign, a previously typed character is erased. For example, let's say you typed whom and realized you had made a mistake. *Before* typing the RETURN, you can type a # to erase the m in whom:

```
$ whom#
pat        tty29     Oct  29  14:40
ruth       tty37     Oct  29  10:54
steve      tty25     Oct  29  15:52
$
```

To the UNIX system, whom# is equivalent to who. A more complicated example follows:

```
$ echo this are###is an exm#ampll#e of the erse##ase
this is an example of the erase
```

Table 4-1 shows some more examples.

TABLE 4-1. Erase character examples

What you type	What the UNIX system "sees"
dateee##	date
whpo##o	who
ddte###ate	date
ddte###atee#	date
whhoom####o	who
eccho###ho	echo
#echo	echo

It's possible to change your erase character to something else. In fact, if the # doesn't work on your system chances are it's already been changed for you. Try the key labeled BACKSPACE instead. If that still doesn't work, ask your system administrator to tell you what the erase character is. At the end of Chapter 5, you'll see how you can change the erase character.

You can also erase, or *kill*, an entire line. If a line is so hopelessly messed up that erasing characters is more trouble than simply starting over, you can type in an *at sign*, '@'. This causes everything typed before the @ to be ignored and starts you on a new line (but does *not* display a new prompt).

```
$ date@
who
pat          tty29      Oct 29 14:40
ruth         tty37      Oct 29 10:54
steve        tty25      Oct 29 15:52
$
```

The Delete Key

On some systems there may be a lot of people logged in at the same time (sometimes as many as forty or fifty), so when you do a who you can get a lot of lines of output at your terminal. To avoid looking at all of that output, which can be annoying if you're using a slow terminal, you can just press the Delete key (labeled DEL or RUBOUT on most terminals). This will stop (or interrupt) the who command and bring back the $ to your terminal without listing the rest of the who command's output. In general the DEL key can be used to interrupt any command and bring you back the prompt. You can even use the DEL instead of the @ to wipe out an incorrect command line. The main difference here is that using the DEL key will cause a $ to be displayed, and the @ won't.

· Logging Off ·

Once you've finished using the system, you can *log off* by simultaneously pressing the key labeled CTRL (for *control*) and the letter d. This key sequence will be denoted hereafter as *CTRL-d* in the text. You will notice that nothing gets displayed at the terminal when this key sequence is typed. However, this is in fact recognized by the system. After *CTRL-d* is typed (and pressing the RETURN key in this case is *not* necessary), the system responds as it did when you first logged in—with a new login: message:

```
$ CTRL-d
login:
```

The new login: message indicates that you are no longer logged into the system. At this point, the terminal is available for use by another user.

The following example shows a sample session with a UNIX system.

HOWARD W. SAMS & COMPANY

Jff

Bookmark

DEAR VALUED CUSTOMER:

Howard W. Sams & Company is dedicated to bringing you timely and authoritative books for your personal and professional library. Our goal is to provide you with excellent technical books written by the most qualified authors. You can assist us in this endeavor by checking the box next to your particular areas of interest.

We appreciate your comments and will use the information to provide you with a more comprehensive selection of titles.

Thank you,

Vice President, Book Publishing
Howard W. Sams & Company

COMPUTER TITLES:

Hardware
- ☐ Apple 140   ☐ Macintosh I01
- ☐ Commodore I10
- ☐ IBM & Compatibles I14

Business Applications
- ☐ Word Processing J01
- ☐ Data Base J04
- ☐ Spreadsheets J02

Operating Systems
- ☐ MS-DOS K05   ☐ OS/2 K10
- ☐ CP/M K01   ☐ UNIX K03

Programming Languages
- ☐ C L03   ☐ Pascal L05
- ☐ Prolog L12   ☐ Assembly L01
- ☐ BASIC L02   ☐ HyperTalk L14

Troubleshooting & Repair
- ☐ Computers S05
- ☐ Peripherals S10

Other
- ☐ Communications/Networking M03
- ☐ AI/Expert Systems T18

ELECTRONICS TITLES:
- ☐ Amateur Radio T01
- ☐ Audio T03
- ☐ Basic Electronics T20
- ☐ Basic Electricity T21
- ☐ Electronics Design T12
- ☐ Electronics Projects T04
- ☐ Satellites T09

- ☐ Instrumentation T05
- ☐ Digital Electronics T11

Troubleshooting & Repair
- ☐ Audio S11   ☐ Television S04
- ☐ VCR S01   ☐ Compact Disc S02
- ☐ Automotive S06
- ☐ Microwave Oven S03

Other interests or comments: _____

_____

_____

Name_____

Title _____

Company _____

Address _____

City _____

State/Zip _____

Daytime Telephone No. _____

A Division of Macmillan, Inc.

4300 West 62nd Street   Indianapolis, Indiana 46268

46268

Bookmark

BUSINESS REPLY CARD

FIRST CLASS PERMIT NO. 1076 INDIANAPOLIS, IND.

POSTAGE WILL BE PAID BY ADDRESSEE

HOWARD W. SAMS & CO.
ATTN: Public Relations Department
P.O. BOX 7092
Indianapolis, IN 46209-9921

fff

HOWARD W. SAMS
& COMPANY

$\mathcal{HH}$

HOWARD W. SAMS & COMPANY
HAYDEN BOOKS

Topics in C Programming
Stephen G. Kochan and
Patrick H. Wood
ISBN: 0-672-46290-7, $24.95

UNIX® Shell Programming
Stephen G. Kochan and
Patrick H. Wood
ISBN: 0-8104-6309-1, $24.95

UNIX® System Security
Patrick H. Wood and
Stephen G. Kochan
ISBN: 0-8104-6267-1, $34.95

UNIX® Text Processing
Dale Dougherty and
Tim O'Reilly
ISBN: 0-672-46291-5, $26.95

UNIX® System Administration
David Fielder and
Bruce H. Hunter
ISBN: 0-8104-6289-3, $24.95

The Waite Group's UNIX® Communications
Bart Anderson, Bryan Costales,
Harry Henderson
ISBN: 0-672-22511-5, $26.95

The Waite Group's UNIX® Primer Plus
Mitchell Waite, Donald Martin,
Stephen Prata
ISBN: 0-672-22028-8, $22.95

The Waite Group's UNIX® Shell Programming Language
Rod Manis and Marc H. Meyer
ISBN: 0-672-22497-6, $24.95

The Waite Group's UNIX® System V Primer, Revised Edition
Mitchell Waite, Donald Martin,
Stephen Prata
ISBN: 0-672-22570-0, $22.95

The Waite Group's Tricks of the UNIX® Masters
Russell G. Sage
ISBN: 0-672-22449-6, $24.95

The Waite Group's UNIX® Papers
The Waite Group
ISBN: 0-672-22578-6, $26.95

The Waite Group's UNIX® System V Bible
Stephen Prata and
Donald Martin
ISBN: 0-672-22562-X, $24.95

The Waite Group's Advanced UNIX®—A Programmer's Guide
Stephen Prata
ISBN: 0-672-22403-8, $24.95

The Waite Group's Inside XENIX®
Christopher L. Morgan
ISBN: 0-672-22445-3, $24.95

To order, return the card below, or call 1-800-428-SAMS. In Indiana call (317) 298-5699.

Please send me the books listed below.

Title	Quantity	ISBN #	Price

☐ Please add my name to your mailing list to receive more information on related titles.

Name (please print) ———————————————

Company ————————————————

City ——————————————————

State/Zip ——————————————

Signature ———————————————
(required for credit card purchase)

Telephone # ———————————————

Subtotal ————

Standard Postage and Handling **$2.50**

All States Add Appropriate Sales Tax ————

TOTAL ————

Enclosed is My Check or Money Order for $————

Charge my Credit Card: ☐ VISA   ☐ MC   ☐ AE

Account No.   Expiration Date ————

☐☐☐☐ ☐☐☐☐ ☐☐☐☐ ☐☐☐☐

46268

```
login: pat
Password: wizard2

Sat Oct 29 16:34:33

*** The system will be shutdown at 19:00 for PM ***

$ who
pat        tty29    Oct 29 16:34
ruth       tty37    Oct 29 10:54
steve      tty25    Oct 29 15:52
$ datet#
Sat Oct 29 16:34:47 EDT 1983
$ date@
who am i
pat        tty29    Oct 29 16:34
$ CTRL-d
login:
```

· Working with Files ·

The UNIX system provides many tools that enable you to work easily
with files. Among these tools are commands that enable you to create
new files, copy files, remove files, move files between directories, examine the contents of files, and so on. In this section you will learn how
to use some of these commands.

Listing Files: the ls Command

Whenever you log into a UNIX system you are automatically placed
inside a special directory known as your HOME directory. Typically,
this directory will be a unique directory that was created for you at the
time you were given an account on the system. To see if you have any
files stored in your directory, you can type the ls command:

    $ ls

If your account has been newly created, then chances are that no
files are stored in your directory. In such a case, you should just get
back another prompt:

```
$ ls
$
```

The UNIX system is typically very terse in response to commands. (As you shall see later in this book, there is a reason for this.) Therefore, if no files are currently stored in your directory, the system does not display a message such as No Files, but instead simply displays *nothing*.

If there *are* some files in your directory, then the names of these files will be displayed, typically one per line, when the ls command is issued:

```
$ ls
READ_ME
rje
$
```

This output indicates that two files called READ_ME and rje are contained in the current directory.

In the sample command sessions that follow, assume that there are *no* files present in the HOME directory.

Creating and Examining Files

Let's create a file on the system. Call the file names and store the five names Susan, Jeff, Henry, Allan, and Ken inside the file. In order to create this file, type the following lines at your terminal, *exactly as they are shown.*

```
$ cat > names
Susan
Jeff
Henry
Allan
Ken
CTRL-d                          CTRL and d keys pressed simultaneously
$
```

This sequence creates a file called names containing the five indicated names. Don't worry about the actual command used to create the file—it will be discussed shortly. Just in case you're wondering, a file name can be composed of just about any character directly available from the keyboard (and even some that aren't) provided the total number of characters contained in the name is not greater than 14.[†] If more than 14 characters are specified, the UNIX system simply ignores the extra characters. The following are all examples of valid file names:

---

† On Berkeley UNIX system 4.2, file names can be any length.

```
print_data
Jul 16. 1955
123
a.out
X
```

Now that you have created a file, you can use the `ls` command
to verify that the file does in fact exist:

```
$ ls
names
$
```

As you can see, the system lists the file `names` in response to the `ls`
command.   This tells you that contained inside your current directory is
a single file called `names`. You can examine the *contents* of this file by
using the `cat` command. The argument to the `cat` command is the
name of the file whose contents you wish to examine.

```
$ cat names
Susan
Jeff
Henry
Allan
Ken
$
```

The command `cat names` results in the display of five names at the
terminal, thus verifying the contents of the `names` file.

Sorting the Contents of a File: the `sort` Command

Now that you have a file stored in our directory, you can begin to perform some basic operations on the file. For example, you can easily *sort*
the contents of the file into alphabetical order using a command called
`sort`. As with the `cat` command, the name of the file to be sorted
must be specified:

```
$ sort names
Allan
Henry
Jeff
Ken
Susan
$
```

The `sort` command sorts the contents of the indicated file line by line and displays the result of the sort at the terminal. The original contents of the `names` files remains unchanged, as can be verified by executing the `cat` command once again:

```
$ cat names
Susan
Jeff
Henry
Allan
Ken
$
```

Counting the Number of Words in a File: the wc Command

Another command that gives some useful information about the contents of a file is the `wc` command. With this command, you can get a count of the total number of lines, words, and characters of information contained in a file. Once again, the name of the file is needed as the argument to this command:

```
$ wc names
        5       5       27 names
$
```

The `wc` command lists three numbers followed by the file name. The first number represents the number of lines contained in the file (5), the second the number of words contained in the file (in this case also 5), and the third the number of characters contained in the file (27). You will notice that a quick count of the characters contained in the five names Susan, Jeff, Henry, Allan, and Ken gives only 22 characters. That leaves you five characters short. Did the `wc` program goof? Hardly. The "missing" five characters are a result of the fact that at the end of each line of data in the file is stored a special "invisible" character called the *newline* character. This character is generated every time you press RETURN on your terminal keyboard. For example, when you typed the name Susan at the terminal and pressed the RETURN key, the characters 'S', 'u', 's', 'a', and 'n' followed immediately by the newline character were written into the file `names`. The same applied to each of the remaining four names that were entered.

Command Options

Suppose you were interested in counting only the number of lines in a file. Well, you know that you can use the `wc` command to obtain this sort of information. Unfortunately, it seems as though if you want a count of the number of lines that you must also get a count of the number of characters and the number of words, since this is what the wc command reports. Is there any way to obtain just a count of the number of lines? The answer to this question is "yes," and the method involves the use of *command-line options*. Most UNIX commands allow the specification of options at the time that a command is executed. These options generally follow the same format:

    -letter

That is, a command option is a minus sign followed immediately by a single letter. For example, in order to count just the number of lines contained in a file, the option -l (that's the letter l) is given to the wc command:

```
$ wc -l names
        5 names
$
```

This time you see that just the number of lines contained in the file is displayed. And as you might have guessed, to count just the number of characters in a file, the -c option is specified:

```
$ wc -c names
       27 names
$
```

Finally, the command option -w can be used to count the number of words contained in the file:

```
$ wc -w names
        5 names
$
```

    The sort command described earlier sorted the lines of data in a file in alphabetical order. But there is a wide assortment of options available with this command. For example, the -r option causes the sort to be performed in *reverse* order:

```
$ sort -r names
Susan
Ken
Jeff
Henry
Allan
$
```

Many UNIX commands are fussy about the ordering of options on the command line. That is, some commands require that the options be listed before the file name arguments. For example, the command `sort names -r` would be quite acceptable; however, the command `wc names -1` would not. Let's generalize by saying that *all* command options should *precede* file names on the command line.

Not only does the UNIX system provide a large number of commands, but each command typically has several different options. When a new command is introduced in this text, every option for that command will not be described. Teaching every option would not only double the size of this book, but would also leave you quite confused. It's much better for you to learn the basic function of the command first and then later explore its options as the need arises. In Section 1 of your *UNIX User's Manual* you will find each command listed with a description of all of its options.

Making a Copy of a File: the `cp` Command

After you have worked with files for a short time, you will realize the need to be able to make a copy of a file. Once a copy of a file has been made, the original file can be modified without fear of loss of the original information . If the original information are ever required, then the file can simply be *restored* from the *backup* copy.

In order to make a copy of a file, the `cp` command is used. The first argument to the command is the name of the file to be copied (known as the *source file*), and the second argument is the name of the file to place the copy into (known as the *destination file*). You can make a copy of the file `names` and call it `saved_names` as follows:

```
$ cp names saved_names
$
```

Execution of this command causes the file named `names` to be copied into a file named `saved_names`. As with many UNIX commands, the fact that a command prompt was displayed after the `cp` command was typed indicates that the command executed successfully. Of course, you can also verify that the new file was in fact created by using the `ls` command:

```
$ ls
names
saved_names
$
```

And you can examine the contents of `saved_names` in the usual manner:

```
$ cat saved_names
Susan
Jeff
Henry
Allan
Ken
$
```

Renaming a File: the mv Command

You sometimes need to change the name of a file. This is accomplished easily with the mv command. The arguments to the mv command follow the same format as the cp command. The first argument is the name of the file to be renamed, and the second argument is the new name. So to change the name of the file saved_names to hold_it, for example, the following command would do the trick:

```
$ mv saved_names hold_it
$
```

Issuing the ls command will still result in the listing of two files, since you did not create a new file but simply renamed an old one:

```
$ ls
hold_it
names
$
```

It is worth noting that the ls command always lists your files in alphabetical order.

A word of caution when using the cp and mv commands: the UNIX system does not care whether the file specified as the second argument already exists. If it does, then in both cases the contents of the file will be lost. So, for example, if a file called old_names exists, then executing the command cp names old_names would copy the file names to old_names, destroying the previous contents of old_names in the process. Similarly, the command mv names old_names would rename names to old_names, even if the file old_names existed prior to execution of the command. (There *is* a way to protect against this sort of thing, and you'll learn about it in a later chapter.)

Removing a File: the rm Command

No system that enabled you to create files would be complete without a command that also allowed you to remove them. Under the UNIX system, this command is called rm. The argument to the rm command is simply the name of the file to be removed:

```
$ rm hold_it
$
```

This command removes the file hold_it from the current directory. The ls command will verify that the file has in fact been removed:

```
$ ls
names
$
```

As you can see, you are now left with only one file in your directory: names.

You can remove more than one file at a time with the rm command by simply specifying all such files on the command line. For example, the following would remove the three files wb, collect, and mon:

```
$ rm wb collect mon
$
```

While the rm command is conceptually one of the simplest UNIX commands, it should be noted that it is one of the most potentially dangerous. It is quite easy to accidentally remove *all* of your files with this command—which is why you must be careful when you use it.

Displaying and Printing Files

You have seen how the cat command is used to display a file at the terminal. So the command

```
cat names
```

would list the contents of names. This approach works fine for relatively small files. Most video terminals can display 24 lines of information, so if your file contains 24 or fewer lines, you're in business. However, if your file is larger than that and you try to cat it, all but the last 24 lines of the file will "fly" right off the screen.

The UNIX system provides a program called pg that allows you to view your file 24 lines at a time. The format of this command is simple enough:

pg *file*

where *file* is the name of the file you want to look at. The program automatically displays enough lines from the file to fill up your entire screen and then waits for you to type a key before continuing. This gives you as much time as you need to read the information on the screen. When you are ready to view the next "screenful," you simply press RETURN. After displaying the next screenful of data, the program once again waits for you to press RETURN. If you decide that you've seen enough, you can type in q instead to stop the display; otherwise, pressing RETURN will once again cause the next screenful to be displayed.

If you're not running UNIX System V Release 2, then you won't have the pg program. However, chances are that you do have a program called more that performs the same function[†]. Unlike pg, more displays the next screenful from the file when you type a "space" and not RETURN. However, it too accepts a q as an indication that you've seen enough of the file.

If you want to get a hard copy printout of your file, you can use the lp command. This command takes as its argument the name of the file to be printed. So

    lp names

will cause the file names to be printed on your line printer. Many installations have special commands that can be used to obtain fancy headings on the printout, or to print your files on other types of printers. You should ask someone about the usual commands that are used at your site to get hard copy printouts of files.

· Working with Directories ·

Now that you are familiar with some of the basic file operations under the UNIX system, it is time to learn how to work with directories. You will recall from Chapter 3 that directories provide a convenient means of organizing files. You will also recall that the UNIX system has what is known as a hierarchical directory structure, meaning that a directory can itself contain directories.

Displaying Your Working Directory: the pwd Command

In order to learn how to work with directories, it is necessary to first learn about the pwd command. This command is used to help you "get your bearings" by telling you the name of your current working directory.

Recall the directory structure from Chapter 3:

---

† This program is actually what's known as a "Berkeley enhancement" since it was added to the UNIX system by the University of California at Berkeley and is not included in the standard UNIX system distributed by AT&T.

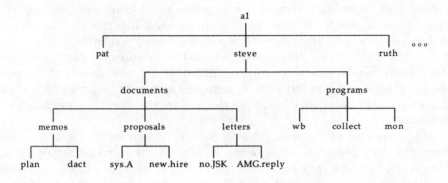

Fig. 4-1. File system a1

The special directory that you are placed in upon logging in to the system is called your HOME directory. You can assume from Fig. 4-1 that the HOME directory for the user steve is /a1/steve. Therefore, whenever steve logs into the system, he will *automatically* be placed inside this directory. To verify that this is the case, the pwd (print working directory) command can be issued:

```
$ pwd
/a1/steve
$
```

The output from the command verifies that steve's current working directory is /a1/steve.

Changing Directories: the cd Command

Now that you know how to find out where you are with the pwd command, let's go "exploring." A very useful command provided by the UNIX system enables you to easily change your current working directory. The command is cd (change directory) and it takes as its argument the name of the directory you wish to change to.

Let's assume that the user steve has just logged into the system and was placed inside his HOME directory, /a1/steve. This is depicted by the ☛ in Fig. 4-2.

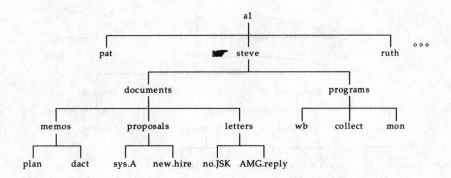

Fig. 4-2. Current working directory is steve

You know from Fig. 4-2 that there are two directories directly "below" steve's HOME directory: documents and programs. In fact, this can be verified at the terminal by issuing the ls command:

```
$ ls
documents
programs
$
```

The ls command lists the two directories documents and programs the same way it listed other files in previous examples. You will see shortly how we can use the ls command to help distinguish directory files from nondirectory files.

In order to make documents your current working directory, you issue the cd command, followed by the name of the directory to change to:

```
$ cd documents
$
```

As with most other commands, the UNIX system lets you know that the cd command executes successfully by "saying nothing." After executing the previous command, you will be placed inside the documents directory, as depicted in Fig. 4-3.

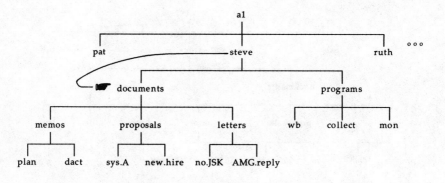

Fig. 4-3. `cd documents`

You can verify at the terminal that the working directory has been changed by issuing the `pwd` command:

```
$ pwd
/a1/steve/documents
$
```

and you can list the files contained in the current directory with the `ls` command:

```
$ ls
letters
memos
proposals
$
```

To continue the exploration, let's change now to the `memos` directory:

```
$ cd memos
$ pwd
/a1/steve/documents/memos
$ ls
dact
plan
$
```

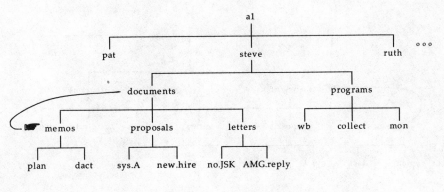

Fig. 4-4. `cd memos`

Now let's try something "illegal":

```
$ cd plan
plan: bad directory
$
```

As you can see, the UNIX system issues an error message when you try to change to a nonexistent directory. (You will recall that the file `plan` is a data file and *not* a directory.)

Now that you know how to work your way down a directory path, let's see how you can get back up. The easiest way to get one level up is to issue the command

```
cd ..
```

since by convention `..` always refers to the directory one level up.

```
$ pwd
/a1/steve/documents/memos
$ cd ..
$ pwd
/a1/steve/documents
$
```

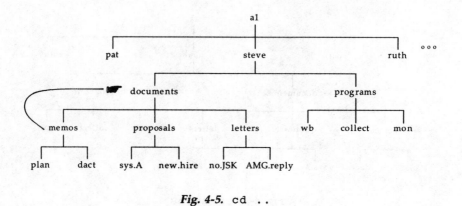

Fig. 4-5. `cd ..`

Issuing the `cd ..` command another time will bring you up one more level to the HOME directory:

```
$ cd ..
$ pwd
/a1/steve
$
```

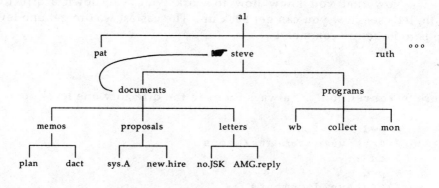

Fig. 4-6. `cd ..`

Suppose now that you wanted to go to the `letters` directory. Well, you know that you can get there by simply issuing two `cd` commands:

```
$ cd documents
$ cd letters
$ pwd
/a1/steve/documents/letters
$
```

Alternatively, you can get to the `letters` directory with a single `cd` command by specifying the relative path `documents/letters`:

```
$ cd documents/letters
$ pwd
/a1/steve/documents/letters
$
```

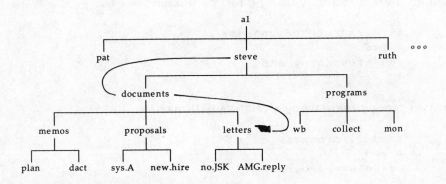

Fig. 4-7. `cd documents/letters`

You can get back up to the `HOME` directory with a single `cd` command as shown:

```
$ cd ../..
$ pwd
/a1/steve
$
```

Or you can get back to the `HOME` directory using a full path name instead of a relative one:

```
$ cd /a1/steve
$ pwd
/a1/steve
$
```

Finally, there is a third way to get back to the `HOME` directory that is also the easiest. Typing the command `cd` *without* an argument will *always* place you back into your `HOME` directory, no matter where you are in your directory path.

```
$ cd
$ pwd
/a1/steve
$
```

Now let's go back to the documents directory:

```
$ cd documents
$
```

What if you now wanted to change to the directory programs? You can go there directly by using a full path name:

```
$ cd /a1/steve/programs
$ pwd
/a1/steve/programs
$
```

or you can get there using a relative path name:

```
$ cd ../programs
$ pwd
/a1/steve/programs
$
```

Remember, you always have a choice between a full and a relative path name. At first, choose the one that's easiest for you to understand; later—once you become more experienced using the UNIX system—you will naturally choose the one that's easiest to type.

More on the 1s Command

By now you know that the 1s command can be used to list your files. To be more specific, whenever you type the command 1s, it is the files contained in the current working directory that are listed. But you can also use 1s to obtain a list of files in other directories by supplying an argument to the command. First let's get back to your HOME directory:

```
$ cd
$ pwd
/a1/steve
$
```

Now let's take a look at the files in the current working directory:

```
$ ls
documents
programs
$
```

If you supply the name of one of these directories to the ls command, then you can get a list of the contents of that directory. So, you can find out what's contained in the documents directory simply by typing the command ls documents:

```
$ ls documents
letters
memos
proposals
$
```

Similarly, you can list the files contained in the programs directory as shown:

```
$ ls programs
collect
mon
wb
$
```

To take a look at the subdirectory memos, you follow a similar procedure:

```
$ ls documents/memos
dact
plan
$
```

If you specify a nondirectory file argument to the ls command, then you simply get that file name echoed back at the terminal:

```
$ ls documents/memos/plan
documents/memos/plan
$
```

There is an option to the ls command that enables you to determine whether a particular file is a directory, among other things. The −1 option (the letter l) provides a more detailed description of the files in a directory. If you were currently in steve's HOME directory as indicated in Fig. 4-6, then the following would illustrate the effect of supplying the −1 option to the ls command:

```
$ ls -l
total 2
drwxr-xr-x    5 steve     DP3725      80 Feb 25 13:27 documents
drwxr-xr-x    2 steve     DP3725      96 Feb 25 13:31 programs
$
```

The first line of the display is a count of the total number of *blocks* (1024 bytes) of storage that the listed files use. Each successive line displayed by the ls -l command contains detailed information about a file in the directory. The first character on each line tells whether the file is a directory. If the character is d, then it is a directory; if it is – then it is an ordinary file; finally, if it is b, c, or p, then it is a special file.

The next nine characters on the line tell how every user on the system can access the particular file. These *access modes* apply to the file's owner (the first three characters), other users in the same *group* as the file's owner (the next three characters), and finally to all other users on the system (the last three characters). They tell whether the user can read from the file, write to the file, or execute the contents of the file. Chapter 10 covers these modes in more detail.

The ls -l command tells who the owner of the file is (it is possible to have a file in your directory that you yourself do not own!), the name of the group owner of the file, how large the file is (i.e., how many characters are contained in it), and when the file was last modified. The information displayed last on the line is the file name itself.

```
$ ls -l programs
total 4
-rwxr--r--    1 steve     DP3725       358 Feb 25 13:31 collect
-rwxr--r--    1 steve     DP3725      1219 Feb 25 13:31 mon
-rwxr--r--    1 steve     DP3725        89 Feb 25 13:30 wb
$
```

The dash in the first column of each line indicates that the three files collect, mon, and wb are ordinary files and not directories.

Creating a Directory: the mkdir Command

In order to be able to create a directory, a special command called mkdir (make directory) must be used. The argument to this command is simply the name of the directory you want to make. As an example, assume that you are still working with the directory structure depicted in Fig. 4-7. Further suppose that you wish to create a new directory called misc *on the same level* as the directories documents and pro-grams. Well, if you were currently in your HOME directory, then typing the command mkdir misc would achieve the desired effect:

```
$ mkdir misc
$
```

Now if you execute an `ls` command, you should get the new directory listed:

```
$ ls
documents
misc
programs
$
```

The directory structure will now appear as shown in Fig. 4-8.

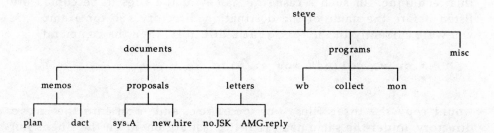

Fig. 4-8. Directory structure with newly created `misc` directory

Since you haven't yet stored any files inside the `misc` directory, the following shows what will happen if you list the contents of the directory.

```
$ ls misc
$
```

Copying a File from One Directory to Another

You have seen how the `cp` command can be used to make a copy of a file. This command can also be used to make a copy of a file from one directory into another. For example, you can copy the file `wb` from the `programs` directory into a file called `wbx` in the `misc` directory as follows:

```
$ cp programs/wb misc/wbx
$
```

Since the two files are contained in different directories, it is not even necessary that they be given different names:

```
$ cp programs/wb misc/wb
$
```

When the destination file will have the same name as the source file (in a different directory, of course), then it is necessary to specify only the destination directory as the second argument:

```
$ cp programs/wb misc
$
```

When this command gets executed, the UNIX system recognizes that the second argument is the name of a directory and copies the source file into that directory. The new file is given the same name as the source file. You can copy more than one file into a directory using this technique. In such a case, the names of the files to be copied are listed before the name of the destination directory. So for example, if you were currently in the programs directory, then the command

```
$ cp wb collect mon ../misc
$
```

would copy the three files wb, collect, and mon into the misc directory, under the same names. If the last argument on the line is not a directory, then you will get the following:

```
$ cp wb collect mon nondir
cp: nondir not found
$
```

To copy a file from another directory into your current one and give it the same name, use the fact that the current directory can always be referenced as '.':

```
$ pwd
/a1/steve/misc
$ cp ../programs/collect .
$
```

The above command copies the file collect from the directory ../programs into the current directory (/a1/steve/misc). Note that this command is identical to

```
$ cp ../programs/collect collect
$
```

The advantage of the first format is that it saves some typing.

Moving Files between Directories

You have learned that the `mv` command can be used to rename a file. However, when the two arguments to this command reference different directories, then the file is actually moved from the first directory into the second directory. For example, first change from the HOME directory to the `documents` directory:

```
$ cd documents
$
```

Suppose now you decide that the file `plan` contained in the `memos` directory is really a proposal and not a memo. So you would like to move it from the `memos` directory into the `proposals` directory. The following would do the trick:

```
$ mv memos/plan proposals/plan
$
```

The `ls` command can be used to verify that the file has indeed been moved:

```
$ ls memos
dact
$ ls proposals
new.hire
plan
sys.A
$
```

As with the `cp` command, if the destination file is to have the same name as the source file, then only the name of the destination directory need be supplied.

```
$ mv memos/plan proposals
$
```

Also like the `cp` command, a group of files can be simultaneously moved into a directory by simply listing all files to be moved before the name of the destination directory:

```
$ pwd
/a1/steve/programs
$ mv wb collect mon ../misc
$
```

This would move the three files wb, collect, and mon into the directory misc.

Remember the difference between the cp and mv commands: after the former command is executed, two copies of the file will exist; after the latter is executed, only a single copy of the file will exist (albeit perhaps under a new name).

Incidentally, you can also use the mv command to change the name of a directory. For example, the following will rename the directory programs to bin.

```
$ mv programs bin
$
```

Removing a Directory: the rmdir Command

Just as you can easily create a directory with the mkdir command, so can you easily remove one with the rmdir command. The only stipulation involved in removing a directory is that no files be contained in the directory. If there *are* files in the directory when rmdir is executed, then you will not be allowed to remove the directory. To remove the directory misc that you created earlier, the following could be used:

```
$ rmdir /a1/steve/misc
$
```

Once again, the above command will work only if no files are contained in the misc directory; otherwise, the following will happen:

```
$ rmdir /a1/steve/misc
rmdir: /a1/steve/misc non-empty
$
```

If this happened and you still wanted to remove the misc directory, then you would first have to remove all of the files contained in that directory before reissuing the rmdir command.

As an alternate method for removing a directory and the files contained in it, you can use the -r option to the rm command. The format is simple:

```
rm -r dir
```

where *dir* is the name of the directory that you want to remove. rm will remove the indicated directory and *all* files in it. Caution! You can easily remove all your files if you're not careful.

· An Introduction to the Editor ed ·

Up to now you've created files using the cat command, and you haven't had any way of altering them without retyping the entire file. The UNIX system provides you with a very helpful tool to change or *edit* your files. It is ed, the *text editor*.

ed is an environment all to itself. It has its own language to control operations on files, and once started is independent of the shell. To start it, you type in ed followed by the name of the file you want to edit:

```
$ ed names
27
```

ed prints out the number of characters contained in the file and then waits for you to type in a command. Note that ed doesn't print any prompt to tell you that it's waiting for you to type something in. In fact, ed is usually very secretive—it says very little to the user, so don't be too worried when ed doesn't say anything; it's probably just waiting for you.

Entering ed Commands

The following examples, that show how the editor works, use the file names that we created earlier. First let's take another look at it so you know what you're going to be working with:

```
$ cat names
Susan
Jeff
Henry
Allan
Ken
$
```

ed commands are single letters, optionally preceded by a line number or range of line numbers. (We'll discuss ranges later.) The ed command n prints out a line or group of lines:

```
$ ed names
27
1n                                      Print line 1
1       Susan
2n                                      Print line 2
2       Jeff
4n                                      Print line 4
4       Allan
1,3n                                    Print lines 1 through 3
1       Susan
2       Jeff
3       Henry
3,9n                                    Print lines 3 through 9
?
```

The first ed command 1n asks the editor to display line 1 of the file. Notice that ed automatically precedes each line that is displayed by its number and some blank spaces. The command 1,3n asks for a *range* of lines to be displayed: from line 1 through line 3. The general format of a range specification is:

starting-line, *ending-line*

The 3,9n command produces a ? from ed. Since there is no line 9 in the file, ed just types back ?. This response is ed's way of saying "I'm sorry, but that doesn't make sense." From time to time, you'll get this response from ed. When you do don't worry about it; just look at what you typed for a possible mistake. Alternatively, type in the "help" command h to ask ed for an explanation:

```
3,9n
?
h                                       Ask ed for an explanation
line out of range
```

There is also another help command in ed: H. This command causes ed to automatically print out explanations of error messages for the remainder of the editing session:

```
H                                       Automatically print explanations
3,9n
?
line out of range
```

You may want to use the H command until you get comfortable with the syntax and use of ed commands. As soon as you start your editing session, type H to "turn on" this automatic help feature.

Returning to the n command, try using it on the file names. You can use the previous example as a starting point. When you're done, if you want to leave the editor and return to the shell, just type in a q. This is the quit command and it tells the editor that you are finished editing the file.

```
$ ed names
27
1,5n
1       Susan
2       Jeff
3       Henry
4       Allan
5       Ken
2n
2       Jeff
q
$
```

When you get back your command prompt, $, you know that you are talking directly to the UNIX system again. Until that time, everything you type in is interpreted by ed.

Now that you've learned how to print the file you're editing, let's see how to make changes to the file. The "delete" command d is used to remove lines:

```
$ ed names
27
1,5n
1       Susan
2       Jeff
3       Henry
4       Allan
5       Ken
3,4d                    Delete lines 3 through 4
1,3n
1       Susan
2       Jeff
3       Ken
```

As you can see, Henry and Allan (lines 3 and 4) were deleted. Also, you should note that Ken is now on line 3. As lines are deleted, the following ones move up to take their place.

```
1,3n
1       Susan
2       Jeff
3       Ken
1d
1,2n
1       Jeff
2       Ken
```

Now there are two names left. So far, you have been making changes to the *editor's copy* of names; the file names has not been altered in any way. To make these changes permanent to names, you must "write" the editor's copy to the file. This is done with the w command:

```
1,2n
1       Jeff
2       Ken
w                          Write the changes to the file
9
q
$ cat names
Jeff
Ken
$
```

When the w command is typed, the number of characters written is displayed at the terminal. The original version of the file is then replaced by the edited copy.

Since you know how to delete lines, you should also know how to add them. The "append" command a allows you to add new lines at any point in a file:

```
$ ed names
9
1,2n
1       Jeff
2       Ken
1a                         Append after the first line
Nancy
George
Bill
.                          Leave append mode
1,5n
1       Jeff
2       Nancy
3       George
4       Bill
5       Ken
```

Note that the command 1a adds the lines *after* line 1. All lines typed in
after the a command are inserted in the file at that point. A single
period tells the editor that you have finished your insertions. The
period must be in the first column and alone on the line. Let's now
write the changed file:

```
w                               Write the changes to the file
27
q                               and quit
$ cat names
Jeff
Nancy
George
Bill
Ken
$
```

Now let's look at a combination of delete and append:

```
$ ed names
27
1,5n
1       Jeff
2       Nancy
3       George
4       Bill
5       Ken
1,2d                            Delete lines 1 and 2
1,3n
1       George
2       Bill
3       Ken
0a                              Append before the first line
Steve
Jim
.                               I'm done with my insertions
1,$n                            Display the entire file
1       Steve
2       Jim
3       George
4       Bill
5       Ken
w                               Write the file
26
q                               and quit
$
```

You should notice two odd things about the previous example. The first is that you are adding `Steve` and `Jim` after line *zero*. There is, of course, no line zero, but you are allowed to use this number to stick lines before the first line of a file. The second oddity is the `$` in `1,$n`. The `$` in `ed` means the *last line* when used with the `n`, `a`, or `d` commands:

```
$ ed names
26
1,$n
1        Steve
2        Jim
3        George
4        Bill
5        Ken
3,$d                              Delete lines 3 through the end
1,$n                              Display the file
1        Steve
2        Jim
w
10
q
$ cat names
Steve
Jim
$
```

`ed` can also be used to enter information into a new file. For example, assume you want to enter data into a new file called `data_file`:

```
$ ed data_file
?data_file                       This file doesn't exist!
a                                Append a few lines
1.24
12
-117.677
199
.
w
21
q
$ cat data_file
1.24
12
-117.677
199
$
```

You'll remember that normally ed displays the number of characters in the file when it first starts. But since data_file didn't exist, ed displayed ?data_file instead.

There are a lot of other ed commands, but the ones shown here are all that are really necessary to create and modify files. The table that follows contains a summary of these commands. In the next chapter we'll cover more of the features in ed.

TABLE 4-2. Basic ed commands

Command	Function
n	Print line
a	Enter append text mode (use . as first and only character on the line to leave append mode)
d	Delete line
h	Explain last error
H	Automatically explain all errors
w	Save editing changes
q	Quit the editor

▪ Command Summary ▪

The following table summarizes all of the commands you have learned so far in this chapter. In this table, *file* refers to a file, *files* to one or more files, and *dir* to a directory.

TABLE 4-3. Command Summary

Command	Description
cat *file*	Display contents of *file*
cd *dir*	Change working directory to *dir*
cp *file₁ file₂*	Copy *file₁* to *file₂*
cp *files dir*	Copy *files* into *dir*
date	Display the date and time
echo *args*	Display *args*
ed *file*	Edit *file*
lp *file*	Print the contents of *file* on the line printer
ls *dir*	List files in *dir* or in current directory if *dir* is not specified
mkdir *dir*	Create directory *dir*
mv *file₁ file₂*	Move *file₁* to *file₂* (simply rename it if both reference the same directory)
mv *files dir*	Move *files* into directory *dir*
pg *file*	Display contents of *file* one screenful at a time
pwd	Display current working directory path
rm *files*	Remove *files*
rmdir *dir*	Remove empty directory *dir*
sort *file*	Alphabetize *file*
wc *file*	Count the number of lines, words and characters in *file*
who	Display who's logged in

5

USING THE UNIX SYSTEM

In this chapter you will learn some more important concepts about the UNIX operating system. These include file name substitution, I/O redirection, and pipes. You will also learn more ed commands that will enable you to make changes to your files more efficiently.

· File Name Substitution ·

The Asterisk

One very powerful feature of the UNIX system is *file name substitution*. It allows you to work with files collectively. For example, let's say your current directory has these files in it:

```
$ ls
chapt1
chapt2
chapt3
chapt4
$
```

Suppose you want to print their contents at the terminal. Well, you could execute four separate cat commands to get the required display:

```
$ cat chapt1
          .
          .
          .
$ cat chapt2
          .
          .
          .
$ cat chapt3
          .
          .
          .
$ cat chapt4
          .
          .
          .
```

Alternatively, you can take advantage of the fact that the cat command allows you to specify more than one file name at a time. When this is done, the contents of the files are displayed at the terminal one after the other.

```
$ cat chapt1 chapt2 chapt3 chapt4
          .
          .
          .
$
```

But you can also type in:

```
$ cat *
          .
          .
          .
$
```

and get the same results. The UNIX system automatically *substitutes* the names of all of the files in the current directory for the *. The same substitution occurs if you use * with the echo command:

```
$ echo *
chapt1 chapt2 chapt3 chapt4
$
```

Here the * is again replaced with the names of all the files contained in the current directory, and the echo command simply displays them

at the terminal. (As you can see, the command echo * provides a good
way to obtain a *horizontal* list of your files.)

    Any place that * appears on the command line, the UNIX system
performs its substitution:

```
$ echo * : *
chapt1 chapt2 chapt3 chapt4 : chapt1 chapt2 chapt3 chapt4
```

    The * can also be used in combination with other characters to
limit the file names that are substituted. For example, let's say that in
your current directory you have not only chapt1 through chapt4
but also files a, b, and c:

```
$ ls
a
b
c
chapt1
chapt2
chapt3
chapt4
$
```

To display the contents of just the files beginning with chapt, you can
type in:

```
$ cat chapt*
      .
      .
      .
$
```

The chapt* matches any file name that *begins* with chapt. All such
file names matched are substituted on the command line by the UNIX
system. Using ch* instead will match the same file names, since the
only file names beginning with ch are chapt1 through chapt4:

```
$ echo ch*
chapt1 chapt2 chapt3 chapt4
$
```

    The * is not limited to the end of a file name; it can be used at
the beginning or in the middle as well:

```
$ echo *t1
chapt1
$ echo *t*
chapt1 chapt2 chapt3 chapt4
$ echo *x
*x
$
```

In the first echo, the *t1 specifies all file names that end in the characters t1. In the second echo, the first * matches everything up to a t and the second everything after; thus, all file names containing a t are printed. Since there are no files ending with x, no substitution occurs in the last case. Therefore, the echo command simply displays *x.

Table 5-1 gives a few examples of how * can be used.

TABLE 5-1. File name substitution examples

Command	Description
echo a*	Print the *names* of the files beginning with a
cat *.c	Print all files ending in .c
rm *.*	Remove all files containing a period
ls x*	List the names of all files beginning with x
rm *	Remove *all* files in the current directory (note: be careful when you use this)
echo a*b	Print the names of all files beginning with a and ending with b
cp ../programs/* .	Copy all files from ../programs into the current directory

Matching Single Characters

The * matches *zero* or more characters, meaning that x* will match the file x as well as x1, x2, xabc, etc. This is usually fine, but sometimes you'll need to match a *single* character. The question mark (?) matches exactly one character. So cat ? will print all files with one-character names, just as cat x? will print all files with two-character names beginning with x.

```
$ ls
a
aa
aax
alice
```

```
b
bb
c
cc
report1
report2
report3
$ echo ?
a b c
$ echo a?
aa
$ echo ??
aa bb cc
$ echo ??*
aa aax alice bb cc report1 report2 report3
$
```

In the last example, the `??` matches two characters, and the `*` matches zero or more up to the end. The net effect is to match all file names of two or more characters.

Another way to match a single character is to give a list of the characters to use in the match inside square brackets [ ]. For example, [abc] matches *one* letter a, b, or c. It's similar to the ?, but it allows you to choose the characters that will be matched.

```
$ echo *
a aa aax alice b bb c cc report1 report2 report3
$ echo [abcd]
a b c
$ echo report[13]
report1 report3
$ echo [ab]*
a aa aax alice b bb
$ echo *[0-9]
report1 report2 report3
$
```

The second `echo` matches any file whose name is a, b, c or d. In the next case, files whose name begin with `report` and end with either 1 or 3 are matched. The fourth case matches any file whose name begins with an a or b. The last case introduces a new twist. The specification [0-9] matches the characters 0 *through* 9. The only restriction in specifying a *range* of characters is that the first character must be alphabetically less than the last character, so that [z-f] is not a valid range specification.

By mixing and matching ranges and characters in the list, you can perform some very complicated substitutions. For example, [a-np-z] will match all files that start with the letters a through n *or* p through z (or more simply stated, any lowercase letter but o).

Here are some more examples of file name substitution:

```
$ ls
a
b
c
chapt1
chapt1.0
chapt1.1
chapt2.0
chapt3
chapt4
chapt4.1
chapt4.2
chapt5
chapt6
chapt7.1
x1
y1
z
$ echo [a-z]
a b c z
$ echo chapt1*
chapt1 chapt1.0 chapt1.1
$ echo chapt1.*
chapt1.0 chapt1.1
$ echo chapt[2-57]*
chapt2.0 chapt4 chapt4.1 chapt4.2 chapt5 chapt7.1
$ echo chapt?
chapt1 chapt3 chapt4 chapt5 chapt6
$ echo chapt*.*
chapt1.0 chapt1.1 chapt2.0 chapt4.1 chapt4.2 chapt7.1
$ echo [abx-z]*
a b x1 y1 z
$ echo [d-f]*
[d-f]*
$
```

The grep Command

One command that is very useful when combined with file name substitution is the grep command.   grep allows you to search one or more files for particular character patterns. The general format of this command is:

grep *pattern* *files*

Every line of each file that contains *pattern* is displayed at the terminal. If more than one file is specified to grep, then each line is also immediately preceded by the name of the file, thus enabling you to identify the particular file that the pattern was found in.

Let's start with an example of searching just a single file for a particular pattern. Let's say you have a directory filled with text files that make up a chapter of a book (this book, perhaps), and you want to find every occurrence of the word shell in the file ed.cmd:

```
$ grep shell ed.cmd
files, and is independent of the shell.
to the shell, just type in a q.
$
```

This output indicates that two lines in the file ed.cmd contain the word shell.

If the pattern does not exist in the specified file(s), then the grep command simply displays a new prompt:

```
$ grep cracker ed.cmd
$
```

Suppose you have a file called phone_book that you use to keep the phone numbers of people you frequently call:

```
$ cat phone_book
Fenson, Eitan          445-4343
Iannino, Tony          937-1232
Levy, Steven           (907) 843-4432
Musa, John             864-5378
Salmon, Ruth           343-2109
Skala, George          723-2205
Swingle, Babs          331-9974
Weather info           976-1212
Wood, Pat              385-3193
Wood, Tom              778-3321
$
```

(We have shown a rather small phone directory here to conserve space.) When you need to look up a particular phone number, the `grep` command comes in handy:

```
$ grep Salmon phone_book
Salmon, Ruth            343-2109
$
```

Look what happens when we look up `Wood`:

```
$ grep Wood phone_book
Wood, Pat               385-3193
Wood, Tom               778-3321
$
```

Two lines are printed, since there are two lines containing `Wood`. If you wanted, you could be more specific in the pattern to obtain only a single match from the directory:

```
$ grep "Wood, Pat" phone_book
Wood, Pat               385-3193
$
```

In this case, quote signs are *required* around the name because of the space that separates the two words `Wood,` and `Pat`. The quotes serve to join the two words together, so that the `grep` command sees them as a *single* pattern. See what happens if you omit the quotes:

```
$ grep Wood, Pat phone_book
grep: can't open Pat
phone_book:Wood, Pat               385-3193
phone_book:Wood, Tom               778-3321
$
```

The `grep` command sees `Wood,` (and *just* `Wood,`) as the pattern and `Pat` and `phone_book` as the files to be searched. Since there is no file called `Pat`, `grep` displays the message `grep: can't open Pat`. `grep` then proceeds to search the file `phone_book` for the pattern `Wood,`. Since this pattern is in the file, the matching lines are displayed at the terminal.

The `grep` command is useful when you have a lot of files and you want to find out which ones contain certain words or phrases. The following example shows how the `grep` command can be used to search for the word `shell` in *all* files in the current directory:

```
$ grep shell *
cmdfiles:shell that enables sophisticated
ed.cmd:files, and is independent of the shell.
ed.cmd:to the shell, just type in a q.
grep.cmd:occurrence of the word shell:
grep.cmd:$ grep shell *
grep.cmd:every use of the word shell.
$
```

When more than one file is specified to grep, each output line is preceded by the name of the file containing that line.

The * can be replaced by any meaningful file list, such as a* or ab?, to determine which files will be searched:

```
$ grep shell *.cmd
ed.cmd:files, and is independent of the shell.
ed.cmd:to the shell, just type in a q.
grep.cmd:occurrence of the word shell:
grep.cmd:$ grep shell *
grep.cmd:every use of the word shell.
$
```

If you want to be really clever, you can even search for every occurrence of shell and Shell with grep:

```
$ grep [Ss]hell *
cmdfiles:shell that enables sophisticated
ed.cmd:files, and is independent of the shell.
ed.cmd:to the shell, just type in a q.
grep.cmd:occurrence of the word shell:
grep.cmd:$ grep shell *
grep.cmd:every use of the word shell.
grep.cmd:occurrence of shell and Shell with grep:
grep.cmd:grep interprets [Ss]hell as Shell or
$
```

As you can see, grep uses the brackets for its pattern search in the same way the UNIX system uses them for file name matching; grep interprets [Ss]hell as Shell *or* shell and goes its merry way through the files looking for the occurrence of either word.

Sifting through the output of grep can be a little tedious sometimes, particularly when there are a lot of occurrences of the pattern and you're interested only in the names of the files. Fortunately, grep has the -1 option to make it print just the names of the files containing the pattern:

```
$ grep -l [Ss]hell *
cmdfiles
ed.cmd
grep.cmd
$ grep -l [Ss]hell *.cmd
ed.cmd
grep.cmd
$
```

As you can see, the name of a file is printed only once if the pattern is found in it no matter how many times it occurs.

One note of caution before we leave this discussion: it's generally a good idea to enclose your grep pattern inside a pair of *single* quotes to "protect" it from the UNIX system. For instance, if you want to find all the lines containing asterisks inside the file stars, then typing

```
grep * stars
```

will not work as expected because the UNIX system will see the asterisk and will automatically substitute the names of all the files in your current directory! Enclosing the asterisk in quotes, however, removes its special meaning from the system:

```
grep '*' stars
```

There are characters other than * that otherwise have a special meaning and must be quoted when used in a pattern. These include brackets ([and]), parentheses ((and)), semicolons (;), dollar signs ($), less-than and greater-than characters (< and >), and vertical bar characters (¦). In the next chapter we'll go into more detail about these characters. For now, just remember to enclose them in quotes.

▪ The Editor ed Revisited ▪

In the last chapter, we went over the basic ed commands n (print text), a (append text), d (delete text), w (write text to file), and q (quit editing session). Now we'll look at some more ed commands that will help you make changes to files faster.

Searching for a String

One very helpful ed command is the *string search*. This is very much like searching with grep, except this command is built into ed. The way you search for a string in ed is to put the string inside slashes (/).

So to search for the string of characters `the`, you would simply type the `ed` command `/the/`:

```
$ ed names
10
1,$n
1        Steve
2        Jim
$a
Pat
George
Carol
Zebediah
.
1,$n
1        Steve
2        Jim
3        Pat
4        George
5        Carol
6        Zebediah
/Geo/                Find the line containing Geo
George
/ebed/               Find the line containing ebed
Zebediah
/Tony/               Find the line containing Tony
?
```

Add some names at the end of the file

As you can see, `ed` prints out the line containing the string. If the string you search for isn't in the file, `ed` prints out its usual I-don't-understand-you question mark.

The Current Line

After you have located a line using the string search command, you can delete it by typing just a `d`.

```
1,$n
1          Steve
2          Jim
3          Pat
4          George
5          Carol
6          Zebediah
/Geo/                          Find the line containing Geo
George
d                              Delete it
1,$n
1          Steve
2          Jim
3          Pat
4          Carol
5          Zebediah
```

Here the d was used without a preceding line number and the line containing George was deleted. This brings up the idea of a *current line*. Every ed command will work without a preceding line number by performing its action on the current line. When you search for a string, the current line is set to the line that contains the string. Typing d at that point will delete the line, typing n will print the line, and typing a will append new lines after the line.

```
1,$n
1          Steve
2          Jim
3          Pat
4          Carol
5          Zebediah
/Steve/                        Find the line containing Steve
Steve
n                              Print the current line
1          Steve
/P/                            Find the line containing P
Pat
a                              Append after the current line
Stan
Debbie
.
n                              Print the current line
5          Debbie
1,$n
1          Steve
2          Jim
```

```
3          Pat
4          Stan
5          Debbie
6          Carol
7          Zebediah
```

As you can see, `Stan` and `Debbie` were appended after `Pat`, which was found in the previous string search. You should also note that the current line was changed to `Debbie` as indicated by the `n` command. Most `ed` commands make the *last line* accessed by the command the current line. For example, the `a` command makes the current line the last line entered; the `n` command makes it the last line printed out; and the `d` command makes it the line after the last one deleted.

The current line can be explicitly referenced with the period (`.`). Sometimes you may want to use the current line in a range. To do that, you use the period as if it were a line number. (Remember how the `$` is used to represent the last line?)

```
1,$n
1          Steve
2          Jim
3          Pat
4          Stan
5          Debbie
6          Carol
7          Zebediah
/P/                          Find the line containing P
Pat
.,$n
3          Pat
4          Stan
5          Debbie                Print from the current line to the end
6          Carol
7          Zebediah
/D/                          Find the line containing D
Debbie
.,$d                         Delete from the current line to the end
n
4          Stan
1,$n
1          Steve
2          Jim
3          Pat
4          Stan
```

Now you've deleted the lines from `Debbie` to the end. Right after the delete the current line is `Stan`, now the last line in the file.

When you perform a string search, the current line is set to the line that contains the string. We should also say that a string search starts on the line *after* the current line, so you can search through a file looking for all the lines containing a string:

```
1n
1        Steve
/t/                          Find the next line containing t
Pat
/t/                          Find the next line containing t
Stan
/t/                          Find the next line containing t
Steve
/t/                          Find the next line containing t
Pat
/t/                          Find the next line containing t
Stan
```

As you can see, the string search goes from one line to the next that contains the string. Also, when it gets to the last line in the file, the search begins again on the first line. This is sometimes referred to as *wraparound*.

Substituting One String with Another

Another useful command in the editor is the substitute command `s`. It allows you to change parts of lines without deleting and retyping them:

```
1,$n
1        Steve
2        Jim
3        Pat
4        Stan
1n
1        Steve
s/ve/phen/                   Change the ve to phen
n
1        Stephen
/Pat/                        Find the line containing Pat
Pat
s/t/trick/                   Change the t to trick
n
3        Patrick
```

Here the s command was used to change Steve to Stephen and
Pat to Patrick. The s command is given two strings separated by
slashes; ed scans the line for the first string and, if it finds it, replaces
it with the second string:

$$s\,/\,string1\,/\,string2\,/$$

If it doesn't find *string1* in the line, ed prints out a ?.
    Like other ed commands, the s command will perform its sub-
stitution on a range of lines:

```
1,$n
1         Stephen
2         Jim
3         Patrick
4         Stan
1,$s/t/xxx/                    Change t to xxx on every line
1,$n
1         Sxxxephen
2         Jim
3         Paxxxrick
4         Sxxxan
1,$s/e/yyy/                    Change e to yyy on every line
1,$n
1         Sxxxyyyphen
2         Jim
3         Paxxxrick
4         Sxxxan
```

Note that when the s command was used to change all e's to yyy that
only the first e on line 1 was changed. This is because the s command
only changes the *first* occurrence of the string that it finds on a line. To
have it change *all* occurrences of the string on the line you have to add
the letter g (for global) at the end of the s command. So

```
s/,/;/g
```

would change all commas to semicolons in the current line, and

```
1,$s/,/;/g
```

would do it for the entire file.
    If you decide that you don't want your editing changes per-
manently recorded, you can leave ed without writing the file:

```
q
?
q
$
```

The first time you type in q, ed prints out a ?. Once changes have
been made to a file, ed considers quitting before writing the changes to
be an error. (And you know what ed types back when it sees an error!).
The second time, however, ed assumes you know what you're doing
and returns to the shell.

The Backslash (\)

Sometimes you'll want to put some special characters in a file. For
example, you might want to have a list of items and prices:

```
hamburger @ $2.89/1b
eggs @ .99/doz
milk @ .59/qt
```

The only problem is getting the @ into the file, since normally it's the
line kill character. If you try to type in the @ while in append mode in
ed, all you'll do is wipe out the line you typed in. Of course since there
are plenty of @'s sprinkled throughout this text, there must be a way of
putting them in files. This is done with the help of the *backslash* (\) also
known as the *reverse slash*. The backslash has a very different meaning to
the UNIX system than the regular slash (/), which is used to separate
directories in a path name. As you can see, the regular slash leans to the
right (/) and the backslash leans to the left (\).

   The purpose of the backslash is to remove the special meaning
that the UNIX system gives to certain characters. This is done by *preceding* the special character with a backslash:

```
$ ed groceries
?groceries
a                                    Add some lines with special characters
hamburger \@ $2.89/1b
eggs \@.99/doz
milk \@ .59/qt
groceries -- check \# 4437      # is erase character
.
1,$n
1       hamburger @ $2.89/1b
2       eggs @ .99/doz
3       milk @ .59/qt
4       groceries -- check # 4437
```

As you can see, the backslash removed the special meaning of the @ and # so they could become part of the file just like any other character. Also note that the backslash disappeared. In the process of removing the special meaning of a character, the backslash goes away. To get a backslash in your file, simply type two in a row. (The first backslash removes the special meaning of the second.)

Writing to a New File

After making some changes to a file, you may decide that you don't want to overwrite the contents of the original file. The w command can also be used to write a *new* file. This is done by simply specifying a file name argument to the w command. As an example, suppose after editing names you wanted to write to a new file names1 and leave names intact:

```
$ ed names
10
1,$n
1       Steve
2       Jim
a
Sam
Bill
.
w names1                    Write to new file names1
19
q
$ cat names
Steve
Jim
$ cat names1
Steve
Jim
Sam
Bill
$
```

This way you can keep both the old and new versions of a file.

Table 5-2 summarizes the ed commands you have learned.

TABLE 5-2. Summary of basic `ed` **commands**

Command	Function
n	Print line
a	Enter append text mode (to leave append mode, use . as first and only character on the line)
d	Delete line
h	Explain last error
H	Automatically explain all errors
/string/	Search for *string* starting from the current line
s/string1/string2/	Change *string1* to *string2*
w *file*	Save editing changes in *file*
q	Quit the editor

• Displaying the End of a File: the `tail` Command •

The `tail` command is an interesting one—its purpose is to display the end of a file. For example, you can use it to display the last ten lines of a file. It seems to be a curiosity, a command that has little use. In time you will see that it is indispensable.

For now, let's see how it works. First, let's make a "big" file for it to work on:

```
$ ed tailfile
?tailfile
$a
now we will
begin to
add a few
lines to
the file
tailfile.
Perhaps five
or
six more
lines will
do the
trick.
```

```
w tailfile
100
q
$
```

Now let's try `tail`:

```
$ tail tailfile
add a few
lines to
the file
tailfile.
Perhaps five
or
six more
lines will
do the
trick.
$
```

As you can see, `tail` displayed the last 10 lines of `tailfile`. You can have it display fewer or more than 10 lines with the *-number* option. For example, to have `tail` display the last five lines of `tailfile`, you can type:

```
$ tail -5 tailfile
or
six more
lines will
do the
trick.
$
```

And to have it display just the last line of `tailfile`, you can type:

```
$ tail -1 tailfile
trick.
$
```

• **Comparing Two Files: the `sdiff` Command** •

Let's use `ed` to create a few files that will be used to illustrate the `sdiff` command:

```
$ ed names
10
1,$d                          Delete all lines
a
Pat
Tony
Ruth                          Put new names in names
Bill
.
w
19
$a
Tom
John
.
w names1
28
4d                            Delete Bill
1,$n
1       Pat
2       Tony
3       Ruth
4       Tom
5       John
w names2
23
q
$
```

Now let's look at the files that were created:

```
$ cat names
Pat
Tony
Ruth
Bill
$ cat names1
Pat
Tony
Ruth
Bill
Tom
John
$ cat names2
Pat
Tony
```

```
Ruth
Tom
John
$
```

So now you have some files that have some lines in common and
some that are unique. This is a good time to introduce the sdiff command.   sdiff prints two files side by side marking the differences:

```
$ sdiff names names1
Pat                                      Pat
Tony                                     Tony
Ruth                                     Ruth
Bill                                     Bill
                               >         Tom
                               >         John
$
```

The > marks a line that appears only in the second file. Similarly, a <
marks a line that appears only in the first file, and a ¦ marks lines that
are in both files but are different.

```
$ sdiff names1 names2
Pat                                      Pat
Tony                                     Tony
Ruth                                     Ruth
Bill                           <
Tom                                      Tom
John                                     John
$ sdiff names names2
Pat                                      Pat
Tony                                     Tony
Ruth                                     Ruth
Bill                           ¦         Tom
                               >         John
$
```

When comparing large files, you can use the -s option with
sdiff; it suppresses the printing of identical lines, considerably reducing the amount of output.

```
$ sdiff -s names names2
4c4,5
Bill                               |          Tom
                                   >          John

$
```

The rather cryptic first line is actually an edit-style command that describes the difference between the two files. Don't worry about it.

```
$ sdiff -s names1 names2
4d3
Bill                               <
$
```

Here you see that the only difference between names1 and names2 is that Bill appears in the former file and not in the latter.

In case you're interested, there's another command similar to sdiff that's called diff. Unlike sdiff, diff does not generate a side-by-side comparison of the two files.

· Standard Input, Standard Output and I/O Redirection ·

Standard Input and Standard Output

Most commands in the UNIX system take input from your terminal and send the resulting output back to your terminal. A command normally reads its input from a place called *standard input*, which happens to be your terminal by default. Similarly, a command normally writes its output to *standard output*, which is also your terminal by default. This concept is depicted in Fig. 5-1.

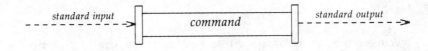

Fig. 5-1. Typical UNIX command

Let's take an example of an actual command. You will recall that executing the who command results in the display of the currently logged-in users. More formally, the who command writes a list of the logged-in users to standard output. This is depicted in Fig. 5-2.

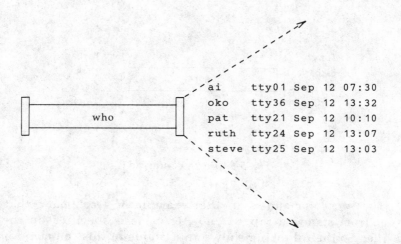

Fig. 5-2. who command

If a `sort` command is executed *without* a file name argument, then the command will take its input from standard input. As with standard output, this is your terminal by default.

When entering data to a command from the terminal, the `CTRL` and `D` keys (denoted *CTRL-d* in this text) must be simultaneously pressed after the last data item has been entered. This tells the command that you have finished entering data. As an example, let's use the `sort` command to sort the following four names: Tony, Barbara, Harry, Dick. Instead of first entering the names into a file as you did before, this time we will enter them directly from the terminal:

```
$ sort
Tony
Barbara
Harry
Dick
CTRL-d
Barbara
Dick
Harry
Tony
$
```

Since no file name was specified to the `sort` command, the input was taken from standard input, the terminal. After the fourth name was typed in, the `CTRL` and `D` keys were pressed to signal the end of the data. At that point, the `sort` command sorted the four names and displayed the results on the standard output device, which is also the terminal. This is depicted in Fig. 5-3.

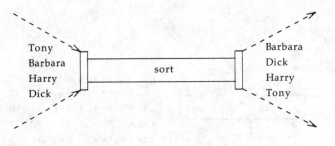

Fig. 5-3. sort command

The wc command is another example of a command that takes its input from standard input if no file name is specified on the command line. So the following shows an example of this command used to count the number of lines of text entered from the terminal:

```
$ wc -l
This is text that
is typed on the
standard input device.
CTRL-d
        3
$
```

You will note that the *CTRL-d* that is used to terminate the input is not counted as a separate line by the wc command. Furthermore, since no file name was specified to the wc command, only the count of the number of lines (3) is listed as the output of the command. (You will recall that this command normally prints the name of the file directly after the count.)

Output Redirection

Under the UNIX system, the output from a command normally intended for standard output can be easily "diverted" to a file instead. This capability is known as *output redirection*.

Suppose you wanted to store the names of the logged-in users inside a file.

If the notation > *filename* is appended to *any* command that normally writes its output to standard output, then the output of that command will be written into the specified file instead of to your terminal:

```
$ who > users
$
```

This command line causes the who command to be executed and its output to be written into the file users. You will notice that no output appears at the terminal. This is because the output has been *redirected* from the default standard output device (the terminal) into the specified file. You can now examine the contents of the users file with the cat command to see if the redirection did in fact work:

```
$ cat users
oko     tty01   Sep 12 07:30
ai      tty15   Sep 12 13:32
ruth    tty21   Sep 12 10:10
pat     tty24   Sep 12 13:07
steve   tty25   Sep 12 13:03
$
```

As another example of output redirection, you can store the current date and time inside a file called now as follows:

```
$ date > now
$ cat now
Tue Oct 4 14:20:26 EDT 1983
$
```

The echo command also writes its output to standard output, which means that it can be redirected:

```
$ echo line 1 > x
$ cat x
line 1
$
```

Consider the following example:

```
$ echo line 1 > x
$ cat x
line 1
$ echo line 2 > x
$ cat x
line 2
$
```

If a command has its output redirected to a file and the file already contains some data, then that data will be lost. Therefore, the contents of x (the line line 1) were lost when the second echo command was executed. Now consider this example:

```
$ echo line 1 > x
$ cat x
line 1
$ echo line 2 >> x
$ cat x
line 1
line 2
$
```

The second echo command uses a different type of output redirection indicated by the characters >>. This character pair causes the standard output from the command to be *appended* to the specified file. Therefore, the previous contents of the file are not lost and the new output simply gets added onto the end.

More on the cat Command

You will recall that the first file in the last chapter was created using the command cat > names. Now you can understand precisely how that command worked. Like most other commands, the cat command takes its input from standard input and writes its output to standard output by default. This means that if no file name is supplied to the cat command then this command will expect its input to come from the terminal. The following example illustrates this idea:

```
$ cat
line one
line one
line two
line two
etc.
etc.
CTRL-d
$
```

Since no file name argument was specified, cat read its input from the terminal. As each line was read, it was written to standard output. The net effect was to simply echo each line typed in. The *CTRL-d* signaled the end of the input to cat. Redirection of the output with a command such as

```
cat > junk
```

would have caused the three lines that were typed to be redirected to the file junk. So you can see how the use of output redirection on the cat command enables you to have text typed in from the terminal stored in a file.

By using the redirection append characters >>, you can use `cat` to append the contents of one file onto the end of another:

```
$ cat file1
This is in file1.
$ cat file2
This is in file2.
$ cat file1 >> file2          Append file1 to file2
$ cat file2
This is in file2.
This is in file1.
$
```

Recall that specifying more than one file name to `cat` results in the display of the first file followed immediately by the second file, and so on:

```
$ cat file1
This is in file1.
$ cat file2
This is in file2.
$ cat file1 file2
This is in file1.
This is in file2.
$ cat file1 file2 > file3      Redirect it instead
$ cat file3
This is in file1.
This is in file2.
$
```

Now you can see where the `cat` command gets its name: when used with more than one file its effect is to *concatenate* the files together.

One thing you should note: a command such as

```
cat file2 file1 > file1
```

will *not* work correctly, and you'll lose the original contents of `file1`. If you want to do this sort of thing, use a temporary file for the output and then `mv` the file where you want it. For example, to concatenate `file1` to the end of `file2` and have the result go to `file1` use the following command sequence:

```
$ cat file2 file1 > temp
$ mv temp file1
$
```

Input Redirection

Just as the output of a command can be redirected to a file, so can the input of a command be redirected from a file. And as the greater-than character > is used for output redirection, the less-than character < is used to redirect the input of a command. Of course, only commands that normally take their input from standard input can have their input redirected from a file in this manner.

In order to redirect the input of a command, you type the < character followed by the name of the file that the input is to be read from. So, for example, to count the number of lines in the file users, you know that you can execute the command wc -l users:

```
$ wc -l users
      5 users
$
```

Or, you can count the number of lines in the file by redirecting the input of the wc command from the terminal to the file users:

```
$ wc -l < users
      5
$
```

You will note that there is a difference in the output produced by the two forms of the wc command. In the first case, the name of the file users is listed with the line count; in the second case, it is not. This points out the subtle distinction between the execution of the two commands. In the first case wc knows it is reading its input from the file users. In the second case, it knows only that it is reading its input from standard input. The shell redirects the input from the terminal to the file users. As far as wc is concerned, it doesn't know whether its input is coming from the terminal or from a file!

Input and Output Redirection

As you might expect, you can simultaneously redirect the input and the output of a command—provided of course the command reads its input from standard input *and* writes its output to standard output.

```
$ cat users
oko     tty01   Sep 12 07:30
ai      tty15   Sep 12 13:32
ruth    tty21   Sep 12 10:10
pat     tty24   Sep 12 13:07
```

```
steve tty25  Sep 12 13:03
$ sort < users > sorted_users
$ cat sorted_users
ai     tty15  Sep 12 13:32
oko    tty01  Sep 12 07:30
pat    tty24  Sep 12 13:07
ruth   tty21  Sep 12 10:10
steve  tty25  Sep 12 13:03
$
```

In this example, the sort command's input was redirected from the file users and its output was redirected to the file sorted_users.

· Pipes ·

As you will recall, the file users that was created previously contains a list of all the users currently logged onto the system. Since you know that there will be one line in the file for each user logged onto the system, you can easily determine the *number* of users logged in by simply counting the number of lines in the users file:

```
$ who > users
$ wc -l < users
       5
$
```

This output would indicate that there were currently five users logged in. Now you have a command sequence you can use whenever you want to know how many users are logged in.

There is another approach to determine the number of logged-in users that bypasses the use of a file. The UNIX system allows you to effectively "connect" two commands together. This connection is known as a *pipe,* and it enables you to take the output from one command and feed it directly into the input of another command. A pipe is effected by the character ¦, which is placed between the two commands. So to make a pipe between the who and wc -l commands, you simply type who ¦ wc -l:

```
$ who ¦ wc -l
       5
$
```

The pipe that is effected between these two commands is depicted in Fig. 5-4.

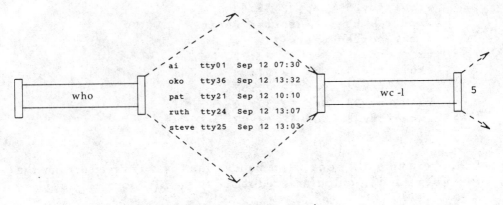

Fig. 5-4. Pipeline process: who ¦ wc -1

When a pipe is set up between two commands, the standard output from the first command is connected directly to the standard input of the second command. You know that the who command writes its list of logged-in users to standard output. Furthermore, you know that if no file name argument is specified to the wc command then it takes its input from standard input. Therefore, the list of logged-in users that is output from the who command automatically becomes the input to the wc command. Note that you never see the output of the who command at the terminal, since it is *piped* directly into the wc command. This is depicted in Fig. 5-5.

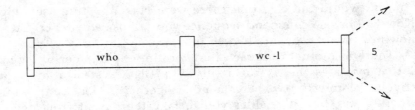

Fig. 5-5. Pipeline process

A pipe can be made between *any* two programs under the UNIX system, provided the first program writes its output to standard output, and the second program reads its input from standard input.

As another example of a pipe, suppose you wanted to count the number of files contained in your directory. Knowledge of the fact that the 1s command displays one line of output per file enables you to use the same type of approach as before:

```
$ ls | wc -l
      10
$
```

The output indicates that the current directory contains 10 files.

The following counts the number of files that end with the characters .c:

```
$ ls *.c | wc -l
       3
$
```

Given the fact that sort takes its input from standard input by default, you can use the following pipeline to get a sorted list of the logged-in users:

```
$ who | sort
adn          tty27        Feb 22 08:56
ai           tty05        Feb 22 09:43
clf          tty11        Feb 22 08:59
console      tty04        Feb 22 09:00
dianne       tty14        Feb 22 08:45
dji          tty20        Feb 22 09:44
fes          tty22        Feb 22 09:31
jcm          tty06        Feb 22 08:19
rcc          tty37        Feb 22 08:27
ruth         tty17        Feb 22 09:44
steve        tty15        Feb 22 08:45
ws           tty13        Feb 22 08:25
$
```

And to save the sorted list of users in a file called users you can use output redirection on the sort command:

```
$ who | sort > users
$ cat users
adn          tty27        Feb 22 08:56
ai           tty05        Feb 22 09:43
clf          tty11        Feb 22 08:59
             .
             .
             .
$
```

Suppose you were interested in finding the *number* of files in your current directory that contained the word `shell`. The first part of the sentence implies that the `wc` command should probably be used, while the latter part indicates that the `grep` command should be used. A command sequence such as:

```
$ grep shell * | wc -l
         6
$
```

is close to what you want, but when you think about it for a while, what this sequence is doing is counting the total number of lines (and not files) that contain the word `shell`—not quite what you want. What you really need is one line of output from `grep` for each file containing `shell`. Recalling the `-l` option to `grep`, this is precisely what you get:

```
$ grep -l shell * | wc -l
         3
$
```

So the output of this pipeline sequence indicates that precisely three files in your current directory contain the word `shell`.

You can use `grep` on the other side of the pipe to quickly scan through the output of a command for something. For example, suppose you want to find out if the user `jim` is logged in. You can type in `who` and scan the output for his id; however, if there are a lot of users logged in or if you're using a slow terminal, you won't want to look at all that output. You do have a faster way to look for him by using `grep`:

```
$ who | grep jim
jim          tty16         Feb 20 10:25
$
```

Note that by not specifying a file to search, `grep` automatically scans its standard input. Naturally, if the user `jim` were not logged in, then you would simply get back a new prompt, because `grep` would not find `jim` in `who`'s output:

```
$ who | grep jim
$
```

It is also possible to form a pipeline consisting of several programs, with the output of one program feeding into the input of the next. Let's take a look at a double pipeline. Suppose every user working on a project called *amps* has a user id in the format

*amps*abc

where *abc* represents the initials of the particular user. Executing a who command might give the following results:

```
$ who
frj          tty04          Feb 27 13:45
kjc123       tty06          Feb 27 13:08
s58411m      tty07          Feb 27 14:10
ampsphw      tty08          Feb 27 09:03
aps          tty10          Feb 27 13:19
ampsoko      tty11          Feb 27 14:39
mack         tty12          Feb 27 14:26
arrizzo      tty14          Feb 27 14:32
ampssgk      tty15          Feb 27 08:40
jam402       tty16          Feb 27 14:20
ampsclf      tty18          Feb 27 10:26
monitor      tty19          Feb 27 14:45
g311bij      tty20          Feb 27 14:24
ruth         tty17          Feb 27 09:14
wl           tty23          Feb 27 14:27
k43htb3      tty29          Feb 27 10:03
s700fwm      tty41          Feb 27 07:29
$
```

So at the time this command was executed there were four users in the *amps* project logged in, with user id's ampsphw, ampsoko, ampssgk, and ampsclf.

By using a pipeline, you can more readily find the *amps* users:

```
$ who | grep amps
ampsphw      tty08          Feb 27 09:03
ampsoko      tty11          Feb 27 14:39
ampssgk      tty15          Feb 27 08:40
ampsclf      tty18          Feb 27 10:26
$
```

To obtain a sorted list of the users in the *amps* project, the following double pipeline could be used:

```
$ who | grep amps | sort
ampsclf      tty18          Feb 27 10:26
ampsoko      tty11          Feb 27 14:39
ampsphw      tty08          Feb 27 09:03
ampssgk      tty15          Feb 27 08:40
$
```

The output of who is fed into the input of grep, which *filters* out only those id's containing the pattern `amps`. These lines are then fed into *sort*, where they are alphabetized and the results displayed at the terminal. This pipeline process is depicted in Fig. 5-6.

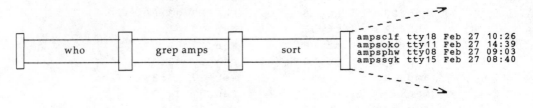

Fig. 5-6. Pipeline `who ¦ grep amps ¦ sort`

(Why can you interchange the `grep` and `sort` commands in this pipeline and still get the same output?)

The term *filter* is often used in UNIX terminology to refer to any program that can take input from standard input, perform some operation on that input, and write the results to standard output. More succinctly, a filter is any program that can be used between two other programs in a pipeline. So in the above pipeline, `grep` and `sort` are both considered filters. `who` is not, since it does not read its input from standard input. As other examples, `cat` and `wc` are filters, while `ls`, `date`, `cd`, `pwd`, `echo`, `rm`, `mv`, and `cp` are not.

As a slight variation on the previous pipeline, consider the task of finding the *number* of logged-in *amps* users:

```
$ who ¦ grep amps ¦ wc -1
    4
$
```

The flow of data through this pipeline is depicted in Fig. 5-7.

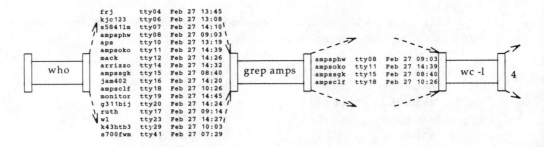

Fig. 5-7. Data flow through pipeline `who ¦ grep amps ¦ wc -1`

Capturing the Output in a Pipe: the `tee` Command

We have stressed the fact that any output from a command that gets piped into another command is not seen at the terminal. Sometimes, you may wish to save the output that is produced in the middle of a pipe. For example, suppose you wanted to save the names of the logged-in *amps* users in a file, as well as count them. The `tee` command enables you to do this easily. The format of this command is simple enough:

`tee` *file*

The `tee` command simply copies the data coming in on standard input to standard output, in the meantime saving a copy in the specified *file*. Figure 5-8 will give you a better understanding of how this command works and where it gets its name.

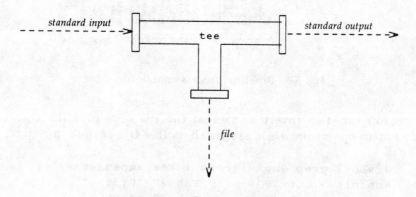

standard input   `tee`   *standard output*

file

Fig. 5-8. The `tee` command

So you can insert the `tee` command right after the `grep` in the previous pipeline to save the user names in a file:

```
$ who | grep amps | tee ampsusers | wc -l
      4
$
```

This pipeline works the same way as the previous one, except in this case the `tee` command saves the output of the `grep` command in the file `ampsusers`:

```
$ cat ampsusers
ampsphw     tty08           Feb 27 09:03
ampsoko     tty11           Feb 27 14:39
ampssgk     tty15           Feb 27 08:40
ampsclf     tty18           Feb 27 10:26
$
```

Operation of this pipeline process is depicted in Fig. 5-9.

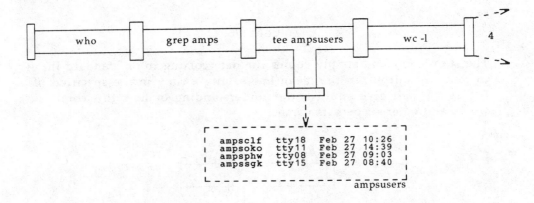

Fig. 5-9. Pipeline process containing tee

You can also insert a tee at the *end* of a pipeline to see the results of an operation while saving them in a file at the same time:

```
$ who ¦ grep amps ¦ sort ¦ tee ampsusers
ampsclf     tty18           Feb 27 10:26
ampsoko     tty11           Feb 27 14:39
ampsphw     tty08           Feb 27 09:03
ampssgk     tty15           Feb 27 08:40
$
```

Here the output from sort is piped into tee, which simultaneously copies its input to the terminal (standard output) and to the file ampsusers.

• Selecting Fields from a Line: the cut Command •

Suppose in the previous examples that you were interested only in the names of the logged-in *amps* users, and couldn't care less about their tty numbers or about the date and time they logged in. So instead of the output that you got, you would really prefer to see the following:

```
ampsclf
ampsoko
ampsphw
ampssgk
```

There is an easy way to just "cut out" the user names from the output of the who command, and this is done with an appropriately named UNIX command called cut.

The basic format of the cut command is:

cut -c*list* *files*

The -c option to cut specifies that you want to cut out specific character positions from *each* line of the specified *files*. *list* tells which character positions to cut. For example, the command

cut -c1 names

would cut out the first character of each line from the file names:

```
$ cat names
Pat
Tony
Ruth
Bill
$ cut -c1 names
P
T
R
B
$
```

And in the following example, the second character is cut from each line of the same file:

```
$ cut -c2 names
a
o
u
i
$
```

Naturally, you can cut more than one character from each line. To do this, you simply list the character positions to be cut, separated by commas:

```
$ cut -c1,2 names
Pa
To
Ru
Bi
$
```

A range of consecutive character positions can also be specified by using the notation:

start–end

The following example cuts the first through third character from each line:

```
$ cut -c1-3 names
Pat
Ton
Rut
Bil
$
```

To specify that a cut is to be made from a specified character position to the end of the line, leave out the ending number:

```
$ cut -c2- names
at
ony
uth
ill
$
```

In this examplem cut is used to cut characters two through the end of the line—in other words, all but the first character.

Of course, the character positions that are cut do not *have* to be consecutive:

```
$ cut -c1,3 names
Pt
Tn
Rt
Bl
$
```

As you might expect, cut takes its input from *standard input* and writes its output to *standard output* by default. This means, of course, that it can be used in a pipeline:

```
$ who | cut -c1-8
frj
kjc123
s58411m
ampsphw
aps
ampsoko
mack
arrizzo
ampssgk
jam402
ampsclf
monitor
g311bij
ruth
wl
k43htb3
s700fwm
$
```

Here you see cut used to extract just the first eight characters from each line of the who command's output. So this pipeline displays just the user ids of the logged-in users. Recalling the problem that was introduced at the start of this section, now you know how to get a list of just the names of the logged-in *amps* people:

```
$ who | cut -c1-8 | grep amps
ampsphw
ampsoko
ampssgk
ampsclf
$
```

Of course, you can also tack a sort onto the end to get a sorted list:

```
$ who | cut -c1-8 | grep amps | sort
ampsclf
ampsoko
ampsphw
ampssgk
$
```

There is a sister command to cut called paste. This command is used to merge characters into single lines. See your *UNIX User's Manual* for details.

Now that you are familiar with pipes you may realize why the UNIX system is typically so terse: so that the output of a program can be easily used as the input to another program. Just think about how much more difficult it would be to do this if the output from commands included "extraneous" information such as headings, for instance. (Think about counting the number of logged-in users if who printed headings; or counting the number of files in your current directory if ls printed headings.) Indeed, most UNIX commands were designed with the realization that the output from the command may very well be the input to another command in a pipe.

• Standard Error •

In addition to standard input and standard output there is another place known as *standard error*. This is where most UNIX commands write their error messages. And as with the other two "standard" places, standard error is associated with your terminal by default. In most cases, you never know the difference between standard output and standard error:

```
$ ls n*                              List all files beginning with n
n* not found
$
```

Here the "not found" message is actually being written to standard error and not standard output by the ls command. You can verify that this message is not being written to standard output by redirecting the ls command's output:

```
$ ls n* > foo
n* not found
$
```

So you see you still got the message printed out at the terminal, even though you redirected standard output to the file foo.

The above example shows the raison d'être for standard error: so that error messages will still get displayed at the terminal even if *standard output* is redirected to a file or piped to another command.

Although it won't be described here, you should note that you can also redirect standard error to a file if you like.

▪ More on Commands ▪

In this section you'll learn some more about the format of the commands you type in.

Typing More Than One Command on a Line

You can type more than one command on a line provided you separate each command with a semicolon. For example, you can find out the current time and also your current working directory by typing in the date and pwd commands on the same line:

```
$ date; pwd
Wed Apr 25 20:14:32 EST 1984
/al/pat/progs
$
```

You can string out as many commands as you like on the line, as long as each command is delimited by a semicolon.

Continuing a Command on the Next Line

Sometimes you may have a command that is too long to fit on a line. Well, you can keep right on typing past the end of the line if you like, or you can insert a backslash character at the end of the line and continue the command on the next line. The backslash at the end of the line (and it must be the *last* character that you type on the line before the RETURN) tells the UNIX system that you want to continue this command on the next line. The following shows a highly manufactured example.

```
$ echo one \
> two \
> three
one two three
$
```

You'll note that the prompt character changed from $ to > on the two continuation lines of the echo command. This is the UNIX system's way of telling you that it's waiting for you to finish typing the command. As soon as you end a line without a backslash, the UNIX system takes this as the end of the command and executes it.

Sending a Command to the Background

Normally, you type in a command and then wait for the results of the command to be displayed at the terminal. For all of the examples you have seen thus far, this waiting time is typically quite short—maybe a second or two. However, you may have to run commands that require many seconds or even minutes to execute. In those cases, you'll have to wait for the command to finish executing before you can proceed further *unless you execute the command in the background.*

If you type in command followed by the ampersand character &, then that command will be sent to the background for execution. This means that the command will no longer tie up your terminal and you can then proceed with other work. The standard output from the command will still be directed to your terminal; however in most cases the standard input will be dissociated from your terminal. If the command does try to read any input from standard input, it will be as if *CTRL-d* were typed.

```
$ sort data > out &        Send the sort  to the background
1258                       Process id
$ date                     Your terminal is immediately available to do other work
Thu Apr 26 17:45:09 EST  1984
$
```

When a command is sent to the background, the UNIX system automatically displays a number, called the *process id* for that command. In the above example, 1258 was the process id assigned by the system. This number uniquely identifies the command that you sent to the background, and can be used to obtain status information about the command. This is done with the `ps` command, described in detail in Chapter 12. Your are also referred to that chapter for more information about the process id.

As noted, sending a command to the background for execution is most often used for commands that require a significant amount of time to execute as it frees up your terminal for other work. However, you shouldn't abuse this feature. Having many commands executing in the background is discourteous to other users since you will be using a disproportionate amount of the computer's resources.

• Changing Your Erase Character •

As promised in Chapter 4, now you'll see how to change your erase character from # to something else. To do this, you must use the `stty` command in the following format:

```
stty echoe erase char
```

where *char* is the character you want as your character erase. Most often, you'll want this to be the BACKSPACE. In fact, if your erase character is not #, then it has probably been changed to BACKSPACE for you. Here's how simple it is to change your erase character:

```
$ stty echoe erase CTRL-h
$
```

The BACKSPACE key has been shown as *CTRL-h* since that's what the system actually "sees" when this key is pressed. Your cursor will probably move back one character when you press BACKSPACE; don't be concerned about this, the stty command will interpret things properly. After the above stty command has been executed, you can use the BACKSPACE key to erase characters. The # key will no longer erase characters—it's special meaning to the system has been removed.

Your newly-defined erase character will remain effective as long as you're logged in. However, next time you log in, it'll be # again. In the next chapter you'll see how you can have your erase character changed automatically whenever you log in.

• Command Files •

One of the most powerful features of the UNIX system is a capability that effectively enables you to define your own commands. For example, you have seen how you to easily determine the number of users currently logged into the system by simply piping the output of the who command into the input of the wc command:

```
$ who ¦ wc -1
      14
$
```

This output indicates that 14 users are currently logged in. It is quite conceivable that you might want to execute this command several times throughout the day. In order to avoid some extra typing, you can first type the above command sequence into a file called perhaps nu (for number of users):

```
$ cat > nu
who ¦ wc -1
CTRL-d
$
```

Now that you have stored this command sequence in the file nu you can simply type in nu at the terminal whenever you want to know the number of logged-in users:

```
$ nu
nu: cannot execute
$
```

Oops! We forgot to mention one thing. Before you can execute the commands contained in the nu file, you must first tell the UNIX system that this file contains commands that can be executed. This is done with the chmod (*change mode*) command. This command is described in more detail in Chapter 10. For now, simply remember its syntax and the fact that it must be used to tell the UNIX system that you have just created a file that contains commands you want to execute.

```
$ chmod +x nu
$
```

The option +x says "make the file executable." This enables you to subsequently execute the commands contained in that file by simply typing the name of the file:

```
$ nu
    14
$
```

That's better! Your newly defined "command" behaves like any other UNIX command. For example, you can redirect its output in the normal fashion:

```
$ nu > out
$ cat out
    14
$
```

The following shows a slight enhancement to the nu command:

```
$ ed nu
12
1,$n
1          who | wc -1
0a
echo Number of users logged in:
.
1,$n
1          echo Number of users logged in:
2          who | wc -1
w
44
q
$ nu
Number of users logged in:
      14
$
```

Edit the command file

Execute it

When nu is typed at the terminal, the commands inside that file are executed in turn. So the echo command is executed first, which displays the phrase Number of users logged in: at the terminal. Then the pipeline who | wc -1 is executed, which displays a count of the number of logged-in users.

You can put any commands at all inside a file, change the mode of the file to make it executable, and then use it like any other command. And as you will see in the next chapter, there even exists a special language in the UNIX system that enables you to create more sophisticated command files.

THE OLD SHELL GAME

This chapter delves into more details about the operation of the shell. It also introduces the unique shell programming language.

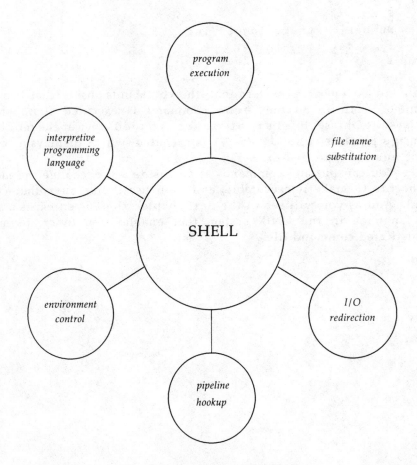

Fig. 6-1. Functions of the Shell

In Chapter 2 you learned that the shell is the UNIX system's command interpreter. But the shell actually does a lot more than just interpret commands. The functions served by the shell are depicted in Fig. 6-1.

Program execution

Just about everything you type in at the terminal is interpreted by the shell. Whenever the shell is waiting for you to type in a command, it displays your command prompt $. After you type in your command and press RETURN, the shell then proceeds to analyze the line you typed in. This line is commonly called the *command line*.

Every command that is executed under the UNIX system has the same general format, as far as the shell is concerned:

command   arguments

The shell treats the first characters on the line up to the first blank (or to the end of the line if there are none) as the name of the command to be executed. Any characters appearing after the command name are interpreted as the command's arguments (except for I/O redirection specifications—see below). Arguments are delimited by blanks. So for example, in the command

```
grep Wood phone_book
```

grep is the command and Wood and phone_book the arguments. As you saw in Chapter 5, quotes can be used to group blank-separated characters together:

```
grep "Wood, Pat" phone_book
```

Here grep also has two arguments: Wood, Pat and phone_book.
The shell is responsible for ensuring that the arguments you type in get properly "handed over" to the program being executed. It then starts execution of the program. After the program has completed execution, control goes back to the shell. At that point, your command prompt is displayed as the shell's way of telling you it is awaiting your next command.

File name substitution

If file name substitution is specified on the command line with the characters *, ?, or [...], then the shell is what performs the substitution. This happens *before* the program gets executed; the program itself never has to worry about it.

I/O redirection

If input and/or output redirection is specified on the command line, then this too is handled by the shell. On input redirection, the shell opens the file for reading and "connects" it to the standard input of the program. Once again, this happens before execution of the program begins, so the program doesn't even know (or care) that its input has been redirected. All it needs to do is read its input from standard input; the shell has taken care of the rest.

If output redirection is specified, then the shell creates the file if necessary and "connects" it to the program's standard output. If the file already exists, then the previous contents of the file are lost, unless the append characters >> are used for the redirection. Just like input redirection, the program itself never has to worry about output redirection; it just writes its output to standard output in the normal fashion.

Pipeline hookup

If the command line contains two programs connected by a pipe, as in

```
who | wc -1
```

then the shell takes responsibility for connecting the standard output of the first program to the standard input of the second. It then starts execution of both programs. As with I/O redirection, the fact that these two programs have been connected by a pipe is unbeknownst to either—the first program simply writes its output to standard output and the second program reads its input from standard input.

Environment control

The shell gives you some flexibility in customizing your "environment" to suit your needs. This environment includes the path name of your HOME directory, the directories that will be searched by the shell whenever you type the name of a program to be executed, and even the particular character that is used by the shell as your command prompt.

Interpretive programming language

The shell provides a powerful programming language. Statements in this language can be typed in directly at the terminal for execution, or they can first be entered into a file. You saw how the latter function is performed at the end of the last chapter when the concept of command files was introduced.

One of the greatest testaments to the power and flexibility of the UNIX system is the fact that the operating system is not tied to a particular command interpreter. Actually, since the shell is a program that runs under the UNIX system just like any other program, several different "flavors" of the shell have evolved. Each differs slightly in the features that it provides and in the syntax of the command language. There are currently three popular shells:

- the "Bourne shell" `sh`
- the "C shell" `csh`
- the "Korn shell" `ksh`

The first and third shells get their names from their inventors, Stephen Bourne and David Korn, respectively. The second shell was developed at the University of California at Berkeley and gets it name from its programming language, which resembles the C programming language in syntax.

The Bourne shell is the shell that is currently distributed with standard AT&T UNIX systems. The Korn shell is compatible with the Bourne shell; the C shell is not. (A good indication that you're running under the C shell is given by your command prompt. If it's a percent sign (%), then you're probably using the C shell.)

The remainder of this chapter introduces you to the command language provided in the standard Bourne shell `sh`. Since the Korn shell is compatible with the Bourne shell, everything you learn here will work with that shell as well. If you're using the C shell, then you may want to check with your system administrator to see if the standard shell `sh` is available. If it is, then you should use that shell while reading through this chapter. Then, after you've learned how to program in the standard shell, you can easily apply what you've learned to the C shell. Appendix E summarizes the main differences between the C shell and the standard shell.

· Shell Variables ·

Variable Names

As with other programming languages, the shell provides the user with the ability to define *variables* and to assign values to them. A shell variable name begins with a letter (upper or lowercase) or underscore character and optionally is followed by a sequence of letters, underscore characters or numeric characters.

```
i5
length
Input_file
HOMEDIR
_cflag
```

are examples of valid shell variable names, whereas the names

```
5i                    Cannot begin with a numeric character
.length               '.' is not a valid character
file name             Embedded spaces not permitted
```

are not for the reasons stated.

Assigning Values to Variables

Values can be assigned to shell variables by writing the variable name followed immediately by the assignment operator = followed by the value to be assigned to the variable:

```
length=80
```

This statement assigns 80 to the shell variable length. Note that embedded spaces are *not* allowed either before or after the equals sign. The shell command

```
file_name=ai.memo
```

assigns ai.memo to the shell variable file_name. When assigning a string of characters to a shell variable, it's generally a good idea to enclose the string within a pair of double quotes, as in:

```
file_name="ai.memo"
```

In fact, if the string of characters contains embedded spaces, then the quotes are *mandatory*:

```
message="The system will be shut down at 18:00 for PM"
```

You should note that unlike other programming languages, there is no "type" associated with a shell variable. Every value that you assign to a variable is simply treated as a string of characters by the shell.

Displaying the Value of a Shell Variable

Now that you know how to assign values to shell variables, let's see how you can use these variables. The first thing you will want to learn is how to access the value that is stored in a shell variable. The shell is unlike most other programming languages in this respect. To access the value stored inside a shell variable, you must immediately precede the name of the variable by a dollar sign, as in $length or $file_name.

To display the value that has been assigned to a shell variable at the terminal, use the echo command. So to assign 80 to the shell variable length and then display its value using the echo command, the following sequence could be used:

```
$ length=80
$ echo $length
80
$
```

The first command assigns the value 80 to the shell variable length. In the next line, the echo command displays the value of this variable. This same technique is used in the next example.

```
$ message="System shutdown in 5 minutes."
$ echo $message
System shutdown in 5 minutes.
$
```

Whenever the shell encounters a dollar sign followed by a variable name, the value of that variable gets substituted at that precise point by the shell. This explains the output from the following sequence of commands.

```
$ length=80
$ echo The length is $length
The length is 80
$
```

Let's see what happens if you try to display a shell variable that was never assigned a value:

```
$ echo $noval

$ echo :$noval:
::
$
```

The last echo demonstrates that an unassigned variable has *no* value. In shell programming terminology, this is known as the *null* value.

Using Shell Variables

Shell variables are frequently used as command arguments:

```
$ file="ai.memo"
$ wc -l $file
     115 ai.memo
$
```

First the string ai.memo is assigned to the shell variable file. Then the wc command is executed. The file name argument to the command is given by the *value* of the shell variable file. Since you assigned the string ai.memo to this variable, the number of lines contained in the file ai.memo is counted and displayed at the terminal, exactly as if the command

```
wc -l ai.memo
```

had been typed in instead. The following provides a further extension to the previous example.

```
$ option="-l"
$ file="ai.memo"
$ wc $option $file
     115 ai.memo
$
```

As a final example along the same lines, consider the following:

```
$ command="wc"
$ option="-l"
$ file="ai.memo"
$ $command $option $file
     115 ai.memo
$
```

The value of a shell variable can be assigned to another shell variable in the expected fashion:

```
$ file="ai.memo"                 Assign ai.memo to file
$ save_file=$file                Assign value of file to save_file
$ echo $save_file                Display the value of save_file
ai.memo
$
```

A shell variable should almost always be preceded by a dollar sign, except if it appears on the left side of an equals sign.

```
$ file="ai.memo"
$ option="-1"
$ command="wc $option $file"
$ echo $command                  Display the contents of command
wc -1 ai.memo
$ $command                       Execute the contents of command
     115 ai.memo
$
```

Another common use for shell variables is for assigning symbolic names to directory paths. For example, recall the directory structure from previous chapters:

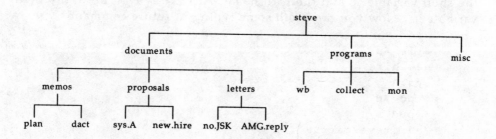

Fig. 6-2. Directory structure

Suppose you had to do a lot of work between two directories, such as between the misc directory and the proposals directory. Your command sequence might include the following types of commands:

```
$ cd /a1/steve/documents/proposals
$ cp sys.A /a1/steve/misc/sys.A_save
$ ls /a1/steve/misc
       .
       .
       .

$ cd /a1/steve/misc
       .
       .
       .
```

Even using relative path names, the typing can get a little tedious when performing operations between directories, such as moving or copying files or simply switching between them.

You can assign path names to shell variables and then use them in subsequent commands to help reduce typing. For example, in

```
$ p=/a1/steve/documents/proposals
$ m=/a1/steve/misc
$
```

the path name /a1/steve/documents/proposals is assigned to the shell variable p and the path name /a1/steve/misc to the shell variable m. Now you can avoid some typing in future commands:

```
$ ls $p
new.hire
sys.A
$ cd $m
$ pwd
/a1/steve/misc
$
```

The next example shows how easily you can move or copy a file between the two directories:

```
$ cp $p/sys.A $m
$ ls $m
sys.A
$
```

It's generally a good idea to use more meaningful variable names than those shown. This is particularly important when writing command files. Meaningful variable names will help make your shell programs more understandable—to both you and others.

▪ The `for` Statement ▪

All programming languages provide mechanisms that enable you to execute repeatedly a group of statements. The shell is no exception, as it provides two such language statements: the `for` and the `while`. This section discusses the `for`, the more widely used of the two. The `while` is discussed later.

The general format of the `for` statement in the shell is:

```
for   variable   in   list
do
        command
        command
        command
        ...
done
```

variable is any shell variable that you choose. It is listed *without* a leading dollar sign. The number of items specified in *list* determines the number of times the *command*s enclosed between the `do` and `done` will be executed. Each time the loop is executed, the next value in *list* is assigned to *variable*.

As an example of the `for`, consider the following:

```
for index in 1 2 3 4 5
do
        echo $index
done
```

In this example, *list* consists of the five values 1, 2, 3, 4, and 5. Therefore, the loop will be executed a total of five times. Each time through the loop, the next value in *list* will be assigned to the shell variable `index`. The "body" of the loop consists of the single command `echo $index`, which has been indented to visually identify it as belonging to the loop.

Let's see what happens if you actually type this `for` loop in at the terminal:

```
$ for index in 1 2 3 4 5
> do
>         echo $index
> done
1
2
3
4
5
$
```

You probably noticed that the prompt changed from `$` to `>` after the first line of the `for` was typed. This is the shell's way of telling you that it is expecting more input. The `>` continues to be displayed by the shell until you type `done`, thus closing the `for` statement. At that point, the shell proceeds to execute the loop.

Execution of the `for` begins with `index` getting assigned the first value in the list: 1. The body of the loop—the `echo` command— is then executed. This results in the display of the value of `index`— 1—at the terminal.

After the `echo` command has been executed, the next value in the list, 2, gets assigned to `index`. The `echo` command is once again executed to display the value of `index` at the terminal, and execution of the loop then continues. The last time through the loop, the value 5 gets assigned to `index`, the `echo` command displays its value at the terminal, and then the loop terminates. At that point the normal `$` command prompt is displayed by the shell.

One of the real uses of the `for` is to apply a command or series of commands to a group of files. Let's assume you have files `names`, `names1`, and `names2` in your current directory and that their contents are as illustrated on pages 74-75.

```
$ ls name*
names
names1
names2
$
```

The following example shows that any values at all can form the *list* in a `for`:

```
$ for file in names names1 names2
> do
>     echo $file
> done
names
```

```
names1
names2
$
```

The next example shows how file name substitution can be used in the list specification:

```
$ for file in name*
> do
>     echo $file
> done
names
names1
names2
$
```

Even though there appears to be only one item in the list, the shell sees the * in name* and expands it into names, names1, and names2. This is verified by the output of the echo commands.

In the following example, the contents of the files names, names1 and names2, are separately sorted:

```
$ for file in name*
> do
>     sort $file
> done
Bill
Pat
Ruth
Tony
Bill
John
Pat
Ruth
Tom
Tony
John
Pat
Ruth
Tom
Tony
$
```

Well, you got the results you wanted, but it's not very readable! The following is certainly an improvement:

```
$ for file in name*
> do
>       echo "========================================="
>       echo "          Sorted contents of $file"
>       echo "========================================="
>       sort $file
>       echo
> done
=========================================
      Sorted contents of names
=========================================
Bill
Pat
Ruth
Tony


=========================================
      Sorted contents of names1
=========================================
Bill
John
Pat
Ruth
Tom
Tony


=========================================
      Sorted contents of names2
=========================================
John
Pat
Ruth
Tom
Tony

$
```

That's more like it. The purpose of the echo that was typed after the
sort is simply to insert a blank line in the display. As you will recall,
this is the effect of executing an echo with no arguments.

· All about Quotes ·

The shell is a unique programming language with respect to the way quote signs work. The shell interprets four different characters on your keyboard as "quote characters":

- the double quote mark "
- the single quote mark '
- the backslash character mark \
- the single *back* quote mark `

Each of these quote marks has a special and *different* meaning to the shell. Understanding the distinctions between them is important.

The Double Quote Mark

Suppose your current directory contained the following files:

```
$ ls
documents
misc
programs
$
```

Now consider the output from the following two `echo` commands:

```
$ echo *
documents misc programs
$ echo "*"
*
$
```

In the first case, the shell substituted * with the names of all of the files in the directory. In the second case, no substitution occurred. Obviously, the double quotes had something to do with this. The fact of the matter is that if the shell sees a pair of double quote marks, then *no file name substitution will occur between the pair of double quotes.*

The following example implies that an even greater generalization can be made:

```
$ echo >
syntax error: `newline or ;' unexpected
$ echo ">"
>
$
```

In the first echo, the shell thought you were redirecting the output from echo and looked for a file name to follow. Since none was specified, the (rather cryptic) error message was generated. In the second case, the double quote marks surrounding the > had the effect of *removing the special meaning of the character to the shell.*

This is the key behind the double quotes: any character that is otherwise special to the shell (such as *, ?, >, <, >>, and ¦) loses its special meaning when it appears between a pair of quote marks. The *exceptions* to this rule are the dollar sign $, the back quote `, and the *backslash* \ (but only if the backslash precedes a $, ", `, or another \; otherwise it *does* lose its special meaning to the shell).

Double quotes also preserve *white-space* characters by removing their special meaning to the shell. These characters are blank spaces, tab characters, and newline characters. You saw double quotes used for this purpose in Chapter 5 when the grep command was taught:

```
$ grep "Wood, Pat" phone_book
```

Without the quotes around "Wood, Pat," the shell thinks that Wood, is the first argument to grep, Pat is the second argument, and phone_book is the third argument. With the quotes, grep sees "Wood, Pat" as the first argument because the special meaning of the space (that is, as argument separator) is removed from the shell.

The Single Quote Mark

Study the output in the following:

```
$ message="hello there"
$ echo $message
hello there
$ echo "$message"
hello there
$
```

In both cases, the value of the shell variable message—hello there—was echoed at the terminal. This is because the shell does substitute the value of shell variables *inside* double quotes. Now look at the following:

```
$ echo '$message'
$message
$
```

As you can see, when a shell variable is enclosed within *single* quote marks, its value is not substituted by the shell. Furthermore, the following example shows that special shell characters enclosed within single quotes also get ignored:

```
$ echo '< > * ? >> ¦'
< > * ? >> ¦
$
```

The shell does not process any characters enclosed within single quotes; that is, they are guaranteed to remain unchanged. Study the following output very carefully to see the subtle differences between no quotes, double quotes, and single quotes.

```
$ echo *
names names1 names2
$ echo * "*" '*'
names names1 names2 * *
$ var=hello
$ echo $var "$var" '$var'
hello hello $var
$
```

The Backslash Character

In Chapter 5 you learned that to enter a special character such as # into a text file using ed it is necessary to precede the character by a backslash \. Preceding any character by a backslash removes the special meaning of that character to the shell. The shell actually treats a character after the \ just as if the character were enclosed in a pair of single quotes. In other words, \ followed by any character *c* is identical to '*c*'. Here are some examples:

```
$ echo \$foo                    Don't treat the $ specially
$foo
$ echo \< \> \" \' \` \$ \¦ \* \?
< > " ' ` $ ¦ * ?
$ echo \\
\
$
```

The last example shows that even a backslash can be preceded by a backslash to remove its special meaning.

The Back Quote Mark

One of the most unusual features of the shell is the way it handles back quote marks. Enclosing a command inside a pair of back quotes causes the command to be executed and its output to be inserted at that precise point. For example, consider the following:

```
$ echo The date is `date`
The date is Sun Mar 11 13:27:33 EST 1984
$
```

When the shell processes the command line, it notices the back quote marks. The shell then proceeds to execute whatever is enclosed between these quotes: the date command. The output from date, Sun Mar 11 13:27:33 EST 1984, is then substituted by the shell at that point on the command line and the echo command is then executed. echo isn't even aware that any of this is happening. In fact, echo sees as its arguments the following characters: The date is Sun Mar 11 13:27:33 EST 1984.

Let's take a look at another example:

```
$ echo Your current working directory is `pwd`
Your current working directory is /a1/steve/programs
$
```

In this case, the pwd command was executed and its output inserted in the command line. To be more precise, it was the standard output of pwd that was inserted by the shell.

You can even have a pipeline executed in this fashion. The entire pipeline must be enclosed inside the back quotes. The following shows a one-line version of the nu program:

```
$ echo There are `who | wc -l` users logged in.
There are 5 users logged in.
$
```

One very powerful feature of the back quote mechanism is the ability to assign the output from a command to a shell variable:

```
$ now=`date`
$ echo $now
Sun Mar 11 13:34:20 EST 1984
$
```

In the first line, the `date` command is executed and its output assigned to the shell variable `now`. In the next line, the value of `now` is displayed. Look at another example:

```
$ users=`who | wc -1`
$ echo There are $users users logged in.
There are 5 users logged in.
$
```

The result of the pipeline `who | wc -1` is assigned to the variable `users` in the first line, and the value of `users` is subsequently displayed with an `echo` command.

Can you explain the output from the following?

```
$ cat names
Pat
Tony
Ruth
Bill
$ list=`cat names`
$ echo $list
Pat Tony Ruth Bill
$
```

The output from `echo` appears on one line because the shell "got to" the newline characters in `list` before `echo` had a chance to see them. Recall that the shell "gobbles" up multiple spaces, newlines and tabs. In order to preserve the newline characters inside `list`, you must enclose `list` inside double quotes (why not single quotes?) so that `echo` can see them:

```
$ echo "$list"
Pat
Tony
Ruth
Bill
$
```

Back-quoted commands can be inserted just about anywhere. For example, here one is used to form the list in a shell `for` statement:

```
$ for name in `cat names`
> do
>     echo Hello, $name
> done
Hello, Pat
Hello, Tony
Hello, Ruth
Hello, Bill
$
```

The following table summarizes the different quoting mechanisms in the shell.

TABLE 6-1. Quote characters

Character	Meaning
"	Removes special meaning of ´, <, >, #, *, ?, &, ¦, ;, (,), [,], ^, blank spaces, newlines, and tabs; $, `, and \ are interpreted (*see* \ *below*)
´	Same as " except also removes special meaning of $, `, and \
\	Removes special meaning of character that follows; inside double quotes, removes special meaning of $, ", `, and \ (but is otherwise not interpreted)
`	Causes enclosed command to be executed and its output inserted at that point

Don't worry if this discussion of quotes seems a bit complicated, because it is! Even experienced UNIX users still have difficulty getting their quotes straight at times. It's only to be expected that you'll experience the same difficulties.

• More on echo •

As of UNIX System III, the echo command gives special meaning to certain characters that are preceded by a backslash \. These characters give you more flexibility and control in your output displays and therefore are quite useful. A complete list of these characters is provided in Section 1 of your *UNIX User's Manual*. Here, three of the most often used characters are discussed.

Moving to the Next Line: \n

If the echo command sees a backslash character followed immediately by the letter n, then at that point a new line will be displayed; that is, the cursor will go to the beginning of the next line. The following examples will help make this point clear. One word of caution before you proceed: in order to remove the special meaning to the shell of the backslash character, any of these special echo characters *must* be quoted (either single or double quotes will do).

```
$ echo "one\ntwo\nthree"
one
two
three
$ echo this is what happens\nif you forget the quotes
this is what happensnif you forget the quotes
$ echo 'skip a\n\nline'
skip a

line
$
```

In the last example, the first \n causes the cursor to move to the beginning of the next line, and the second one causes it to go down another line. The net effect is to insert a blank line between skip a and line.

Staying on the Same Line: \c

Normally, after echo displays its last argument it goes to the beginning of the next line. This is usually what you want. However, suppose you wanted to display one part of a message and then later in the program display another part of the message *on the same line*. Or, as you'll see later, suppose you wanted to display a message and then have the user enter some data right after that message on the same line.

If you tack the characters \c to the end of an echo command, then echo will *not* automatically go to the beginning of the next line; instead, it will stay right where it is. Once again, some examples will help you understand:

```
$ echo "stay on this line\c"
stay on this line$
```

The \c causes the echo command to suppress the newline. Therefore, the shell's prompt was printed right after the last character displayed by echo.

Type the following commands into a file called `testx`:

```
echo "one\c"
echo "two\c"
echo "three"
```

Now change the mode on the file so that it can be executed and then run it.

```
$ chmod +x testx
$ testx
onetwothree
$
```

As a final example, type the lines

```
for i in 0 1 2 3 4 5 6 7 8 9
do
      echo "$i\c"
done

echo
```

into a file called `test2` and then execute it:

```
$ chmod +x test2
$ test2
0123456789
$
```

The string `$i\c` was enclosed in double quotes rather than single quotes so that the value of the shell variable `i` would be substituted by the shell. (Of course, `$i"\c"` or `$i'\c'` could have been used instead.)

The purpose of the last `echo` is simply to go to the next line. If it hadn't been included, then the shell's prompt, `$`, would have appeared right after the `9`.

If you are running Berkeley UNIX, or a release of the UNIX system prior to System III, then `echo` can be given the option `-n` to achieve the same result as the `\c` (e.g.,

```
echo -n "stay on this line"
```

).

Moving to the Next Tab Stop: \t

Try pressing the key labeled TAB at your terminal and see what happens. (If your terminal doesn't have this key, simultaneously type CTRL and I instead.) If your terminal is like most others, then each time you press this key, the cursor will move across the screen. On most terminals, the cursor moves over eight character positions each time the TAB key is pressed. The "first" tab position is column 1, the second column 9, the third column 17 and so on. Tabs are useful for aligning data in columnar format. You can move to the *next* tab position on the line in an echo command by using the characters \t:

```
$ echo "1\t2\t3\t4\t5"
1       2       3       4       5
$
```

As mentioned, tabs are useful for aligning data. Type the following lines into the file inventory:

```
echo
echo "Item\tNumber"
echo "----\t------"
echo "Widgets\t1,020"
echo "Pipes\t5,730"
echo "Filters\t3,097"
echo "Tees\t2,912"
echo
```

and then execute it:

```
$ chmod +x inventory
$ inventory

Item    Number
----    ------
Widgets 1,020
Pipes   5,730
Filters 3,097
Tees    2,912

$
```

I think you get the idea of how the tab character works. The phone book shown on page 61 was created with tab characters so that the phone numbers all lined up. Each name and number is separated by two tab characters.

If your echo command does not support the \t characters, or if you don't want to use this feature, then you can just type the tabs directly (inside quotes, of course).

• Passing Arguments to Shell Programs •

Arguments greatly increase the flexibility and usefulness of any program. You can have your shell programs take arguments the same way other UNIX commands take them. When the program is executed, you simply list the arguments on the command line in the normal fashion:

```
add Pennino 985-0987
```

This indicates to the shell that the program add is to be executed and that it has two arguments: Pennino and 985-0987. To reference arguments from inside a shell program, the notation

$$\$i$$

is used, where i is an integer from 1 through 9 that identifies the first through ninth arguments, respectively. So typing the line

```
add Pennino 985-0987
```

would cause the add program to be executed with the arguments Pennino and 985-0987 assigned to $1 and $2 respectively. The add program would treat these arguments like any other shell variables. For instance, to display the value of the second argument (985-0987) the following line might appear inside add:

```
echo $2
```

To search the file phone_book for the occurrence of the first argument (Pennino), this line might appear inside add:

```
grep $1 phone_book
```

Suppose you type the following shell program into a file called arg1:

```
# shell command file to display argument 1

echo "Argument one is :$1:"
```

The first line is known as a *comment* and its sole purpose is to document

the purpose of this shell program.[†] Whenever the shell encounters a #
character, it simply ignores the remainder of the line; therefore, you can
type whatever you please. (Recall that to enter the # character into a
file using ed you must first enter a \ so that the # is not interpreted
as a character erase.)

```
$ ed arg1
?
a
\#  shell command file to display argument 1

echo "Argument one is :$1:"
.
w
73
q
$
```

Remember what has to be done before you can execute the commands contained in arg1?

```
$ chmod +x arg1
$
```

That's right! You have to explicitly tell the UNIX system that this file
contains commands to be executed. Now let's experiment with this file
to see exactly what the shell considers to be the first argument.

```
$ arg1 abc
Argument one is :abc:
$
```

The colons were placed around the display of $1 in arg1 to see pre-
cisely what characters are included. For example:

```
$ arg1
Argument one is ::
$
```

If no argument is supplied, then the value of $1 is null.

```
$ arg1 one two three
Argument one is :one:
$
```

---

† This feature is not supported in UNIX Version 7.

The shell always delimits arguments by blank spaces. Therefore, only one is assigned to $1. As is the case with standard UNIX commands, if you want to include blanks in an argument, then it must be surrounded by a pair of quotes (either single or double):

```
$ arg1 "one two three"
Argument one is :one two three:
$
```

You can even assign just blanks to an argument, as long as they are quoted:

```
$ arg1 "    "
Argument one is :    :
$
```

Again, as with standard UNIX commands, file name substitution can be used:

```
$ ls
arg1
collect
mon
nu
wb
$ arg1 c*
Argument one is :collect:
$ arg1 ??
Argument one is :nu:
$
```

In the last example, ?? gets expanded to the names of all files that are exactly two characters long: nu and wb. Since the shell separates these by a blank, only the first name in the list, nu, gets assigned to $1.

Now let's see a practical use of a shell program that takes an argument. Recall the phone directory file called phone_book:

```
$ cat phone_book
Fenson, Eitan          445-4343
Iannino, Tony          937-1232
Levy, Steven           (907) 843-4432
Musa, John             864-5378
Salmon, Ruth           343-2109
Skala, George          723-2205
Swingle, Babs          331-9974
```

```
Weather info              976-1212
Wood, Pat                 385-3193
Wood, Tom                 778-3321
$
```

You saw how the grep command could be used to look up an entry in
this file:

```
$ grep "Iannino, Tony" phone_book
Iannino, Tony             937-1232
$
```

Here's a simple shell program that takes a name as its argument and
does a lookup of the name inside the file phone_book:

```
# lookup a person's phone number

grep "$1" phone_book
```

The quotes around $1 are needed so that grep sees a name with
embedded blanks as a single argument.

   If you type these lines into a file called lu (for lookup) and
change the mode on the file to make it executable, then the following
would depict typical operation of the program:

```
$ lu "Iannino, Tony"
Iannino, Tony             937-1232
$ lu "Maggio, Rick"
$
```

The last example shows what happens when a name isn't found in the
phone book: you just get back your command prompt.

   Now that you have a shell program to look up someone's
number, it might be nice also to have a program to add a new entry to
the phone book, as well as one to remove an entry from the phone book.
Call the former program add and the latter rem. The add program
will be developed in the text; it's left as exercise for you to write the
rem program (hint: read the description of sed at the end of this
chapter).

   Before proceeding, it might be a good idea to make a separate
directory for the phone book file and its associated programs. Call the
directory phone and create it at the same level as the documents,
programs, and misc directories (refer to Fig. 6-2):

```
$ cd                                        Return to HOME directory
$ mkdir phone                               Make the new directory
$ mv misc/phone_book misc/lu phone          Move the two files in
$ cd phone                                  Change to the new directory
$ ls                                        and take a look
lu
phone_book
$
```

After executing this sequence of commands, the directory structure will appear as shown in Fig. 6-3:

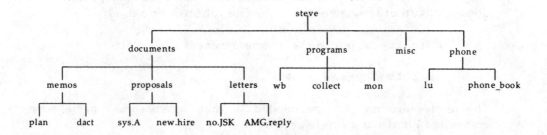

Fig. 6-3. Directory structure with the new phone directory

Now that your files are better organized, let's develop the add program. The program should be straightforward enough. You can have it take two arguments: the name and the number to be added. These two arguments can then simply be appended to the end of the phone_book file:

```
#
# add a name and number to the phone book
#

echo "$1\t\t$2" >> phone_book
echo "$1 has been added to the phone book."
```

Type the above shell program into the file add, change its mode, and execute it:

```
$ add "Gunderman, Dick" 867-5394
Gunderman, Dick has been added to the phone book.
$ lu Gunderman
Gunderman, Dick          867-5394
$
```

It seems to be working just fine. Let's take a closer look at the new phone_book file:

```
$ cat phone_book
Fenson, Eitan           445-4343
Iannino, Tony           937-1232
Levy, Steven            (907) 843-4432
Musa, John              864-5378
Salmon, Ruth            343-2109
Skala, George           723-2205
Swingle, Babs           331-9974
Weather info            976-1212
Wood, Pat               385-3193
Wood, Tom               778-3321
Gunderman, Dick         867-5394
$
```

Gunderman was added to the end of the file, as we intended. However, you'll notice that the file is no longer in alphabetical order. This isn't necessarily a problem, but you could modify your add program to sort the phone book after adding a new entry. This change is shown next:

```
#
#   add a name and number to the phone book
#

echo "$1\t\t$2" >> phone_book        # add name and number
sort phone_book > temp               # sort the phone book
mv temp phone_book                   # replace the old one
echo "$1 has been added to the phone book."
```

You can't have the output of the sort go directly to phone_book using a statement such as

```
sort phone_book > phone_book
```

because of the way output redirection works. If the designated file already exists, then any previous contents get destroyed. So the shell would first "zero out" the phone_book file and then execute the sort.   sort would then try to sort phone_book, which would not contain any information. The net result of the entire operation would be a phone_book file that did not contain any data. This explains why you must have the output of sort go to a "temporary" file first. After the sort is finished, we then change the name of the temporary file temp to phone_book.

Let's see what happens when you add another entry to the phone book:

```
$ add "Benson, Harry" 338-7776
Benson, Harry has been added to the phone book.
$ cat phone_book
Benson, Harry          338-7776
Fenson, Eitan          445-4343
Gunderman, Dick        867-5394
Iannino, Tony          937-1232
Levy, Steven           (907) 843-4432
Musa, John             864-5378
Salmon, Ruth           343-2109
Skala, George          723-2205
Swingle, Babs          331-9974
Weather info           976-1212
Wood, Pat              385-3193
Wood, Tom              778-3321
$
```

$# and $*

The shell has two "variables" that are automatically set whenever you execute a shell program. The first one is $# and it is set to the *number* of arguments that were passed to the program. The second one is $* and it is set to *all* of the arguments that were passed.

To see how $# gets set, type the following into a file called num and make it executable:

```
echo Number of arguments is $#.
```

Now let's experiment:

```
$ num one
Number of arguments is 1.
$ num one two three
Number of arguments is 3.
$ num "one two three"
Number of arguments is 1.
$ num
Number of arguments is 0.
$
```

So you see that $# tells you the number of arguments that were passed to the program. This information is useful when you write a shell program that expects a precise number of arguments. You'll see shortly how you can test the value of this variable to see if the correct number were supplied to the program.

Now it's time to turn your attention to $*. As you'll recall, this variable contains the *entire* list of arguments passed to a program.

Edit the num program and add the following line at the end:

```
echo They are :$*:
```

So the file num should now look like this:

```
echo Number of arguments is $#.
echo They are :$*:
```

Let's try it out:

```
$ num one
Number of arguments is 1.
They are :one:
$ num one two three
Number of arguments is 3.
They are :one two three:
$ num "one two three"
Number of arguments is 1.
They are :one two three:
$ num
Number of arguments is 0.
They are ::
$ num *
Number of arguments is 5.
They are :arg1 collect mon nu wb:
$ num ??
Number of arguments is 2.
They are :nu wb:
$
```

$* is useful in shell programs that take a variable number of arguments. In such programs it's not unusual to see $* used as the list specification in a for statement, for instance, to sequence through each of the arguments. As an example, the following shell program takes a variable number of file arguments. Each argument is the name of a file that is to be sorted, preceded by an appropriate heading:

```
#
#  shell program to sort some files
#

for file in $*
do
        echo "========================================="
        echo "         Sorted contents of $file"
        echo "========================================="
        sort $file
        echo
done
```

If you type this program into a file called sortf, then the following shows the types of results you might get from executing the program:

```
$ sortf names
=========================================
         Sorted contents of names
=========================================
Bill
Pat
Ruth
Tony

$ sortf name*
=========================================
         Sorted contents of names
=========================================
Bill
Pat
Ruth
Tony


=========================================
         Sorted contents of names1
=========================================
Bill
John
Pat
Ruth
Tom
Tony
```

```
==========================================
        Sorted contents of names2
==========================================
John
Pat
Ruth
Tom
Tony

$ sortf
$
```

The last example shows what happens when no arguments are supplied. In that case, the value of $*$ is *null*, so the `for` statement inside `sortf` has an "empty" list. The shell simply ignores the entire `for` statement if the list is empty, thus explaining the output.

• The `if` Statement •

Every programming language provides at least one statement that lets you conditionally perform some actions based on the results of a question. In the shell, the `if` statement performs this function. The general format of the `if` is:

```
if condition
then
        command
        command
        ...
fi
```

If the value of *condition* is valid or *TRUE*, then the commands enclosed between the `then` and the `fi` will be executed; otherwise they will be skipped. *condition* might be a test to determine if a shell variable has a particular value or if a certain file exists, for example. These tests are enclosed inside a pair of brackets. So the general format is

[*test-expression*]

As an example, the following command sequence will display the message `Hello, steve` if the value of the variable `user` is equal to `steve` (assume here that it *is*):

```
$ if [ $user = steve ]
> then
>       echo Hello, steve
> fi
Hello, steve
$
```

The *condition,* [$user = steve], (and note that the blanks after the [, around the = and before the] are all required) tests if the shell variable user is equal to the character string steve. If it is, then the echo command is executed; otherwise, it is ignored.

There are other *relational operators* that you can use besides the equality operator =. The more commonly used operators are summarized in Table 6-2.

TABLE 6-2. Summary of relational operators

Operator	Used to test if	Example
=	two strings are equal	"$user" = steve
!=	two strings are not equal	"$group" != GP
-n	a string has nonzero length	-n "$file"
-z	a string has zero length	-z "$name"
-eq	two integers are equal	"$count" -eq 10
-ne	two integers are not equal	"$line" -ne 0
-lt	one integer is less than another	"$i" -lt 100
-le	one integer is less than or equal to another	"$i1" -le "$i2"
-gt	one integer is greater than another	"$count" -gt 0
-ge	one integer is greater than or equal to another	"$a" -ge "$b"
-f	a file is an ordinary file	-f data_file
-d	a file is a directory	-d "$DATADIR"
-s	a file has nonzero length	-s grepout

In addition, an expression can be joined with either the *and* operator -a or the *or* operator -o. So the expression

```
[ $i -gt 5  -a  $i -le 100 ]
```

will be *TRUE* only if the value of the shell variable i is greater than 5 *and* less than or equal to 100. The expression

```
[ $env = UNIX  -o  $group = GP ]
```

will be *TRUE* if the shell variable env equals UNIX *or* the variable group equals GP.

(There are also other operators that have not been described here. For more information, look under the program test in Section 1 of your *UNIX User's Manual*.)

In general, you should enclose shell variables used on either side of a relational operator within a pair of double quotes. Otherwise, in most cases the shell will issue an error message if the variable is null or contains blanks:

```
$ user=""                        Intentionally set user null
$ if [ $user != steve ]
> then
>     echo I was expecting steve
> fi
test: argument expected
$
```

Executing an if statement directly from the terminal is usually quite useless. However, this statement is very useful inside command files.

The else Clause

The shell provides an else clause to the if that can be used to cause execution of statements to occur if the specified test proves *FALSE*. The general format of the if-else is:

```
if condition
then
        command
        command
        . . .
else
        command
        command
        . . .
fi
```

If the result of *condition* is *TRUE*, then the commands enclosed between the then and else get executed; otherwise, the statements between the else and fi get executed. In either case, only one set of commands get executed, never both.

As an example of the use of the else and also of the $# variable, let's modify the lookup program lu to include a test to ensure that exactly one argument is supplied on the command line:

```
# lookup a person's phone number in the phone book

if [ $# -ne 1 ]
then
        echo "\nUsage: lu name\n"
else
        grep "$1" phone_book
fi
```

If the number of arguments does not equal 1, then the echo command displays the proper command usage to the user; otherwise the grep gets executed to search phone_book for the specified name.

```
$ lu

Usage: lu name

$ lu Iannino, Tony

Usage: lu name

$ lu "Iannino, Tony"
Iannino, Tony              937-1232
$ lu "Maggio"
$
```

The last example reminds you that the program doesn't display anything if a name is not found in the phone book. It might be nice to change the program to display a message if it couldn't find someone's name.

You know that grep simply produces no output when it doesn't find any lines that match the given pattern. Using this fact and the back quoting mechanism, you can assign the output of the grep to a shell variable and then test the variable to see if it is null (i.e., has zero length) or not. If it is null, then you know that grep couldn't find the name in the file. In that case, you can display a message to this effect at the terminal. If it isn't null, then the variable will contain the result of the grep; so you can simply display its value at the terminal.

Here's the (once again) modified lu program:

```
# lookup a person's phone number in the phone book

if [ $# -ne 1 ]
then
      echo "\nUsage: lu name\n"
else
      output=`grep "$1" phone_book`

      if [ -z "$output" ]
      then
            echo "I couldn't find $1 in the phone book"
      else
            echo "$output"
      fi
fi
```

It's perfectly valid to include ifs inside other ifs. In fact, the nesting can go as deep as you like. Just remember that for each if you must include a corresponding fi.

```
$ lu Salmon
Salmon, Ruth              343-2109
$ lu Archer
I couldn't find Archer in the phone book
$ lu Wood
Wood, Pat                 385-3193
Wood, Tom                 778-3321
$
```

The output from the last example explains why you had to include $output inside double quotes in the echo command of the program. Had you not done so, then the shell would have removed the newline character from output before being passed as an argument to echo, thus resulting in the display of the two Wood entries on the same line.

The elif Construct

Suppose you wanted to create a shell program that displayed the salutation "Good morning." if it's anytime after midnight but before noon; the phrase "Good afternoon." if it's from noon to 6 P.M.; and the phrase "Good evening." if it's anytime from 6 P.M. to midnight.

If you think about writing a shell program to perform this task, you will realize that its structure should look something like this:

```
if    it's after midnight and before noon
then
        display Good morning.
else
        if  it's after noon and before 6 PM
        then
                display Good afternoon.
        else
                display Good evening.
        fi
fi
```

You can directly translate the above into a shell program. First you have to figure out how to make the tests on the time of day. Well, you know that the date command gives you the time (plus some other information):

```
$ date
Sun Mar 18 13:43:00 EST 1984
$
```

For this program, all you really need to know is the hour of the day. You can use the cut command to get the hour of the day out of date given the fact that the hour always appears in columns 12-13 of date's output:

```
$ date ¦ cut -c12-13
13
$
```

Now that you have this technique, you can write the program. Before proceeding, however, let's introduce the elif construct. As the name implies, this construct is actually a marriage of the else and if. Its general format is:

```
if condition
then
    command
    command
    . . .
elif condition
then
    command
    command
    . . .
fi
```

You can include as many `elifs` as you need. At the end of it all you can place an `else` so that a set of commands can be executed if none of the preceding test expressions is *TRUE*. Now here is a shell program to print the salutation. Call the program `salute`:

```
#
# shell program to execute date and then display
# Good morning, Good afternoon, or Good evening, as
# appropriate
#

hour=`date | cut -c12-13`

if [ $hour -ge 0  -a  $hour -1t 12 ]
then
      echo "Good morning."
elif [ $hour -ge 12  -a  $hour -1t  18 ]
then
      echo "Good afternoon."
else
      echo "Good evening."
fi
```

Let's see if it works for the present time:

```
$ date
Sun Mar 18 13:59:11 EST 1984          We know it's afternoon
$ salute
Good afternoon.                        Seems okay
$
```

• Arithmetic Operations with Shell Variables •

The standard shell does not provide any built-in mechanisms to enable you to perform arithmetic operations on shell variables. You may think this quite unusual for a programming language. It is unusual; but then, no one ever claimed that the shell was your usual programming language!

Suppose you had a shell variable called `count` and you set it equal to 0 with the statement:

```
count=0
```

If you attempted to add 1 to count, this is what you'd get:

```
$ count=$count+1
$ echo $count
0 + 1
$
```

Once again, the shell doesn't know how to add 1 to a variable in the manner akin to most programming languages. All is not lost, however, as there is a program called expr that is used by UNIX shell programmers to evaluate expressions in shell programs. Let's experiment with this program:

```
$ expr 1 + 2
3
$ expr 5 "*" 10
50
$ expr 1+2
1+2
$ count=100
$ expr $count + 1
101
$
```

The expr program evaluates the expression given by its arguments and writes the result to standard output. In the first case, expr is given three arguments, 1, +, and 2. The result of the addition, 3, is then displayed.

In the second example the * operator—used to multiply two integers—*must* be quoted to prevent the shell from substituting the names of all of the files in the current directory on the command line. You could not place quotes around the entire expression, as in

```
expr "5 * 10"
```

since this would only be seen by expr as *one* argument and not three. (Try it and see what happens.)

The third example shows that expr does not interpret

```
1+2
```

as you might expect. This has to do with the same point made in the previous sentence: expr expects to see each term and operator as separate arguments.

The fact that `expr` writes its result to standard output is the key to performing arithmetic operations in the shell. By using the back-quote mechanism, you can assign `expr`'s result to a shell variable:

```
$ result=`expr 1 + 2`
$ echo $result
3
$
```

And the following shows how you can use `expr` to add 1 to a shell variable:

```
$ count=100
$ count=`expr $count + 1`          Add 1 to count
$ echo $count
101
$
```

You should note that the Korn shell `ksh` *does* provide built-in integer arithmetic operations.

▪ The `while` Statement ▪

The `while` is another looping statement provided by the shell. It enables you to repeatedly execute a set of commands *while* a specified condition is *TRUE*. The format of the `while` is:

```
while condition
do
        command
        command
        ...
done
```

The *condition* part is the same as it is for the `if` statement. It is tested first when the `while` loop starts. If it is *TRUE*, then the commands enclosed between the `do` and `done` are executed. Each time after the commands are executed, *condition* is again tested. The commands enclosed between the `do` and `done` will continue to be executed until *condition* proves *FALSE*. At that time, the `while` loop will be terminated.

The following illustrates use of the `while` and also the method that was outlined for performing arithmetic with shell variables.

```
$ count=1
$ while [ "$count" -le 10 ]
> do
>      echo $count
>      count=`expr $count + 1`
> done
1
2
3
4
5
6
7
8
9
10
$
```

Before leaving this brief discussion of the `while` statement, you should note that the shell also provides a statement called `until` that is very similar in operation to the `while`. Consult your UNIX documentation for more details.

· Reading Data from the Terminal ·

When writing shell programs you may come across the need to have the user enter some data from the terminal. The shell statement `read` exists for this purpose. Its general format is simple enough:

read variable-list

Execution of this statement causes the shell to read in a line from the terminal and assign the values read to the shell variables specified in *variable-list*. If only one variable is listed, then the entire line is assigned to that variable. Values typed in are delimited by blanks or tabs. Let's experiment with `read` at the terminal:

```
$ read a b c
one two    three
$ echo :$a:$b:$c:
:one:two:three:                         Blanks got removed
$ read line                             Only one variable
this is a line of text        !!!
$ echo $line
this is a line of text        !!!       Entire line was assigned
```

```
$ read a b
first and then the rest
$ echo :$a:$b:
:first:and then the rest:              Extra data gets stored in last variable
$
```

Now let's put the `read` statement to work in an actual program. The purpose of this program is to show how you can develop your own commands that prompt the user for information. You'll create a program called `copy` to copy files. The program will not take any arguments but instead will prompt the user for the names of the source and destination files. After this information has been entered, then the `copy` program will simply call the `cp` command to perform the copy.

```
#
# Program to copy files
#

echo "Source file: \c"
read source

echo "Destination file: \c"
read destination

cp $source $destination
```

The `\c` characters were placed in the two `echo`s so that the user can enter the data on the same line as the prompt message.
   Now to test it:

```
$ ls                          Let's see what's around
names
names1
names2
$ copy
Source file: names
Destination file: test
$ ls
names
names1
names2
test                          The new file is there
$ sdiff -s names test         and it's identical to the original
$
```

A subtle point worth noting about the `copy` program: since you were careful *not* to enclose the shell variables destination and source inside quotes in the cp command, the shell will perform file name substitution on these arguments if specified:

```
$ ls *2
names2
$ copy
Source file: *2
Destination file: test2
$ sdiff -s names2 test2
$
```

Some interesting modifications can be made to the copy program to make it more useful. One might be to allow the user to enter the arguments on the command line if desired. The program could then test for this condition and then directly call the cp command with the arguments typed on the line (remember $* ?).

Another worthwhile change might test to see if the destination file already existed. If it did, then the user could be asked if he wanted to proceed with the copy. If he didn't, the program could simply ignore the copy request. This would be helpful for novice UNIX users, as it could help keep them from accidentally overwriting their files. (You can even make your own version of the mv command to do the same type of check.)

Thef main point to be remembered from all of this is that the UNIX system provides you with the power and flexibility to effectively customize UNIX commands. The fact that cp is a built-in UNIX command while copy is a custom-written command can remain unknown to other users. (In fact, you could even call your version of the command cp if you wanted to.)

• The case Statement •

The shell case statement is useful when you want to compare a value against a whole series of values. You know that this can be done with an if-elif statement chain, but the case statement is more concise and also easier to write and to read. The general format of this statement is:

```
case value
in
        pattern₁ )      command
                        command
                        . . .
                        command;;
```

```
pattern₂ )      command
                command
                . . .
                command;;
. . .
patternₙ )      command
                command
                . . .
                command;;
esac
```

Operation of the case proceeds as follows: *value* is successively compared against *pattern₁*, *pattern₂*, ..., *patternₙ*. As soon as a match is found, the commands listed after the matching pattern are executed, until a double semicolon (;;) is reached. At that point, the case statement is terminated. If *value* does not match any of the specified patterns, then no action is taken, and the entire case is effectively "skipped." If the special pattern * is included as the *last* pattern in the case, then the commands that follow will be executed whenever none of the preceding patterns match.

As a simple example of the use of the case, the following program displays the English equivalent of a number from 0 through 9. This number is given as an argument to the command. If a value other than 0 through 9 is specified, then the program displays the message Invalid argument.

```
#
# Display the English equivalent of a digit
#

case "$1"
in
     0 )     echo zero;;
     1 )     echo one;;
     2 )     echo two;;
     3 )     echo three;;
     4 )     echo four;;
     5 )     echo five;;
     6 )     echo six;;
     7 )     echo seven;;
     8 )     echo eight;;
     9 )     echo nine;;
     * )     echo Invalid argument;;
esac
```

If you call this program digit, then the following represents some sample uses:

```
$ digit 5
five
$ digit x
Invalid argument
$ digit 8
eight
$
```

The case statement is frequently used by shell programmers in writing programs that take options. For example, the following shell statements might appear in a program that took options -1, -c, and -w, plus a list of file name arguments. The for that surrounds the case enables you to supply a variable number of options and arguments, in any order.

```
loption=""
coption=""
woption=""
filelist=""

for arg in $*
do
        case $arg
        in
                -1)    loption=1;;
                -w)    woption=1;;
                -c)    coption=1;;
                 *)    filelist="$filelist $arg";;
        esac
done
```

This code sequence assumes that any argument typed on the command line that's not -1, -w, or -c is a file name. At the end of execution of these statements, the shell variable loption will be set to 1 if -1 were typed on the command line, the variable woption to 1 if -w were typed, and the variable coption to 1 if -c were typed. The shell variable filelist will contain a list of the files typed on the command line.

If this sequence of statements occurred in a program called coop, for instance, then the following shows sample command lines that would get properly interpreted:

```
coop -w -c file1
```

```
coop -w f* -c -l
coop -l
coop file1 file2 name*
```

The patterns that are specified inside a `case` statement are expanded by the shell the same way file names are. This means, for example, that the pattern

```
na*
```

would match any value that begins with `na`; the pattern

```
?x
```

would match any two-character value that ends in `x`; and the pattern

```
[a-z]
```

would match any lower-case letter.

An *or*ing of patterns is effected by separating patterns with a vertical bar `¦`. So, for example, the following pattern will match the value `hp` *or* `hp-2624` *or* `2624`:

```
hp ¦ hp-2624 ¦ 2624
```

And as a final example, the following pattern matches any values that begin with the characters `fig` *or* `tbl`:

```
fig* ¦ tbl*
```

· Your Environment ·

Whenever you log onto the system, you are given your own copy of the shell program. You are also set up in your own little world known as your *environment*. Included in this environment are special shell variables that are specific to you. For example, there is a shell variable `HOME` that contains the path to your `HOME` directory; another variable called `PATH` describes to the UNIX system the directories that are to be searched whenever a command is executed; two shell variables called `PS1` and `PS2` describe your first and second "level" command prompts.

There's No Place Like HOME

The shell variable HOME is automatically set to your HOME directory path as soon as you log into the system. Try printing out the value of this variable at your terminal and see what happens:

```
$ echo $HOME
/a1/steve
$
```

The HOME variable is used by several UNIX commands to locate your HOME directory. For example, you will recall that typing just the command cd with no argument places you in your HOME directory. The cd command determines where this directory is by examining your HOME variable. Study the following example:

```
$ pwd
/a1/steve/documents
$ cd                              Change to HOME directory
$ pwd
/a1/steve
$ HOME=/a1/steve/misc            Change the value of HOME
$ cd                              Now see what happens
$ pwd
/a1/steve/misc
$
```

As you can see, changing the value of the shell variable HOME has an effect on the execution of the cd command. Be careful—operation of other commands may be affected as well.

PS1 and PS2

By now you're used to getting a dollar sign prompt printed whenever the shell is waiting for you to type a command. But what if you don't want your prompt to be a dollar sign? Well, you can easily change your prompt character at any time simply by changing the value of the shell variable PS1. First, let's see what value this variable currently has:

```
$ echo prompt is $PS1
prompt is $
$
```

Now let's see what happens when you change it:

```
$ PS1=">"
>date
```

```
Mon Mar  5 16:16:05 EST 1984
>
```

(You will recall from the discussion on quotes that you must include >
in quotes when assigning it to PS1; otherwise, the shell thinks you're
trying to redirect output.) As you can see, as soon as you change the
value of PS1, the value it is changed to becomes your new prompt
character for *all* subsequent commands. You can change the command
prompt to any characters at all, as the next few examples illustrate:

```
>PS1="> "                                  Add an extra blank space to the end
> date
Mon Mar  5 16:19:55 EST 1984
> PS1="=> "
=> PS1="Enter your command: "
Enter your command: date
Mon Mar  5 16:20:25 EST 1984
Enter your command:
```

The last prompt, Enter your command: , may seem a little extreme,
but it does illustrate the point.

As you probably guessed, the prompt that is printed whenever
the shell is expecting more input (normally >) can also be changed.
This prompt character is stored in the variable PS2:

```
Enter your command: echo $PS2
>
Enter your command: PS1="$ "                Change this back
$
```

Now that you've changed your PS1 prompt to something more reason-
able, change the value of PS2:

```
$ PS2="====> "
$ for n in 1 2 3
====> do
====> echo $n
====> done
1
2
3
$
```

Any value that is assigned to either PS1 or PS2 remains in effect
throughout your login session. Next time you log in, the default values

of $ and > will be used. You'll see shortly how you can keep these changes across login sessions.

Your PATH

Probably the most important shell variable is the one called PATH. This variable tells the shell exactly *where* to look to find *any* command that you execute. Whenever you log in, your PATH variable is set to some default value. See what it is set to now:

```
$ echo $PATH
:/bin:/usr/bin
$
```

The PATH variable contains a list of *all* directories that will be searched whenever you type in the name of a program to be executed. It also specifies the order in which this search will be performed. The directories listed in the PATH variable will be searched by the shell from left to right. A colon (:) separates one path from the next in the list. A colon at the start of the list means that the current directory is to be searched first.

The value of the PATH variable shown indicates that three directories are to be searched whenever you type in the name of a program to be executed: first the current directory, then the directory /bin, and finally the directory /usr/bin. As soon as the shell finds the program in one of these directories, it executes it. However, if it doesn't find it in any of these directories, then it prints the message *command*: not found.

The nice thing about the PATH variable is that you can change its value to control the order of the search, or to add new directories to be searched. For example, the directory structure depicted in Fig. 6-3 contains a directory called programs that you can assume contains programs that can be executed. So you probably would place your nu (to count the number of users) and salute (to print "Good morning," "Good afternoon," or "Good evening,") programs inside this directory (see Fig. 6-4).

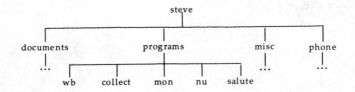

Fig. 6-4. Local program directory programs

Without using the PATH mechanism, whenever you want to find out how many users are logged in, you have to explicitly tell the shell where it can find the nu program.

```
$ pwd
/a1/steve/documents/memos
$ nu                              Execute the program nu
nu: not found                    The shell couldn't find it
$ /a1/steve/programs/nu
There are 9 users logged in.
$
```

The first time you tried to execute nu, the shell used the PATH variable to determine where to search for the program. So first it looked inside the current directory /a1/steve/documents/memos for nu. Since no executable file of that name was to be found in that directory, it continued its search with the directory /bin and then with the directory /usr/bin. Since nu couldn't be found in either of these two directories either, the shell printed its not found message at the terminal.

The next time, a full path to the nu program was specified (a relative path could have been used as well). So the shell went directly to the directory /a1/steve/programs to find nu, since specifying a path to a program always overrides the PATH variable.

Instead of having to explicitly tell the shell where to find nu each time you want to use it, you can add the programs directory to your PATH so that the shell will automatically search this directory. To do this, you can explicitly assign the new search path to PATH:

```
PATH=:/bin:/usr/bin:/a1/steve/programs
```

or you can equivalently "tack" your new directory onto the end of the existing PATH:

```
PATH=$PATH:/a1/steve/programs
```

This last method saves some typing. Now you can execute a program contained in your programs directory from *anywhere*:

```
$ pwd
/a1/steve/documents/memos
$ PATH=$PATH:/a1/steve/programs        Add programs  to the PATH
$ echo $PATH
:/bin:/usr/bin:/a1/steve/programs
$ nu
There are 9 users logged in.          This time the shell found it
$ salute
Good morning.
$
```

Recall the programs lu, add and rem to look up, add and
remove entries, respectively, from the phone book. We stored these programs, together with the phone_book file in a directory that we called
phone. It would be nice if you could execute the lu, add and rem
programs from anywhere in your directory path. So let's add
/a1/steve/phone to your PATH:

```
$ PATH=$PATH:/a1/steve/phone
$ echo $PATH
:/bin:/usr/bin:/a1/steve/programs:/a1/steve/phone
$
```

Now let's go back to the HOME directory /a1/steve and try to look
someone up in the phone book:

```
$ cd
$ lu Gunderman
grep: couldn't open phone_book
I couldn't find Gunderman in the phone book
$
```

What happened? The output says that grep couldn't open the file
phone_book. This happened because grep looked for this file only
in the *current working directory* /a1/steve and couldn't find it there.
Remember, PATH only specifies directories to be searched for programs,
and not for other files. And unless a relative or full path name is specified for a file, only the current working directory will be searched for
that file.
      As you might expect, add and rem probably have the same
problem as the lu program. These programs will work only if executed
from inside the phone directory, since that is where the phone_book
file resides.
      There are two ways to solve this problem. The first is to edit
each program to specify a full path to the phone_book file wherever
it is used. So, for example, the lu program would now appear as
shown:

```
# lookup a person's phone number in the phone book

if [ $# -ne 1 ]
then
      echo "Usage: lu name"
else
      output=`grep "$1" /a1/steve/phone/phone_book`

      if [ -z "$output" ]
      then
            echo "I couldn't find $1 in the phone book"
      else
            echo "$output"
      fi
fi
```

Now this program will work from anywhere:

```
$ pwd                           See where we are
/a1/steve
$ lu Gunderman
Gunderman, Dick       867-5394
$
```

Another solution is to have each program change its working directory
to the phone directory as soon as it begins execution. In this way, the
phone_book file *will* be found in the current directory:

```
# lookup a person's phone number in the phone book

if [ $# -ne 1 ]
then
      echo "Usage: lu name"
else
      cd /a1/steve/phone

      output=`grep "$1" phone_book`

      if [ -z "$output" ]
      then
            echo "I couldn't find $1 in the phone book"
      else
            echo "$output"
      fi
fi
```

It is interesting to note that executing a cd from inside a shell program, only changes the working directory for that program. It has no effect on *your* current working directory. The following verifies this fact:

```
$ pwd
/a1/steve
$ lu Benson
Benson, Harry               338-7776
$ pwd
/a1/steve                        It didn't change
$
```

The second technique for solving our problem—namely cd'ing to the phone directory is very useful when dealing with shell programs that need to reference many files in a particular directory. By changing to that directory, you are saved from the "bother" of having to fully qualify all of these files in the program.

Before leaving this discussion, you should note that the shell uses the PATH variable to find standard UNIX commands as well. These are stored in the directories /bin and /usr/bin. If you did something naughty such as assigned the null string to PATH, then the system would not be able to find *any* command:

```
$ PATH=""                        "Wipe out" the PATH
$ date
date: not found
$ who                            The shell can't find anything now
who: not found
$ PATH=:/bin:/usr/bin            Set it back
$ date
Tue Mar  6 09:41:23 EST 1984     That's better!
$
```

As with the PS1, PS2, and HOME shell variables, any changes made to PATH will not be there next time you log in.

Exported Variables

Whenever you execute a shell program, the shell creates an entirely separate environment for that program to run in. This means that the program gets its own distinct set of variables. Any variables that you assigned values to before executing the program cannot be accessed or changed by the program. And when the program finishes execution, its environment goes away with it. So any variables set by that program do not exist after that program has completed execution. The following illustrates an example:

```
$ cat > foo
echo :$x:              ⎫
CTRL-d                 ⎬ Create a program to display the value of x
$ chmod +x foo         ⎭
$ x=100
$ echo $x
100
$ foo
::
$
```

The foo program couldn't access the value of x. Furthermore, if foo had assigned a value to a variable called x, then that would have had no effect on the variable x that was assigned the value 100 before foo was executed—its value would still be 100 after execution of foo was completed.

There *is* a way to access the value of a shell variable from another program. A shell statement called export must be used; its format is

$$\text{export} \quad \textit{variable-list}$$

where *variable-list* is a blank-separated list of variables (*not* preceded by dollar signs). Any program that subsequently gets executed can access the value of the exported variables—but it still cannot permanently change them.

Let's go back to the foo program:

```
$ echo $x
100                    It's still there
$ export x
$ foo
:100:                  This time foo knows about x
$
```

Now add a line to the beginning of foo so that it looks like this:

```
x=50
echo :$x:
```

Here's what happens when you execute foo:

```
$ echo $x
100
$ foo
:50:
$ echo $x
100
$
```

So you see that foo could not permanently change the value of x; it
merely changed its own copy of x that existed in its environment.

Your .profile

Suppose you've made several changes to your environment and you
would like to have them saved; that is, you want these changes to still
be there the next time you log in. In order to be able to do this, the
shell has adopted the following convention: Every time you log in, the
shell automatically looks in your HOME directory for a file called
.profile. If the file is there, then the shell automatically executes it.
And since this file gets executed in a different way from other shell programs, any variables that get set or exported inside the .profile
remain in effect even after execution of the .profile has completed.
      You may have a .profile right now without even being aware
of it! First, go to your HOME directory:

```
$ cd
$ pwd
/a1/steve
$
```

Now see if there's a .profile file there:

```
$ ls .profile
.profile
$
```

Apparently, steve does have one. But look what happens if he does
an ls to list all the files in his directory:

```
$ ls
documents
misc
phone
programs
$
```

The .profile file is *not* listed when the ls command is executed. This is because the ls command does not normally list file names that begin with a period. You can explicitly list such "hidden" files with a command such as ls .profile, or you can use the -a option to the ls command:

```
$ ls -a
.
..
.profile
documents
misc
phone
programs
$
```

You see that the directory file .. as well as the current directory file . are both listed when the -a option is used.

Getting back to the .profile file, let's assume that you don't have one. Let's set one up to include the programs and phone directories in your PATH, change PS1 to "=> ", change your erase character from # to BACKSPACE (*CTRL-h*), print a salutation, and then tell us how many users are logged in:

```
# Add "programs" and "phone" to the search path and
# export it so other programs know about it

PATH=$PATH:/a1/steve/programs:/a1/steve/phone
export PATH

# Now change PS1

PS1="=> "

# Set erase character to Backspace

stty echoe erase CTRL-h

# Print salutation

echo
salute

# Tell how many people are logged in

nu
```

The shell will be able to find the `salute` and `nu` programs since your
`PATH` will be changed by the time you execute these programs.

If you typed the above lines into a `.profile` file in your
`HOME` directory, the following shows what would happen *whenever* you
subsequently logged in.

```
login: steve
Password: iop098

Good morning.
There are 5 users logged in.
=>
```

▪ The Stream Editor `sed` ▪

It's worthwhile taking a slight diversion at this point to describe a program that's commonly used when writing shell programs. The `sed`
program allows you to perform a one-pass edit on a file. The general
format of sed is

$$sed \quad ed\text{-}command \quad file$$

where *ed-command* is an `ed`-style command that is to be applied to the
contents of *file*. Unless explicit line numbers are referenced by this command, the command will be sequentially applied to every line of *file*.
The output of `sed` goes to standard output, which as you know may be
redirected if desired.

As an example, consider the following file called `test`.

```
$ cat test
Unix used to be a trademark of Bell
Laboratories.  Unix is now a trademark
of AT&T Bell Laboratories.
$
```

The following shows how `sed` can be used to change all occurrences of
the string `Unix` to the string `UNIX` in the file `test`:

```
$ sed s/Unix/UNIX/g test
UNIX used to be a trademark of Bell
Laboratories.  UNIX is now a trademark
of AT&T Bell Laboratories.
$
```

The g was placed at the end of the substitute command just in case the string Unix occurred more than once on any line. (Remember from the discussions of ed that the s command will only change the first occurrence of a string on a line unless the "global" option g is used.)

You don't have to specify a line range to the s command (as in 1,$s/Unix/UNIX/g) since sed automatically applies the editor command to every line of the file by default.

If you wanted to *permanently* change all occurrences of Unix to UNIX in the file test, then you would have to redirect sed's output to a file and then mv the file back:

```
$ sed s/Unix/UNIX/g test > foo     Make the edit changes
$ mv foo test                      Replace the old file with the new one
$ cat test                         Verify that it worked
UNIX used to be a trademark of Bell
Laboratories.  UNIX is now a trademark
of AT&T Bell Laboratories.
$
```

Redirecting the output of sed directly to test would have messed things up royally. This two step process must be used.

The following example shows how line 3 from the file test can be deleted:

```
$ sed 3d test
UNIX used to be a trademark of Bell
Laboratories.  UNIX is now a trademark
$
```

Remember that in order to get this change reflected back in the file test you have to go through the redirection and moving scheme outlined above.

To delete all lines from test that contain the string UNIX, you can use the following sed command:

```
$ sed /UNIX/d test
of AT&T Bell Laboratories.
$
```

sed is often used to "edit" the value stored in a shell variable. For example, the following takes the value of the shell variable VAL and changes all minus signs to plus signs:

```
$ echo $VAL
a--b--c
$ echo $VAL ¦ sed s/-/+/g
a++b++c
$
```

The echo is used to write the value of the shell variable VAL to standard output so that it can be piped into the sed command, which takes its input from standard input if no file name is supplied.

You can assign the output of the above command sequence back to VAL by using the shell's back-quoting mechanism:

```
$ echo $VAL
a--b--c
$ VAL=`echo $VAL ¦ sed s/-/+/g`
$ echo $VAL
a++b++c
$
```

This works as before, except the result of the sed is stored back in the shell variable VAL.

The cut command is also commonly used to "edit" shell variables. In the following example, the first character contained in the shell variable filename is extracted and assigned to the variable ch1:

```
$ echo $filename
s.main.c
$ ch1=`echo $filename ¦ cut -c1`
$ echo $ch1
s
$
```

As previously mentioned, this chapter has not attempted to cover all of the features provided by the shell. Rather, it has attempted to introduce you to its wonderfully rich and powerful programming language. A thorough treatment requires an entire book. Among the features not covered here are subshells, more advanced types of parameter substitutions, and the special shell commands ., break, continue, eval, exec, exit, set, shift, trap, and wait. If you turn to the appropriate pages in your *UNIX User's Manual,* you will find a concise summary of each of these features.

7

SCREEN EDITING WITH VI

Editing is one of the most frequently used functions of a general purpose computer. No matter what you're planning to do, basic editing is
sure to be the first step. Currently, the UNIX system supports a line editor, ed, which was discussed in Chapters 4 and 5. Many prefer to use a
screen editor to create or modify their files. The only restriction of a
screen editor is that the user must have a video (screen) terminal.

A screen editor allows you to see portions of your file on the
terminal's screen and to modify characters and lines by simply typing at
the current *cursor* position. The cursor is the little blinking line or box
that shows you where the next character will be printed, either by you
or the system. In a screen editor, you move the cursor around your file
until you find the part you want to modify, then you add or change the
text to your liking.

Two screen editors are supplied with UNIX System V Release 2.0.
Of the two, we will discuss vi, which is the more popular. vi was
developed by the University of California at Berkeley and is also supplied with the Berkeley distribution of the UNIX system.

This chapter is divided into three parts. The first is an introduction to vi. It is meant to get you started using vi and to familiarize
you with cursor motions and simple editing. The second section is more
advanced and is meant to teach many of the more useful vi commands
that can make you more effective at using vi. There are fewer examples and more "meat" in the second section. The third section is
devoted to advanced and miscellaneous vi commands that can greatly
improve your editing speed. It covers the commands quickly, and it
should be read after you've spent a few hours using the commands in
the first two sections. We have also put a vi command summary at the
end of this chapter.

• Introduction to vi •

Before you can use vi, you must let it know what type of terminal you
are using. The way you let vi know about your terminal is with the
shell variable TERM. By setting TERM to your terminal type, vi will
know what features, capabilities, and quirks your terminal has:

```
$ echo $TERM              Is it already set?
                          I guess not
$ TERM=hp2621             A popular terminal made by Hewlett-Packard
$ export TERM             Make the variable TERM available to vi
$
```

For vi, just remember that you *must* set TERM to the terminal type
you're using, and you *must* export it as well. If you want, you can put
the TERM= and export in your .profile as well. You will find a
discussion of shell variables, the export command, and the .pro-
file in Chapter 6.

There is a table at the end of this chapter of the terminals that
vi can be used with. This list is hardly complete, as some UNIX
administrators will add terminals at the request of users. If you don't
recognize your terminal in the list, ask your system administrator
whether your terminal is supported.

Entering vi

Now you can run vi just like any other UNIX command. When you
start vi, it will print out the file name, number of lines, and number of
characters at the *bottom* of your screen:

```
$ date
Sat Mar 10 14:46:38 EST 1984
$ cat names
John
Jim
Pat
Steve
$ vi names




"names" 4 lines, 19 characters▢
```

Then it will clear your screen and fill it with the file you're editing:

```
▢ohn
Jim
Pat
Steve
~
~
~
~
~
~
~
~
~
~
~
~
~
~
"names" 4 lines, 19 characters
```

The four lines from the file names and a message line at the bottom
are listed. A ~ in the first column means that the file doesn't have
enough lines to fill up the screen. The cursor is depicted by a box (▢

and is placed in the upper left corner when vi starts. The bottom line is the *message line*. It will sometimes print things, but this depends on the command. There will be more about the message line as the chapter progresses.

Conventions Used in this Chapter

The screens shown previously are only 20 lines long and about 60 characters wide. Most video terminals are at least 24 lines by 80 characters, but in the interest of saving space and giving clearer examples, our windows will be 8 lines by about 23 characters.

The way we'll show vi commands and responses is as follows. Two screens will be shown side by side. The first shows the screen before the vi command is entered; listed between the screens is the vi command that is entered; and the second shows the screen after the command:

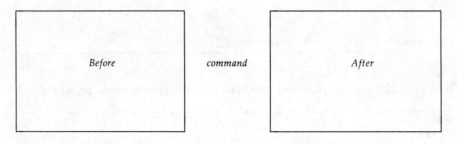

When running vi, the RETURN key is seldom used except when entering text. For all of the following vi screens, the RETURN key is *not* entered at the end of a command or line unless it is explicitly shown with CR (see Table 7-1). vi uses control characters extensively (remember the *CTRL-d*?), so the shorthand *^LETTER* will be used in place of *CTRL-LETTER*.

TABLE 7-1. Special characters for vi

Character	vi representation
cursor	☐
RETURN	CR
ESCAPE	ESC
CTRL-u	^U
CTRL-d	^D
CTRL-b	^B
CTRL-f	^F
CTRL-l	^L

Moving Around

The first thing you need to learn about using vi is how to move the cursor around on the screen. Once you know how to do that, you can position it where you want to make additions or changes.

Let's start by running vi on the file names:

```
$ vi namesCR




"names" 4 lines, 19 cha
```

So you will have a screen that looks like this:

```
John
Jim
Pat
Steve
~
~
~
"names" 4 lines, 19 cha
```

The basic screen motion commands are h, j, k, and 1. You might notice they are situated next to each other on the right side of the keyboard. The motions for h, j, k, and 1 are left, down, up, and right, respectively (see Fig. 7-1).

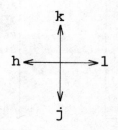

Fig. 7-1. Basic Cursor Motions

Here are a few examples; note that the commands are not echoed on the screen—the only thing `vi` shows on the screen (except for the message line) is *the contents of the file.*

```
┌──────────────────────────────┐         ┌──────────────────────────────┐
│ John                         │         │ John                         │
│ Jim                          │         │ Jim                          │
│ Pat                   j      │ Pat     │
│ Steve            move down   │ Steve   │
│ ~                            │         │ ~                            │
│ ~                            │         │ ~                            │
│ ~                            │         │ ~                            │
│ "names" 4 lines, 19 cha      │         │ "names" 4 lines, 19 cha      │
└──────────────────────────────┘         └──────────────────────────────┘
```

```
┌──────────────────────────────┐         ┌──────────────────────────────┐
│ John                         │         │ John                         │
│ Jim                          │         │ Jim                          │
│ Pat                   j      │ Pat     │
│ Steve            move down   │ Steve   │
│ ~                            │         │ ~                            │
│ ~                            │         │ ~                            │
│ ~                            │         │ ~                            │
│ "names" 4 lines, 19 cha      │         │ "names" 4 lines, 19 cha      │
└──────────────────────────────┘         └──────────────────────────────┘
```

```
┌──────────────────────────────┐         ┌──────────────────────────────┐
│ John                         │         │ John                         │
│ Jim                          │         │ Jim                          │
│ Pat                   l      │ Pat     │
│ Steve            move right  │ Steve   │
│ ~                            │         │ ~                            │
│ ~                            │         │ ~                            │
│ ~                            │         │ ~                            │
│ "names" 4 lines, 19 cha      │         │ "names" 4 lines, 19 cha      │
└──────────────────────────────┘         └──────────────────────────────┘
```

```
┌──────────────────────────────┐         ┌──────────────────────────────┐
│ John                         │         │ John                         │
│ Jim                          │         │ Jim                          │
│ Pat                   k      │ Pat     │
│ Steve            move up     │ Steve   │
│ ~                            │         │ ~                            │
│ ~                            │         │ ~                            │
│ ~                            │         │ ~                            │
│ "names" 4 lines, 19 cha      │         │ "names" 4 lines, 19 cha      │
└──────────────────────────────┘         └──────────────────────────────┘
```

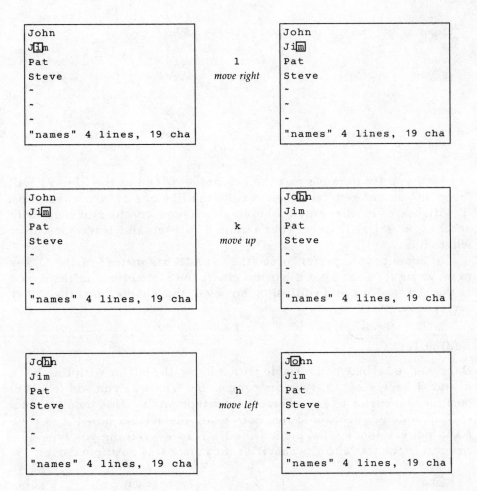

You can precede these keys with numbers, which allows you to move more than one column or line at a time:

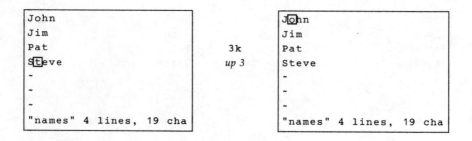

```
John                              John
Jim                               Jim
Pat               3k              Pat
Steve            up 3             Steve
~                                 ~
~                                 ~
~                                 ~
"names" 4 lines, 19 cha           "names" 4 lines, 19 cha
```

If you try to move past the beginning or end of the file, vi will "beep" at you. In general, when vi doesn't like one of your commands, it will beep. In the previous example, if you try to move up with another k, vi will cause your terminal to beep and leave the cursor where it is.

Some people prefer to use the SPACE bar instead of the 1 key to move right. The SPACE bar has *exactly* the same effect on the cursor as the 1 key. To avoid confusion, however, this chapter uses the 1 key exclusively.

Adding Text

Once you've become comfortable with moving the cursor with the h, j, k, and 1 keys, you can try adding some text. The way you add text is to position the cursor over a character and type an a. This puts you in a special mode of operation called *insert mode*. (Remember how the a command put you in a special mode in ed?) Now everything you type in is *appended* to the text *after* the character the cursor was positioned over:

```
John                              Joxxyyzzhh
Jim                               Jim
Pat            axxyyzz            Pat
Steve          add xxyyzz         Steve
~                                 ~
~                                 ~
~                                 ~
"names" 4 lines, 19 cha           "names" 4 lines, 19 cha
```

When you're done adding text, you press the ESC key.

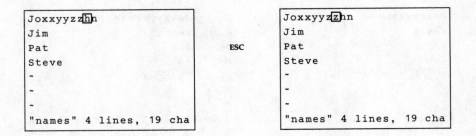

```
Joxxyyzzhn                           Joxxyyzzhn
Jim                                  Jim
Pat                     ESC          Pat
Steve                                Steve
~                                    ~
~                                    ~
~                                    ~
"names" 4 lines, 19 cha              "names" 4 lines, 19 cha
```

When you press the ESC key, the cursor moves back to the last character
you entered. This way, you know that you are no longer in insert mode.

You can even put RETURNs in the added text, and new lines
appear, almost magically:

```
Joxxyyzzhn                           Joxxyyzzone
Jim                                  twohn
Pat                     aoneCR       Jim
Steve                   twoESC       Pat
~                    embedded CR     Steve
~                                    ~
~                                    ~
"names" 4 lines, 19 cha              "names" 4 lines, 19 cha
```

The appending started between the z and hn of the first line, causing
the hn to be carried to the next line when the CR was pressed.

There's another way of adding text. It's with the i command.
i works like the a command, but it *inserts* instead of appending, meaning the characters you type in are placed *before* the current character
position. (You might have noticed that it's impossible to add text at the
beginning of a line with the a command.)   i also puts you in insert
mode, requiring an ESC to finish inserting.

```
Joxxyyzzone                          Joxxyyzzone
twohn                                twohn
Jim                     3j           Jim
Pat                    down 3        Pat
Steve                                Steve
~                                    ~
~                                    ~
"names" 4 lines, 19 cha              "names" 4 lines, 19 cha
```

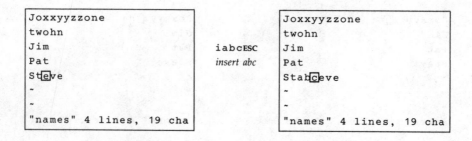

After the ESC is pressed, the cursor moves back to the last character inserted, just as with the a command.

Deleting Text

Now that you can add text to a file, the next thing to learn is how to delete text. Basically, there are two commands that delete text in vi: x and d.

To delete one character, you use the x command.   x deletes the character at the current cursor position, moving the rest of the line left into the void created by the deleted character:

```
Joxxyyzzone                          Joxxyyzzone
twohn                                twohn
Jim                        x         Jim
Pat                    delete "c"    Pat
Stabceve                             Stabeve
~                                    ~
~                                    ~
"names" 4 lines, 19 cha              "names" 4 lines, 19 cha
```

```
Joxxyyzzone                          Joxxyyzzone
twohn                                twohn
Jim                        x         Jim
Pat                    delete "e"    Pat
Stabeve                              Stabve
~                                    ~
~                                    ~
"names" 4 lines, 19 cha              "names" 4 lines, 19 cha
```

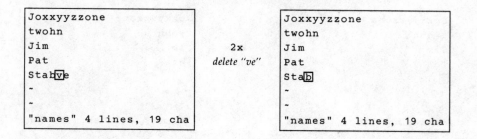

As you can see, the **x** command can be preceded by a number to indicate how many characters you want to delete. If you get rid of all the characters on a line and keep hitting **x**, you will get beeps because you are trying to delete nonexistent characters:

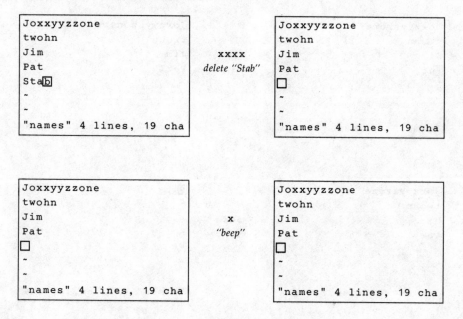

Note that each **x** of the **xxxx** is done at the end of the line. When **x** is used at the end of a line, it deletes the character at the current cursor position and then moves the cursor *left* to what is now the new end of the line.

Deleting characters is all well and good, but sometimes you want to delete an entire line. The **x** command will get rid of all the characters on a line, but it won't get rid of the line itself. To delete a line, you use the **dd** command. (That's two **d**'s in a row.) The **dd** command is just a special case of a more general delete that is discussed in the second half of this chapter. It can be preceded by a number to indicate the number of lines to delete.

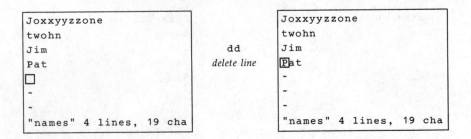

Here the last line was deleted and replaced on the screen with a ~ (meaning nothing's there).

Now move up to the top and delete a few lines. Notice how the lines following those deleted move up:

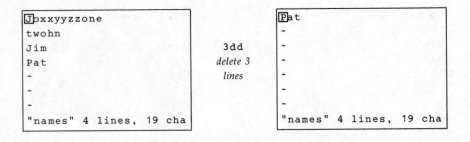

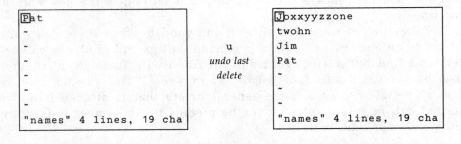

OOPS!! We really didn't want to delete all those lines! We need to *undo* that delete command:

That's better. As you can see, if you make a mistake with vi, you can just type a u and undo the change. The u will undo the last x or dd command. It also works with other commands that change the file.

Saving the File

Like ed, vi also changes a copy of the file (sometimes referred to as a *buffer*) that must be written before the file is actually changed. There are several ways to write files in vi, but the easiest is with the ZZ command. When you type in two capital Z's, vi will automatically write the file *and* quit, putting you back in the shell. (Notice how the top line scrolls off the top of the screen when the $ is printed.)

```
Jbxxyyzzone
twohn
Jim
Pat
~
~
~
"names" 4 lines, 19 cha
```

ZZ
write "names"
and quit

```
twohn
Jim
Pat
~
~
~
"names" 4 lines, 26 cha
$ □
```

Once you're back in the shell, all the special screen editing features go away.

TABLE 7-2. **Summary of basic vi commands**

Command	Operation
h	← Move cursor left
j	↓ Move cursor down
k	↑ Move cursor up
l	→ Move cursor right
a	Append after cursor (end with ESC)
i	Insert before cursor (end with ESC)
x	Delete character at Current cursor position
dd	Delete current line
ZZ	Write file and quit

• Using vi •

This part of the chapter covers some of the more advanced features of vi. The next section covers some advanced vi commands that aren't as widely used but are very useful to users who have gained some proficiency with vi.

Scrolling

The term *scrolling* refers to the property of video terminals that makes the top line leave the screen as each new line is displayed at the bottom. If you are listing a file at your terminal, the top of it will disappear from the screen as more of the file is displayed. Screen editors use scrolling to edit large files. Only the first 23 lines are displayed by vi when you start it on a large file. As you work with the file and move about in it, the top lines will sometimes scroll up off the screen as more lines are displayed at the bottom; sometimes the lines at the bottom will scroll down off the screen as more lines are listed at the top.

The following example illustrates how simple scrolling works in vi:

```
$ cat jokes
A few years ago,
Quasimodo (the
hunchback of Notre
Dame) was looking
for a replacement.
He put an ad in the
paper, and this guy
showed up to apply
for the job.
The only problem was
this guy had no arms
so Quasi asked him
how he was going to
ring the bells.
The guy said "I run
up and hit the bells
with my head," and
ran right into a
bell with his fore-
head.   Then he took
a step back and went
for the BIIIIG bell;
tripping, he fell
headlong to the
pavement.  A crowd
gathered in front of
the church, as a
```

```
police inspector
came by and asked
Quasi "who is this
guy?"
Quasi replied, "I
don't know, but his
face rings a bell."
$
```

<table>
<tr>
<td>

```
police inspector
came by and asked
Quasi "who is this
guy?"
Quasi replied, "I
don't know, but his
face rings a bell."
$ vi jokesCR
```
</td>
<td>start vi</td>
<td>

```
A few years ago,
Quasimodo (the
hunchback of Notre
Dame) was looking
for a replacement.
He put an ad in the
paper, and this guy
"jokes" 34 lines, 625 c
```
</td>
</tr>
<tr>
<td>

```
A few years ago,
Quasimodo (the
hunchback of Notre
Dame) was looking
for a replacement.
He put an ad in the
paper, and this guy
"jokes" 34 lines, 625 c
```
</td>
<td>6j
down 6 lines</td>
<td>

```
A few years ago,
Quasimodo (the
hunchback of Notre
Dame) was looking
for a replacement.
He put an ad in the
paper, and this guy
"jokes" 34 lines, 625 c
```
</td>
</tr>
<tr>
<td>

```
A few years ago,
Quasimodo (the
hunchback of Notre
Dame) was looking
for a replacement.
He put an ad in the
paper, and this guy
"jokes" 34 lines, 625 c
```
</td>
<td>j
down 1 line</td>
<td>

```
Quasimodo (the
hunchback of Notre
Dame) was looking
for a replacement.
He put an ad in the
paper, and this guy
showed up to apply
```
</td>
</tr>
<tr>
<td>

```
Quasimodo (the
hunchback of Notre
Dame) was looking
for a replacement.
He put an ad in the
paper, and this guy
showed up to apply
```
</td>
<td>j
down 1 line</td>
<td>

```
hunchback of Notre
Dame) was looking
for a replacement.
He put an ad in the
paper, and this guy
showed up to apply
for the job.
```
</td>
</tr>
</table>

As you can see, when you try to move past the bottom of the screen, vi scrolls the screen up a line. After a scroll, the text on the message line usually gets clobbered. As you might expect, you can precede the command with a number to scroll the screen several lines:

```
hunchback of Notre
Dame) was looking
for a replacement.
He put an ad in the
paper, and this guy
showed up to apply
for the job.
```
                    4j
                down 4 lines
```
paper, and this guy
showed up to apply
for the job.
The only problem was
this guy had no arms
so Quasi asked him
how he was going to
```

Similarly, you can scroll up the screen with the k command.

vi also supplies you with commands for scrolling several lines at a time. The ˆD and ˆU scroll half a screen down or up if there are enough lines in the file to do so:

```
paper, and this guy
showed up to apply
for the job.
The only problem was
this guy had no arms
so Quasi asked him
how he was going to
```
                    ˆD
                down 1/2
                screen
```
this guy had no arms
so Quasi asked him
how he was going to
ring the bells.
The guy said "I run
up and hit the bells
with my head," and
```

```
this guy had no arms
so Quasi asked him
how he was going to
ring the bells.
The guy said "I run
up and hit the bells
with my head," and
```
                    ˆD
                down 1/2
                screen
```
The guy said "I run
up and hit the bells
with my head," and
ran right into a
bell with his fore-
head.  Then he took
a step back and went
```

```
The guy said "I run
up and hit the bells
with my head," and
ran right into a
bell with his fore-
head.  Then he took
a step back and went
```
                    ˆU
                up 1/2 screen
```
this guy had no arms
so Quasi asked him
how he was going to
ring the bells.
The guy said "I run
up and hit the bells
with my head," and
```

You also have the commands `F` and `B` that scroll forward and back one full screen, respectively.

String Searching

`vi` can search for strings just like `ed` does. You type in a `/` followed by the string you want to search for followed by a `CR`. `vi` then scans for the next occurrence of the string:

```
this guy had no arms
so Quasi asked him
how he was going to
ring the bells.
The guy said "I run
up and hit the bells
with my head," and
```

/Quasi`CR`
search for
"Quasi"

```
police inspector
came by and asked
Quasi "who is this
guy?"
Quasi replied, "I
don't know, but his
face rings a bell."
```

```
police inspector
came by and asked
Quasi "who is this
guy?"
Quasi replied, "I
don't know, but his
face rings a bell."
```

/Quasi`CR`
search for
"Quasi"

```
police inspector
came by and asked
Quasi "who is this
guy?"
Quasi replied, "I
don't know, but his
face rings a bell."
/Quasi
```

When you type in a `/`, `vi` puts a `/` on the message line at the bottom of the screen. As you type in the characters you want to search for, `vi` puts these characters on the message line, so you can see the string you're searching for. As you can see, the second search didn't scroll the screen because the next "Quasi" was already on the screen. `vi` simply moved the cursor down two lines. Since the screen wasn't scrolled, the message line remained intact with `/Quasi`.

The `/` command searches *forward* or down through a file, finding the next occurrence of a string. If you want to find the *previous* occurrence of a string, you can use the `?` command. It works the same as `/`, but it searches up through the file for the string:

```
police inspector
came by and asked
Quasi "who is this
guy?"
Quasi replied, "I
don't know, but his
face rings a bell."
/Quasi
```

?QuasiCR
search for
previous "Quasi"

```
police inspector
came by and asked
Quasi "who is this
guy?"
Quasi replied, "I
don't know, but his
face rings a bell."
?Quasi
```

To facilitate searching through a file more than once for a particular string, vi provides you with the n command. After you search for a string with the / command, you can use the n command to look for the next occurrence of that string without typing in the string again. This allows you to search down through a file quickly. If you used the ? instead of the /, then n would search up for the previous string. You might say that n repeats the most recent / or ?.

Words

vi knows about objects called *words* that are simply letters and numbers separated by blanks, tabs, or punctuation marks.   vi allows you to move from word to word, delete them, and change them with simple commands. The w command moves the cursor to the next word, the b command moves the cursor backward a word, and the e command moves the cursor to the end of a word:

```
police inspector
came by and asked
Quasi "who is this
guy?"
Quasi replied, "I
don't know, but his
face rings a bell."
?Quasi
```

w
go to
next word

```
police inspector
came by and asked
Quasi "who is this
guy?"
Quasi replied, "I
don't know, but his
face rings a bell."
?Quasi
```

```
police inspector
came by and asked
Quasi "who is this
guy?"
Quasi replied, "I
don't know, but his
face rings a bell."
?Quasi
```

e
go to
end of word

```
police inspector
came by and asked
Quasi "who is this
guy?"
Quasi replied, "I
don't know, but his
face rings a bell."
?Quasi
```

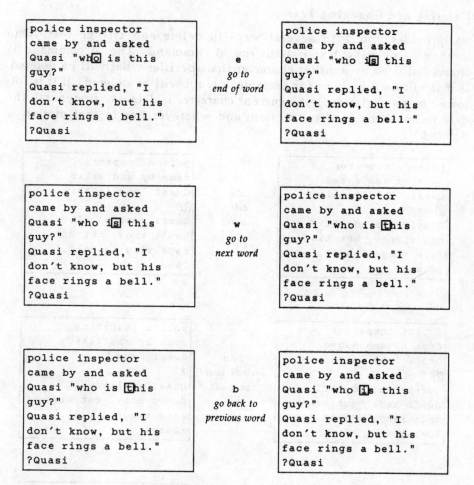

(You might notice that since none of the previous commands scrolled the screen, the `?Quasi` remains on the command line.) The w command goes to the next line when you move past the end of a line and the b command goes to the previous line when you move past the beginning of a line:

Deleting and Changing Text

vi provides you with several ways to delete and change text. One method of deleting text is with the d command. The d command is *always* followed by another character that specifies what will be deleted. If it is followed by a w, for example, a word will be deleted. If it is followed by an 1 (letter l), the current character is deleted. In general, the d is followed by a cursor motion, and whatever lies in that motion is deleted:

```
police inspector
came by and asked
Quasi "who is this
guy?"
Quasi replied, "I
don't know, but his
face rings a bell."
?Quasi
```

dw
*delete
word*

```
police inspector
came by and asked
Quasi "who is this
?"
Quasi replied, "I
don't know, but his
face rings a bell."
?Quasi
```

```
police inspector
came by and asked
Quasi "who is this
?"
Quasi replied, "I
don't know, but his
face rings a bell."
?Quasi
```

2db
*delete backward
two words*

```
police inspector
came by and asked
Quasi "who
?"
Quasi replied, "I
don't know, but his
face rings a bell."
?Quasi
```

```
police inspector
came by and asked
Quasi "who
?"
Quasi replied, "I
don't know, but his
face rings a bell."
?Quasi
```

dh
*delete previous
character*

```
police inspector
came by and asked
Quasi "wh
?"
Quasi replied, "I
don't know, but his
face rings a bell."
?Quasi
```

The dd is a special case of the d command that deletes the current line. Other commands that use cursor motions to determine what is to be affected often use two command letters in a row to "do it to the current line." One of these commands is the c command.

The c command *changes* whatever lies in the specified motion. It puts you in input mode so you can type in your changes. Of course, you must hit the ESC key to get back into command mode. As you might guess, cc changes the entire line. Here is an example of the c command:

```
police inspector
came by and asked
Quasi "who is [t]his
?"
Quasi replied, "I
don't know, but his
face rings a bell."
?Quasi
```
cw
change
a word
```
police inspector
came by and asked
Quasi "who is [t]hi$
?"
Quasi replied, "I
don't know, but his
face rings a bell."
?Quasi
```

Note that a $ is placed at the last character affected by the change.

```
police inspector
came by and asked
Quasi "who is [t]hi$
?"
Quasi replied, "I
don't know, but his
face rings a bell."
?Quasi
```
a testESC
enter change
```
police inspector
came by and asked
Quasi "who is a tes[t]
?"
Quasi replied, "I
don't know, but his
face rings a bell."
?Quasi
```

Control Commands

There are certain commands in vi that are preceded by a colon (:). These are control commands that have to do with external file manipulation (reading and writing files) and some special functions of vi.

The file manipulation commands include :q, which quits vi; :w, which writes the file without quitting vi (unlike ZZ); and :q!, which quits vi without writing, discarding all changes (:q won't quit if changes have been made to the file).

The control commands that perform special functions include :*number*, which moves the cursor to the specified line number, scrolling if necessary (for example, :1 moves the cursor to the beginning of the file) and :*ed-command*, which causes the ed command *ed-command* to be executed. As you can see, the :w and :q commands come from ed. Here are a few examples of these special control commands:

```
police inspector
came by and asked              :1CR
Quasi "who is a test          go to
?"                            line 1
Quasi replied, "I
don't know, but his
face rings a bell."
```

```
A few years ago,
Quasimodo (the
hunchback of Notre
Dame) was looking
for a replacement.
He put an ad in the
paper, and this guy
```

```
A few years ago,
Quasimodo (the
hunchback of Notre             :5CR
Dame) was looking             go to
for a replacement.            line 5
He put an ad in the
paper, and this guy
```

```
A few years ago,
Quasimodo (the
hunchback of Notre
Dame) was looking
for a replacement.
He put an ad in the
paper, and this guy
```

```
A few years ago,
Quasimodo (the
hunchback of Notre         :s/a/is/CR
Dame) was looking          change "a"
for a replacement.          to "is"
He put an ad in the
paper, and this guy
```

```
A few years ago,
Quasimodo (the
hunchback of Notre
Dame) was looking
for is replacement.
He put an ad in the
paper, and this guy
```

```
A few years ago,
Quasimodo (the
hunchback of Notre             u
Dame) was looking         undo change
for is replacement.
He put an ad in the
paper, and this guy
```

```
A few years ago,
Quasimodo (the
hunchback of Notre
Dame) was looking
for a replacement.
He put an ad in the
paper, and this guy
```

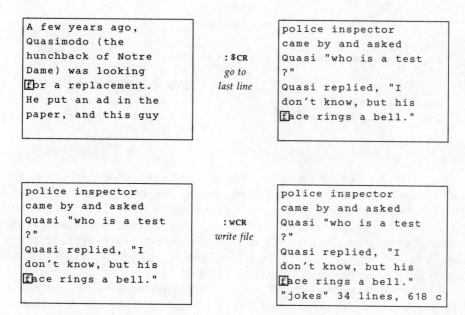

```
A few years ago,
Quasimodo (the                            police inspector
hunchback of Notre                        came by and asked
Dame) was looking        :$CR             Quasi "who is a test
■or a replacement.       go to            ?"
He put an ad in the      last line        Quasi replied, "I
paper, and this guy                       don't know, but his
                                          ■ace rings a bell."


police inspector                          police inspector
came by and asked                         came by and asked
Quasi "who is a test     :wCR             Quasi "who is a test
?"                       write file       ?"
Quasi replied, "I                         Quasi replied, "I
don't know, but his                       don't know, but his
■ace rings a bell."                       ■ace rings a bell."
                                          "jokes" 34 lines, 618 c
```

▪ Odds and Ends ▪

vi provides many commands that are not really necessary. You can use other commands or combinations of other commands to perform the same functions. (Actually, almost all of the commands are unnecessary except for x, dd, i, and a.) For example, you have the o and O commands. o creates a new line after the current one, places the cursor at the beginning of that line, and puts you in insert mode. O does the same, but the new line is *above* the current one.

```
police inspector                          police inspector
came by and asked                         came by and asked
Quasi "who is a test      O               Quasi "who is a test
?"                        create line above ?"
■uasi replied, "I         current line    ▯
don't know, but his                       Quasi replied, "I
face rings a bell."                       don't know, but his
"jokes" 34 lines, 618
```

```
police inspector                    police inspector
came by and asked                   came by and asked
Quasi "who is a test    new textESC  Quasi "who is a test
?"                      put text     ?"
□                       on new line  new tex[t]
Quasi replied, "I                   Quasi replied, "I
don't know, but his                 don't know, but his
```

The D command deletes from the current cursor position to the *end* of the current line. The C command changes the text from the current cursor position to the *end* of the current line. The A command appends at the *end* of the current line, and the I command inserts at the *beginning* of the current line. To move the cursor to the beginning of the line, you just type in a 0 (that's a zero, not an oh), and to move the cursor to the end of the line, you type in a $.

Two commands, r and R, are sometimes very helpful in reducing keystrokes. The r command allows you to replace the next character with one of your choosing. The first character you type after an r replaces the character under the cursor:

```
police inspector                    police inspector
came by and asked                   came by and asked
Quasi "who is a test    r9           Quasi "who is a test
?"                      replace "t"  ?"
new tex[t]              with "9"     new tex[9]
Quasi replied, "I                   Quasi replied, "I
don't know, but his                 don't know, but his
```

Note that r does not put you in insert mode. It just changes *one* character.

The R command is similar to the r command, but it places you in insert mode and allows you to change as many characters as you want. The characters you type in replace the ones already there, but they don't affect the rest of the line. The R command simply overwrites text until you hit ESC.

```
police inspector                    police inspector
came by and asked                   came by and asked
Quasi "who is a test    0            Quasi "who is a test
?"                      move to      ?"
new tex[9]              first column [n]ew tex9
Quasi replied, "I                   Quasi replied, "I
don't know, but his                 don't know, but his
```

```
┌─────────────────────────┐                    ┌─────────────────────────┐
│ police inspector        │                    │ police inspector        │
│ came by and asked       │                    │ came by and asked       │
│ Quasi "who is a test    │   R1234ESC         │ Quasi "who is a test    │
│ ?"                      │  replace text      │ ?"                      │
│ ⬚new tex9               │                    │ 123⬚4⬚tex9              │
│ Quasi replied, "I       │                    │ Quasi replied, "I       │
│ don't know, but his     │                    │ don't know, but his     │
└─────────────────────────┘                    └─────────────────────────┘
```

The s command is equivalent to a c1 command. It changes one or more characters. For example, 4s is the same as 4c1. S is the same as cc (change the whole line).

A RETURN as a cursor motion will move the cursor to the beginning of the first *word* on the next line. It's useful for indented text or program blocks.

Some commands simply don't fall into the typical categories of moving the cursor or deleting, changing, and adding text. One of these is the ι command, which redraws the screen. If something messes up your screen (perhaps some static on your telephone line), you can use the ι command to have your entire screen redrawn. The ι command doesn't change the current cursor position.

Remember the undo command (u)? vi saves deleted text and u puts it back. vi also saves the previous state of a line *before any changes were made to it*. The U command will bring back that original state:

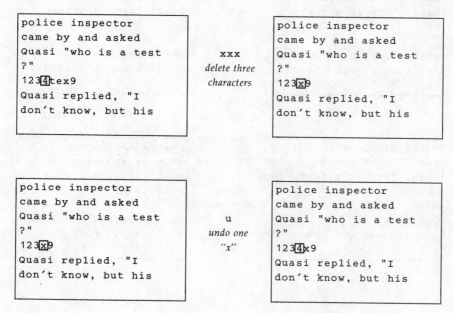

```
┌─────────────────────────┐                    ┌─────────────────────────┐
│ police inspector        │                    │ police inspector        │
│ came by and asked       │                    │ came by and asked       │
│ Quasi "who is a test    │   xxx              │ Quasi "who is a test    │
│ ?"                      │  delete three      │ ?"                      │
│ 123⬚4⬚tex9              │  characters        │ 123⬚x⬚9                 │
│ Quasi replied, "I       │                    │ Quasi replied, "I       │
│ don't know, but his     │                    │ don't know, but his     │
└─────────────────────────┘                    └─────────────────────────┘

┌─────────────────────────┐                    ┌─────────────────────────┐
│ police inspector        │                    │ police inspector        │
│ came by and asked       │                    │ came by and asked       │
│ Quasi "who is a test    │   u                │ Quasi "who is a test    │
│ ?"                      │  undo one          │ ?"                      │
│ 123⬚x⬚9                 │   "x"              │ 123⬚4⬚x9                │
│ Quasi replied, "I       │                    │ Quasi replied, "I       │
│ don't know, but his     │                    │ don't know, but his     │
└─────────────────────────┘                    └─────────────────────────┘
```

```
police inspector
came by and asked
Quasi "who is a test
?"
123█k9
Quasi replied, "I
don't know, but his
```

U
*undo whole
line*

```
police inspector
came by and asked
Quasi "who is a test
?"
█234tex9
Quasi replied, "I
don't know, but his
```

The p command also puts deleted text back, but it allows you to control text placement.   p puts the last deleted text *after* the current cursor position. (P puts it before.)

```
police inspector
came by and asked
Quasi "who is a test
?"
█234tex9
Quasi replied, "I
don't know, but his
```

dw
delete word

```
police inspector
came by and asked
Quasi "who is a test
?"
█
Quasi replied, "I
don't know, but his
```

```
police inspector
came by and asked
Quasi "who is a test
?"
█
Quasi replied, "I
don't know, but his
```

k
up a line

```
police inspector
came by and asked
Quasi "who is a test
█"
Quasi replied, "I
don't know, but his
```

```
police inspector
came by and asked
Quasi "who is a test
█"
Quasi replied, "I
don't know, but his
```

p
*put text
after cursor*

```
police inspector
came by and asked
Quasi "who is a test
?1234tex█"
Quasi replied, "I
don't know, but his
```

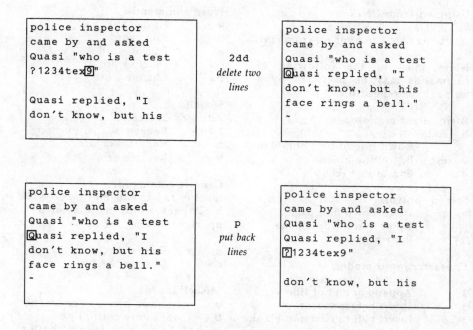

```
police inspector
came by and asked
Quasi "who is a test        2dd        police inspector
?1234tex9"               delete two    came by and asked
                            lines      Quasi "who is a test
Quasi replied, "I                      Quasi replied, "I
don't know, but his                    don't know, but his
                                       face rings a bell."
                                       ~
```

```
police inspector                       police inspector
came by and asked                      came by and asked
Quasi "who is a test         p         Quasi "who is a test
Quasi replied, "I        put back      Quasi replied, "I
don't know, but his        lines       ?1234tex9"
face rings a bell."
~                                      don't know, but his
```

As you can see, p puts back whole lines as well.

The y and Y commands allow you to take (yank) the text without deleting it, so that you can later put it somewhere else with the p or P command. yobject yanks whatever object happens to be (yw, yl, ye, y$, etc.). yy yanks the current line. Y is the same as yy. You can precede y and Y with numbers to determine the number of objects or lines you want to yank. The key sequence YP is often referred to as "copy line." The Y yanks the current line, and P puts the yanked text above the current line.

```
police inspector                       police inspector
came by and asked                      came by and asked
Quasi "who is a test        YP         Quasi "who is a test
Quasi replied, "I        copy line     Quasi replied, "I
?1234tex9"                             ?1234tex9"
                                       ?1234tex9"
don't know, but his
```

The following list summarizes the vi commands we covered in this chapter:

Using vi from UNIX:
$ **vi** *file*   edit *file*
$ **vi -r** *file*   recover *file* from crash

Note: most of the following vi commands may be preceded by a number for repetition.

Basic cursor motions:
h j k l ← ↓ ↑ →
CR   Down line to first non-blank
0 (zero) Beginning of line
$ End of line (EOL)

Screen control:
^U ^D   Up or down half page
^B ^F   Up or down whole page
^L   Reprint page

Character input modes:
†a   Append after cursor
†A   Append at end of line
†i   Insert before cursor
†I   Insert before first non-blank
†o   Add lines after current line
†O   Add lines before current line

Delete and change:
dd   Delete line
†cc   Change line
D   Delete from cursor to EOL
†C   Change from cursor to EOL
x   Delete character
†s   Change character
†S   Change line
r*chr*   Replace current chr with *chr*
†R   Overprint change

Word commands:
w   Next word
b   Back word
e   End of word
dw   Delete word
†cw   Change word

Search:
/*string*/   Search for *string*
?*string*?   Reverse search for *string*
n   Repeat last / or ?
N   Reverse of n

Generic commands:
object **is any cursor motion: w for word; b for back word; h,j,k,l for left, down, up, right;** /*string* **for up to** *string* **etc.**

d*object*   Delete *object*
†c*object*   Change *object*

Miscellaneous:
u   Undo previous command
U   Restore entire line
y*object* Save *object* in temp buffer
Y   Save line(s) in Temp buffer
p   Put saved buffer after cursor
P   Put saved buffer before cursor

Control commands:
:w   Write file
:wq   Write file and quit
:q   Quit
:q!   Quit (override checks)
:*ed-cmd* Run the ed command *ed-cmd*
:*num*   Go to line *num*
ZZ   Same as :wq

Now that you know about vi, you can use it for just about everything you need to type. Letters, programs, electronic mail, and even recipes can be created and edited with vi without any difficulty at all, once you've learned just a few basic commands. You shouldn't consider this chapter a complete description of vi; vi is much too complex to cover in one chapter. If you want more information on vi, there are several references listed in Appendix A as well as in the *UNIX User's Manual* (System V Release 2.0 and later).

---

† Note: all commands marked with † enter input mode and are exited with the escape (ESC) character.

TABLE 7-3. Partial list of terminals supported for `vi`

TERM	Terminal	TERM	Terminal
a980	Adds Consul 980	i400	Infoton 400
regent	Adds Regent series	adm2	Lear Siegler ADM-2
viewpoint	Adds Viewpoint	adm3	Lear Siegler ADM-3
aa	Ann Arbor 4080	adm31	Lear Siegler ADM-31
aaa	Ann Arbor Ambassador	adm3a	Lear Siegler ADM-3a
c100	Concept 100	adm42	Lear Siegler ADM-42
c108	Concept 108	adm5	Lear Siegler ADM-5
dm1520	Datamedia 1520	microterm	Microterm ACT-IV
dm2500	Datamedia 2500	microterm5	Microterm ACT-V
dm3025	Datamedia 3025a	mime	Microterm Mime I, Mime II
3045	Datamedia 3045a	mime2a	Microterm Mime IIa
dt80	Datamedia dt80/1	fox	Perkin-Elmer 1100
gt40	DEC gt40	owl	Perkin-Elmer 1200
gt42	DEC gt42	bantam	Perkin-Elmer 550
vt100	DEC vt100	tek4012	Tektronix 4012
vt132	DEC vt132	tek4013	Tektronix 4013
vt50	DEC vt50	tek4014	Tektronix 4014
vt52	DEC vt52	tek4015	Tektronix 4015
ep40	Execuport 4000	tek4023	Tektronix 4023
ep48	Execuport 4080	tek4025	Tektronix 4024, 4025, 4027
h1000	Hazeltine 1000	tek4112	Tektronix 4110 series
h1420	Hazeltine 1420	t1061	Teleray 1061
h1500	Hazeltine 1500	t3700	Teleray 3700
h1510	Hazeltine 1510	t3800	Teleray 3800 series
h1520	Hazeltine 1520	tty4424	Teletype 4424M
h1552	Hazeltine 1552	tty40	Teletype Dataspeed 40/2
h2000	Hazeltine 2000	tty5620	Teletype 5620
h19	Heathkit h19	tty5420	Teletype 5420
hp2621	HP 2621A, 2621P	tvi912b	Televideo 912
hp2624	HP 2624B, 2623A	tvi920b	Televideo 920
hp2626	HP 2626A, 2626P	tvi925	Televideo 925
hp2640A	HP 2640A	tvi950	Televideo 950
hp2640B	HP 2640B, 2544A	vc303a	Volker-Craig 303a
hp2645	HP 2645	vc303	Volker-Craig 303
hp2648	HP 2648A	vc404	Volker-Craig 404
i100	Infoton 100		

8

UNIX IN THE OFFICE

This chapter shows how useful a UNIX system can be in an office environment. We'll discuss how you can use the UNIX system to communicate to other users, set up an automatic appointment reminder service, and perform simple desk calculations. We'll also discuss how to format documents and have these documents checked for spelling and punctuation mistakes, as well as have their style analyzed.

· "Talking" to Other Users ·

Sometimes you may want to send a message to a user who is logged in on another terminal. That terminal may be located in another office on the floor, or even in another plant location, making it inconvenient for you to talk directly to that person. As an alternative to calling the person on the telephone, you can use the `write` command. `write` allows you to send a message to any other logged-in user. The message that you send will appear on that user's screen. The user will then have the option to send you a reply by initiating a `write` command from his or her own terminal. With this technique, two users can effectively have a "conversation" through their terminals.

The general format of the `write` command is

> `write` *user tty*

where *user* is the user id of the logged-in user and *tty* is an optional tty number. This latter information is needed when there is more than one logged-in user with the same user id—the *tty* number designates the terminal that the message is to be sent to.

As an example, the command

> **write pat**

tells the UNIX system that you wish to start a conversation with the user pat. If pat is not currently logged in, then the following will occur:

```
$ write pat
pat is not logged on.
$
```

If pat is logged in, then the write command will print the following on pat's terminal (it will also "beep" pat's terminal a few times to alert him in case he fell asleep):

```
Message from bob tty15 ...
```

(Here we assume that the write command was initiated by the user bob.) The actual format of this line may differ slightly on your system (for example, System V also includes the date and time on the line).

After initiating the write, the system will wait for you to type your message. This message can contain as many lines as you like. Each line that you type will get displayed on pat's terminal. When you have finished typing your message, enter *CTRL-d* as the first and only character on the line. This will terminate the write and display the line <EOT> on pat's terminal to tell him you are finished.

If pat decides to answer your message, he can initiate his own write command from his terminal:

```
$ write bob
```

Any lines that pat now types will automatically be displayed on bob's terminal. When pat has finished his message, he too must type in *CTRL-d* to terminate his write.

With write commands simultaneously active on both pat's and bob's terminals, you can see how these two users can effectively carry on a conversation. As a matter of convention, most UNIX users typically end their message lines with the characters -o to tell the other user that their message line is finished and that they are (possibly) awaiting a reply (as in "over"). The characters -oo are often used to signal the end of the conversation (as in "over and out").

The following sequence of screens depicts a typical conversation. On the left-hand side of the page we show bob's screen, and on the right-hand side we show pat's screen.

```
$ date
Sat Mar 24 14:32:30 EST 1984
$ who
mblc tty06    Mar 24 08:53
pat  tty08    Mar 24 13:01
bob  tty15    Mar 24 13:19
$
```

bob checks to make sure pat is logged in

```
$ date
Sat Mar 24 14:32:30 EST 1984
$ who
mblc tty06    Mar 24 08:53
pat  tty08    Mar 24 13:01
bob  tty15    Mar 24 13:19
$ write pat
```

Now he initiates a conversation with him

Here's what happens on pat's terminal

```
$ pwd
/a1/pat/tp
$

Message from bob tty15 ...
```

```
$ date
Sat Mar 24 14:32:30 EST 1984
$ who
mblc tty06    Mar 24 08:53
pat  tty08    Mar 24 13:01
bob  tty15    Mar 24 13:19
$ write pat
Hello, pat
I'm trying to find the file
fopen.c.  Do you know what
directory it's in?     -o
```

bob *types his question and*
waits for pat *to answer*

pat *gets the question and sends his response*

```
/a1/pat/tp
$

Message from bob tty15 ...
Hello, pat
I'm trying to find the file
fopen.c.  Do you know what
directory it's in?     -o
write bob
Yes.  You can find it in
/usr/src/lib/libc/port/stdio -o
```

```
$ write pat
Hello, pat
I'm trying to find the file
fopen.c.  Do you know what
directory it's in?     -o

Message from pat tty08 ...
Yes.  You can find it in
/usr/src/lib/libc/port/stdio -o
Thank you    -oo
$
```

bob *gets the answer, thanks*
pat, *and then terminates*
the conversation from his end

Although not shown above, bob typed in a *CTRL-d* after thanking pat.
This terminated the write that he initiated and returned his command

prompt. Let's see what happens on pat's terminal:

Now pat *terminates the conversation from his end by typing CTRL-d*

```
Message from bob tty15 ...
Hello, pat
I'm trying to find the file
fopen.c.  Do you know what
directory it's in?      -o
write bob
Yes.  You can find it in
/usr/src/lib/libc/port/stdio -o
Thank you     -oo
<EOT>
$
```

```
Hello, pat
I'm trying to find the file
fopen.c.  Do you know what
directory it's in?      -o

Message from pat tty08 ...
Yes.  You can find it in
/usr/src/lib/libc/port/stdio -o
Thank you     -oo
$
<EOT>
```

The conversation has now been terminated from both ends

Inhibiting Messages with the mesg Command

Sometimes you may decide that you don't want to receive any messages. For example, you may be running a particular program and you don't want your screen to get all messed up when someone writes to you. The perfect example is when using a screen editor such as vi. If someone tries to write to you while you're in the middle of editing a file, the incoming text will simply overwrite information on your screen, turning your screen into a royal mess! Don't be alarmed, however, as this problem is only temporary; all you have to do to restore your screen to its previous state is type in the screen refresh command *CTRL-l.*

You can tell the UNIX system that you don't want to receive any messages by using the command `mesg`. This command takes a single argument: n or y. The former specifies that you don't want to receive any messages; the latter specifies that you do. So to inhibit incoming messages while you are editing a file, type the command

```
mesg n
```

before you enter the editor. Then, after your edits are complete, you can tell the system that you're willing to once again receive messages by typing the command

```
mesg y
```

If anyone tries to write to you while you have messages inhibited, they will get `Permission denied.` printed at their terminal:

```
$ write steve
Permission denied.              steve is not receiving messages
$
```

Incidentally, you can find out your current message-receiving status by simply typing `mesg` with no arguments:

```
$ mesg n                        No messages, please
$ mesg                          Let's verify it
is n
$ mesg y                        I changed my mind
$ mesg
is y
$
```

• Electronic Mail •

One of the phrases you will hear most often when someone talks about office automation is *electronic mail*. Electronic mail gives you the ability to send messages, memos, or any types of documents to other users electronically—that is, without the use of paper.

The main difference between sending a message to someone using the electronic mail facility and the `write` command is that the latter requires that the person be logged in at the time that the message is sent. With electronic mail, the mail is automatically kept by the system until the user issues the necessary command to read his or her mail. Some people send electronic messages using the following approach: if the user is logged in, then they use the `write` command to talk to the user directly. If the user isn't logged in, then they instead use the `mail` command to send the message.

Under the UNIX system, the `mail` command handles the sending and receiving of electronic mail. The format of the command to send mail to a user is simple:

`mail` *user*

where *user* is the user id of the person you want to send the mail to. Once this command line has been typed, the `mail` program will then wait for you to type your message to be sent to *user*. You can then type in as many lines as you like. When you are done, type *CTRL-d* to tell the `mail` program that the message is completed. The `mail` program will then take your message and "mail" it to the specified user.

Periodically, the shell automatically checks to see if you have received any new mail. If you have, then you will get the following message displayed at your terminal:

`you have mail`

This check is also performed automatically every time you log in.

If you get the message telling you that you have mail, you will then want to read your mail. Reading mail is even easier than sending it—you simply type the command `mail` with *no* arguments. This causes the `mail` program to display any mail that has been sent to you. As each item of mail is displayed at your terminal, the `mail` program displays a `?` and then waits for you to give a "filing disposition" for that piece of mail. Normally, after you type in your disposition, the next piece of mail will then be displayed. After reading your last piece of mail, the `mail` program will return you to the shell command level.

The most commonly used mail dispositions are summarized in Table 8-1. For more information, look under the `mail` command in Section 1 of your *UNIX User's Manual*.

TABLE 8-1. Common `mail` dispositions

Option	Meaning
RETURN	No disposition on this piece of mail; it will still be there next time `mail` is read; next piece of mail is then displayed
d	Delete this piece of mail; next piece of mail is then displayed
s *file*	Save this piece of mail in *file*; next piece of mail is then displayed
*	Print a list of disposition commands
q	Quit reading mail; any unread pieces will be there next time mail is read

Note that on some systems the disposition ? is used to obtain a list of commands rather than * (and some systems accept both!).

Let's take a look at an example of mail. We'll assume here that the user pat wants to send some mail to ruth. We'll also assume that ruth is not logged in at the time that pat sends the mail. We'll show pat's terminal on the left side of the page and ruth's on the right side.

```
$ mail ruth
```

Send mail to ruth

After pat has typed the command mail ruth, he can then enter his message to ruth. The mail command takes every line that he types in up to the *CTRL-d* as the message to be mailed.

```
$ mail ruth
ruth,
    I wanted to remind you that
we have a meeting scheduled for
Monday (3/26) at 1pm.
              pat
$
```

pat *types in his message*

Typing *CTRL-d* causes pat's message to be mailed to ruth. It also returns his command prompt as an indication that the mail command has finished execution.

Now let's assume `ruth` arrives at work and logs in:

Upon logging in, `ruth` is automatically told that she has mail

```
login:ruth
Password:
you have mail

Good morning.
There are 4 users logged in.
$
```

To read her mail, all that `ruth` has to do is type in the command `mail`:

`ruth` reads her mail; the `mail` program then waits for her to enter a disposition

```
Good morning.
There are 4 users logged in.
$ mail
From pat Fri Mar 23 13:27 EST 1984
ruth,
    I wanted to remind you that
we have a meeting scheduled for
Monday (3/26) at 1pm.
                        pat

?
```

she decides not to save it so she types in a d (for delete)

```
There are 4 users logged in.
$ mail
From pat Fri Mar 23 13:27 EST 1984
ruth,
    I wanted to remind you that
we have a meeting scheduled for
Monday (3/26) at 1pm.
                        pat


? d
$
```

The `mail` program inserts a "postmark" at the front of each piece of mail telling where the mail came from and the time and date that it was sent.

If `ruth` had more mail, then the next piece would have been displayed after she entered her `d` disposition. Since she got back her command prompt instead, she obviously had no more mail.

There are some additional points worth noting about the `mail` command. First, you can simply type `mail` at your terminal at any time to see if you have mail. If you don't have any mail, then the message `No mail.` will be displayed:

```
$ mail
No mail.
$
```

You can send the same piece of mail to more than one user by simply listing each user on the command line, as in:

```
$ mail tony fred leela alice
...
```

Since `mail` reads the message to be sent from standard input, you can redirect its input from a file. So to send the contents of the file `reminder` to `ruth`, the following could be used:

```
$ mail ruth < reminder
$
```

If you have to send a long message to someone, this technique comes in handy. You can first enter your message into a file using a text editor such as `ed` or `vi`, make any necessary changes, and then mail the contents of the file. That way you can even keep a copy of the message for yourself!

A final point: Unlike the `write` command, you can send messages to users on *other* computer systems with the `mail` command. This is discussed in more detail in Chapter 11.

▪ Calendar Commands ▪

Two commands are provided that help you keep track of your days. One of these is a command to display a calendar at the terminal and another to remind you of things you have to do on certain dates.

Displaying a Calendar: the `cal` Command

Type in the command `cal` 1985 at your terminal. This is what you'll get:

```
$ cal 1985
```

```
                                 1985

           Jan                    Feb                    Mar
   S  M Tu  W Th  F  S     S  M Tu  W Th  F  S     S  M Tu  W Th  F  S
         1  2  3  4  5                    1  2                    1  2
   6  7  8  9 10 11 12     3  4  5  6  7  8  9     3  4  5  6  7  8  9
  13 14 15 16 17 18 19    10 11 12 13 14 15 16    10 11 12 13 14 15 16
  20 21 22 23 24 25 26    17 18 19 20 21 22 23    17 18 19 20 21 22 23
  27 28 29 30 31          24 25 26 27 28          24 25 26 27 28 29 30
                                                  31

           Apr                    May                    Jun
   S  M Tu  W Th  F  S     S  M Tu  W Th  F  S     S  M Tu  W Th  F  S
      1  2  3  4  5  6              1  2  3  4                       1
   7  8  9 10 11 12 13     5  6  7  8  9 10 11     2  3  4  5  6  7  8
  14 15 16 17 18 19 20    12 13 14 15 16 17 18     9 10 11 12 13 14 15
  21 22 23 24 25 26 27    19 20 21 22 23 24 25    16 17 18 19 20 21 22
  28 29 30                26 27 28 29 30 31       23 24 25 26 27 28 29
                                                  30

           Jul                    Aug                    Sep
   S  M Tu  W Th  F  S     S  M Tu  W Th  F  S     S  M Tu  W Th  F  S
      1  2  3  4  5  6              1  2  3     1  2  3  4  5  6  7
   7  8  9 10 11 12 13     4  5  6  7  8  9 10     8  9 10 11 12 13 14
  14 15 16 17 18 19 20    11 12 13 14 15 16 17    15 16 17 18 19 20 21
  21 22 23 24 25 26 27    18 19 20 21 22 23 24    22 23 24 25 26 27 28
  28 29 30 31             25 26 27 28 29 30 31    29 30

           Oct                    Nov                    Dec
   S  M Tu  W Th  F  S     S  M Tu  W Th  F  S     S  M Tu  W Th  F  S
         1  2  3  4  5                    1  2     1  2  3  4  5  6  7
   6  7  8  9 10 11 12     3  4  5  6  7  8  9     8  9 10 11 12 13 14
  13 14 15 16 17 18 19    10 11 12 13 14 15 16    15 16 17 18 19 20 21
  20 21 22 23 24 25 26    17 18 19 20 21 22 23    22 23 24 25 26 27 28
  27 28 29 30 31          24 25 26 27 28 29 30    29 30 31
```

```
$
```

As you can see, typing the command `cal` 1985 resulted in the display of a calendar for the year 1985. And you can get a calendar for any year you want, simply by typing `cal` followed by the year. So, `cal 1968` would display a calendar for the year 1968, and `cal 2000` would display one for the year 2000.

In case you're not interested in getting a full year's calendar displayed at your terminal, `cal` gives you the option to display just a single month of any given year. To do this, the format of the `cal` command is

<code>cal</code> month year

where *month* is a numerical month number from 1 through 12 and *year* is as before.

Here are some examples:

```
$ cal 1 2001                          Calendar for January 2001
    January 2001
 S   M Tu  W Th   F   S
     1   2   3   4   5   6
 7   8   9  10  11  12  13
14  15  16  17  18  19  20
21  22  23  24  25  26  27
28  29  30  31

$ cal 7 1955                          Calendar for July 1955
    July 1955
 S   M Tu  W Th   F   S
                  1   2
 3   4   5   6   7   8   9
10  11  12  13  14  15  16
17  18  19  20  21  22  23
24  25  26  27  28  29  30
31

$
```

As you can see, operation of `cal` is simple; just remember that the full year must always be spelled out (so `cal 7 55` would display a calendar for July 55 and not July 1955!)

A note about the `cal` program: if you're running UNIX System V Release 2 or later, then you can type in `cal` without any arguments to get a calendar printed for the current month.

Calendar Reminder Service: `calendar`

Many busy people keep track of their scheduled appointments by recording them in a book. At the beginning of each day, they may consult their book to see what appointments are scheduled for that day. At the end of the day, they might also consult the book to see what's in store for the next day.

The UNIX system provides a similar type of facility that enables you to automatically keep track of your appointments. This is done with the `calendar` command. Instead of recording your appointments in a book, you write them into a file called `calendar` instead. Along with each appointment you must also record the date—in any suitable format as long as both the month and the day of the appointment are recorded. Suitable date formats include Feb. 4, February 4, 2/4, etc.

At the beginning of each day, most UNIX systems will automatically check your `calendar` file to see if you have any appointments entered for that day *or* for the following day (and if it's Friday, then the following day extends through Monday).

If you do have some appointments scheduled for these days, then the system will automatically mail you a list of your appointments.

If your system does not perform this automatic check each day, then you can do it yourself! In fact, you can get a list of your appointments for the current and following day at any time by simply typing the command `calendar` at your terminal. If you want, you can add this command to your `.profile` to cause your appointments to be checked every time you log in.

But enough talk; let's see how it works. For starters, let's assume that today is July 15, and that it's a Thursday. Further assume that you have entered a list of appointments into a file called `calendar` in your HOME directory. Now to the example:

```
$ date
Thu Jul 15 19:38:14 EST 1988
$ cd                            Go to the HOME directory
$ cat calendar                  and look at the calendar file
7/14: 9:50am        PFS Meeting

7/15: 10:30am       Call EK&F to get estimate.
7/15: 1:30pm        Meet with Pat to discuss outline

7/16: 11:00am       Computer Center User's Meeting
7/16:               in Room 3A-108
7/16: 4:30pm        Call Purchasing about 5620 order

7/17: noon          lunch with Tony
$ calendar                      See what's scheduled
7/15: 10:30am       Call EK&F to get estimate.
7/15: 1:30pm        Meet with Pat to discuss outline
7/16: 11:00am       Computer Center User's Meeting
7/16:               in Room 3A-108
7/16: 4:30pm        Call Purchasing about 5620 order
$
```

Don't confuse the `calendar` command with the file of the same name. The `calendar` file must reside in your `HOME` directory in order to get automatic once-a-day processing of the file (if supported on your system). However, when you execute the `calendar` command, it looks for the file `calendar` *only in the current directory*. This means that you should be in your `HOME` directory whenever you execute this command.

The `calendar` command is not very intelligent about appointments. When the command is executed, it sequentially searches through the `calendar` file for lines that contain either today's or tomorrow's date (and remember, "tomorrow" extends through Monday if "today" is Friday). Whenever it finds such a line, it simply displays it at the terminal. This means that if you have an appointment that spans more than one line then you must include the date on every line. This explains why you had to write the date 7/16 on the second line of the Computer Center User's Meeting reminder.

The `calendar` file must be completely maintained by you. You have to add and remove appointments from the file; the system does not do it for you. Of course, with the help of a text editor such as `ed` or `vi`, this is not a difficult thing to do.

· A Desk Calculator Program ·

The UNIX system has two programs that enable you to effectively convert your multimillion dollar computer into a handy desktop calculator! One program is called `bc`, and the other is called `dc`. We'll only briefly describe the former here. (The latter program operates using so-called "Reverse Polish Notation." Hewlett-Packard calculator owners will be quite familiar with this, so they may wish to learn how to use that program instead.)

To start up the desk calculator program you simply type in `bc`:

```
$ bc
```

As is typical, `bc` does not display any command prompt to let you know it has started—it simply sits there and waits for you to type in your calculations. `bc` continues to operate this way until you enter *CTRL-d* to terminate the program.

Once you've started up `bc`, it's very easy to use it:

```
2 + 5                          Add 2 and 5
7
```

`bc` automatically displays the result of each operation; there's no need to hit an equals key or anything like that.

The symbol recognized as the multiplication operator by bc is the asterisk *:

```
753.25 * 2
1506.50
1 + 2 * 10
21
```

Multiplication and division operations are done before addition and subtraction operations, if they appear in the same expression. You can always use parentheses if you want to change that:

```
(1 + 2)*10
30
```

The division operator is the slash /. See what happens if you try to divide 1 by 2:

```
1 / 2
0
```

Normally, bc automatically selects the number of decimal places for displaying results. However, for division operations, it won't display any decimal places unless you tell it to. This is done by setting scale to the desired number of places.

```
scale=3                    Accuracy to three decimal places
1 / 2
0.500                      That's better
```

If you want to save the result of an operation, you can temporarily store it in any one of 26 "memories," identified by the letters a-z:

```
a=1749.23 * 12             Save the result in a
```

The value stored in a can be subsequently "recalled" by simply typing a:

```
a                          Show me what's stored in a
20990.76
```

You can even use its value in subsequent expressions:

```
a * 30
629722.80
```

There are many other features provided by bc that we won't describe here. There is a math library for calculating logs, sines, cosines, etc.;

and the program even has some built-in programming capabilities. For more details, read BC—*An Arbitrary Precision Desk-Calculator Language* by L. L. Cherry and R. Morris, Bell Laboratories, Inc.

• Word Processing •

Nowhere is there more evidence of the computer's influence in the office than in the area of word processing. As a result of word processing, memos, reports and documents are prepared in much less time and at greatly reduced costs. This is particularly true when dealing with documents that go through many rounds of revisions. Formerly, these documents were either partially or fully retyped. Now, we simply make the changes to the document and the word processor takes care of the rest—it prints the document, paginates it, justifies it, and even checks for spelling mistakes!

The UNIX system provides a multitude of word-processing tools. These tools are logically divided into two groups: format control and analysis. The first group allows you to control the physical appearance of the document; i.e., how the document will look when it's printed. The second is for analyzing the text contained in the document, i.e., proofreading the document and describing its style. This analysis includes checking for spelling and punctuation mistakes, overused words, misused phrases, and split infinitives.

Document formatting is done with a program called `nroff`; document analysis is done with a set of programs collectively called the WRITER'S WORKBENCH system.

• Formatting Text with `nroff` •

As we mentioned, the `nroff` program is used to control the way a document will look when it's printed. This is done by interspersing `nroff` "commands" throughout the actual text wherever such control is desired. There are about 90 different `nroff` commands that enable you to specify everything from the length of each line to the spacing to use between each line of the document. It is our intention to give you a brief introduction to `nroff` in this section by describing a dozen or so basic commands. With this small set of commands, you will be able to use `nroff` to format letters, memos, and even small documents.

Setting Up the Page

One of the first things you need to learn is how to tell `nroff` about the page that you want the document printed on. Specifically, you should tell `nroff`

- where to set the left margin
- where to set the right margin
- what the length of the page is

Setting of the left margin is done with the page offset command `.po` (*all* `nroff` commands start with a `.` and must be typed in the first column of the line). Immediately after the `.po` you type the distance from the left edge of the paper you want the margin to be set at, followed by the letter *i* to tell `nroff` that this distance is expressed in *inches* (`nroff` can also take distances expressed in other units such as centimeters or *ems*). Thus, to set the left margin in at 1 inch, the following `nroff` command would be used:

    .po 1i

To set it to 2½ inches, the following would work:

    .po 2.5i

You get the picture.

Setting the right margin is a little different. Instead of specifying the distance from the right margin, you specify the total length of a line of text. This is done with the line length command `.11`. For example, suppose you're dealing with 8½-by-11-inch paper. If you want your left and right margins both to be 1 inch wide, then your line length should be set to 8½ - 2 = 6½ inches. So to set up both margins on the page, the following two commands would appear in your document:

    .po 1i   *1-inch margin on the left*
    .11 6.5i   *1-inch margin on the right*

Now we come to the last command for specifying the physical layout of the page: the `.pl` command. This command is used to specify the length of the page. So, for 8½-by-11-inch paper, you would write:

    .pl 11i

Filling and Adjusting Text

In order for a document to look nice, you usually try to make each line appear as uniform as possible. That means that you try to align your right margin as precisely as you can. With the `nroff` program, there are basically three choices available to you for controlling this alignment. You can have

(1) no alignment done;

(2) each line filled with as many words as possible, taking words from the following lines if necessary; or

(3) each line filled as in (2) and also padded with blanks so that every line is aligned at the right margin.

The second option is known as *filling* the text, whereas the third is known as *adjusting* the text. You can't have the latter without the former; that is, if you select the adjust option, then filling is included.

Let's take a small sample of text to see the difference between the three options. Here's the sample:

```
$ cat sample
Here is some sample text.
In the first case,
we'll show the default:
adjust and fill on.
Then, we'll turn
adjust off.  Finally,
we'll see  what happens
when both adjust and
fill are turned off.
$
```

Before we can proceed with our example, we must digress slightly to discuss the mechanisms for processing a document through `nroff`.

The general format of the `nroff` command is

`nroff` **-T***dev file*

where *dev* is an abbreviation for a terminal or printer that the output from `nroff` is to be sent to (see Table 8-2), and *file* is the name of the document to be printed.

TABLE 8-2. Device abbreviations for `nroff`

Abbreviation	Used for
37	TELETYPE® Model 37 terminal
tn300	GE TermiNet 300
300	DASI 300
382	DTC-382
450	DASI 450
832	Anderson Jacobson 832
2631	Hewlett-Packard 2631
4000A	Trendata 4000A
lp	ASCII line printer
X	EBCDIC line printer

In the remaining examples in this section, we'll assume that the output is going to a standard ASCII line printer; therefore, we'll use the -Tlp option. (In fact, if you can't figure out what abbreviation to use from Table 8-2, try 1p—it's a good guess.)

`nroff` writes its output to standard output. This means that if you want to get a document printed on the printer then you should pipe `nroff`'s output into a line printer program like `lp`:

```
nroff -Tlp sample | lp
```

This represents the complete command sequence to get the contents of the file `sample` formatted and then printed on the line printer.

If you don't pipe `nroff`'s output anywhere then it will get displayed at the terminal by default. This is how you can check out your format requests before they get printed. However, we do recommend that you use one of the "paging" programs such as `pg` or `more` to prevent your document from "flying" off the screen. Therefore, the command sequence

```
nroff -Tlp sample | pg
```

would enable you to view the results of the `nroff` at the terminal one screenful at a time. Then once you're satisfied with the results, you can pipe the output to `1p` instead.

Now back to the example. For the first case we'll see what happens by default; that is, if we don't explicitly insert any line adjust or fill commands. For purposes of this example, we'll assume that we'll set the line length to 3½ inches, and the page length to 1½ inches. We won't bother setting the left margin.

```
$ cat sample
.ll 3.5i                            Set the line length to 3½ inches
.pl 1.5i                            and the page length to 1½ inches
Here is some sample text.
In the first case,
we'll show the default:
adjust and fill on.
Then, we'll turn
adjust off.  Finally,
we'll see  what happens
when both adjust and
fill are turned off.
$ nroff -Tlp sample                 Process the file through nroff
Here is some sample  text.  In  the
first case, we'll show the default:
adjust and fill  on.   Then,  we'll
turn  adjust  off.   Finally, we'll
see  what happens when both  adjust
and fill are turned off.



$
```

We had the output of nroff go directly to the terminal, without feeding it through a paging program first since we're only dealing with a very small file. You'll notice that nroff printed three blank lines at the end. This was done to "fill up" the lines on our 1½-inch page (most printers print six lines per inch, so 1½-inches would represent nine lines of text).

As you can see, nroff filled and adjusted the lines in sample. Now let's see what happens if we use the .na command to turn off line adjusting.

```
$ cat sample
.ll 3.5i
.pl 1.5i
.na                              No line adjusting
Here is some sample text.
In the first case,
we'll show the default:
adjust and fill on.
Then, we'll turn
adjust off.  Finally,
we'll see  what happens
when both adjust and
fill are turned off.
$ nroff -Tlp sample
Here is some sample text. In the
first case, we'll show the default:
adjust and fill on.  Then, we'll
turn adjust off.  Finally, we'll
see  what happens when both adjust
and fill are turned off.



$
```

nroff still tries to fit as many words on a line as possible; however, with adjust turned off, the lines are not padded with spaces.

To turn off line fill mode, the nroff "no fill" command .nf is used. Since adjusting can only be done with filling, lines that are not filled will not be adjusted.

The next example shows what happens when fill mode is turned off with the .nf command.

```
$ cat sample
.ll 3.5i
.pl 1.5i
.nf                              No fill (that also means no adjust)
Here is some sample text.
In the first case,
we'll show the default:
adjust and fill on.
Then, we'll turn
adjust off.  Finally,
we'll see  what happens
when both adjust and
fill are turned off.
$ nroff -Tlp sample
Here is some sample text.
In the first case,
we'll show the default:
```

```
adjust and fill on.
Then, we'll turn
adjust off.  Finally,
we'll see  what happens
when both adjust and
fill are turned off.
$
```

As you can see, `nroff` really did nothing at all to the text. The `.nf` command is useful when you want `nroff` to leave a portion of your text alone. It simply "writes it as it sees it."

After you've turned off fill mode, you may later decide to turn it back on again. This is readily accomplished with the fill command `.fi`. And if you turned adjust mode off with a `.na` command and wanted to turn it back on, the command to use is `.ad`. Of course, turning adjust back on automatically turns fill back on.

Related to the notion of filling and adjusting text is the hyphenation of words at the end of lines. Normally, `nroff` does not do this for you. However, you can use the `.hy` command to have `nroff` automatically hyphenate your text. This can improve the appearance of your formatted text. (This book was produced using the automatic hyphenation feature.)

Skipping Lines

To skip a line in your text, you can simply insert a blank line at the appropriate point in your file:

```
$ cat sample
.pl 1.5i
Skip a line

here
$ nroff -Tlp sample
Skip a line

here



$
```

To skip more lines, you simply insert more blank lines in the file:

```
$ cat sample
.pl 1.5i
Skip 4 lines



here
$ nroff -Tlp sample
Skip 4 lines




here



$
```

Alternatively, you can use an nroff command designed specifically for skipping lines: .sp. The number of lines to skip is typed right after the .sp or may be omitted if you just want to skip a single line. The following shows how a .sp 4 command is used to skip four lines.

```
$ cat sample
.pl 1.5i
Skip 4 lines
.sp 4
here
$ nroff -Tlp sample
Skip 4 lines




here



$
```

Centering Text

It's very easy to center text on the page with nroff. To center a single line, you simply place the .ce command before the line to be centered:

```
$ cat sample
.ll 3.5i
.pl 1.5i
.ce
Center this line
xxxxxxxxxxxxxxxxxxxxxxxxxxxxxxxxxxxxx
$ nroff -Tlp sample
        Center this line
xxxxxxxxxxxxxxxxxxxxxxxxxxxxxxxxxxxxx
```
Center the line that follows

```
$
```

To center more than one consecutive line of text, it is not necessary to include separate .ce commands before each line. Instead, you can use a single .ce immediately before the group of lines to be centered. In that case, the .ce command takes the form

$$.ce\ n$$

where *n* is the number of lines to be centered.

```
$ cat sample
.ll 3.5i
.pl 1.5i
.ce 4
Stephen Kochan & Patrick Wood
AT&T Bell Laboratories
1 Whippany Road
Whippany, New Jersey  07981
$ nroff -Tlp sample
   Stephen Kochan & Patrick Wood
      AT&T Bell Laboratories
         1 Whippany Road
      Whippany, New Jersey  07981
```
Center the next four lines

```
$
```

Underlining Text

To underline some text in nroff, you simply use the .ul command. On the next line after this command, you type the word or words that are to be underlined. It's that simple.

```
$ cat text
.ll 3.5i
.pl 1.5i
Underlining a
.ul
word
in the middle of a sentence is easy.
.ul
Underlining an entire sentence is just as easy.
$ nroff -Tlp text
Underlining a word in the middle of
a sentence is easy.  Underlining an
entire sentence is just as easy.
$
```

Whatever text gets typed on the line following the .ul will get under-lined by nroff. Beware that some printers may not directly support this capability. You may have to use a special filter program to get your text printed properly. See your system administrator if you run into problems.

Getting Double-Spaced Output

To get double-spaced output, you can place the command

```
.ls 2
```

at the beginning of your text. You can actually supply any number you desire after the .ls. So .ls 3 would give you triple-spaced output, whereas .ls 1 would produce single-spaced output (this is what you get by default).

Indenting Text

The .in command makes it easy to indent text. The number that immediately follows .in specifies the distance to indent from the left margin. The indentation remains in effect until another .in command is issued.

```
$ cat sample
.ll 3.5i
.pl 1.5i
Indentation is useful for setting off
```

```
certain portions of text.
.in .5i
Here we indent in a half-inch from the
left margin.
.in 0i
And then we go back.
$ nroff -Tlp sample
Indentation is useful  for  setting
off certain portions of text.
     Here we indent in a  half-inch
     from the left margin.
And then we go back.



    $
```

Going to a New Page

Sometimes you may want to start some text at the top of a new page. To force this situation, use the .bp command, which stands for *break page*.

Give Me a Break

Normally, when nroff is operating in fill mode, it tries to fit as many words on a line as it can by bringing in words from subsequent lines. However, there are times when nroff will not do this, even while operating in fill mode. Certain commands cause this; in nroff terminology, these commands are said to cause a *break*. For example, the line space command .sp causes a break. nroff will not use words that follow the .sp to fill the line before the break. And since this line will not be filled, it won't be adjusted either. Let's look at an example.

```
$ cat sample
.ll 3.5i
.pl 1.5i
Here is some text to show the effect
of causing a break.
.sp
Notice that words from this line were
not used to fill in the previous line.
Also notice that the line before
the .sp was not filled or adjusted.
$ nroff -Tlp sample
Here  is  some  text  to  show  the
effect of causing a break.

Notice that words  from  this  line
were   not  used  to  fill  in  the
previous line.  Also  notice  that
the  line  before  the  .sp was not
filled or adjusted.


$
```

Breaks can also be caused in other ways: A blank line in your text causes a break, as does any line that *begins* with a blank space (but *not* a tab).

Sometimes you may want to force a break. To do this you can use the .br command. This command causes a break but otherwise has no effect.

Command Summary

To refresh your memory, we have summarized each of the nroff commands described in this section in the following table. In the third column we have identified whether the command causes a break.

TABLE 8-3. Basic `nroff` **commands**

Command	Description	Breaks?
`.ad`	Adjust text (provided fill mode hasn't been turned off)	*no*
`.bp`	Go to top of next page	*yes*
`.br`	Cause a break	*yes*
`.fi`	Fill text (and also adjust it provided adjust hasn't been turned off with a `.na` command)	*yes*
`.ce` *n*	Center next *n* lines of text (or just next line if *n* is omitted)	*yes*
`.hy`	Hyphenate text	*no*
`.in` *ni*	Indent *n* inches from the left margin	
`.ll` *ni*	Set line length to *n* inches	*no*
`.ls` *n*	Set line spacing to *n*; *n* = 2 for double-spaced output	*no*
`.na`	Don't adjust text	*no*
`.nf`	Don't fill or adjust text	*yes*
`.pl` *ni*	Set page length to *n* inches	*no*
`.po` *ni*	Set left margin to *n* inches	*no*
`.sp` *n*	Skip *n* lines (or just 1 if *n* is omitted)	*yes*
`.ul` *n*	Underline next *n* lines of text (or just next line if *n* is omitted)	*no*

A Small Example

Now we are ready to take a look at a small, complete example. We'll show how a letter can be formatted using the `nroff` commands covered in this section.

Let's assume that we have letterhead that is only 5 inches wide and 5 inches long. We'll leave ½-inch margin on both sides of the page.

Here is the `nroff` input for the sample letter:

```
.po  .5i                              ½-inch left margin
.ll  4i                               ½-inch right margin
.pl  5i                               Length of page is 5 inches
.hy                                   Hyphenate words
.nf                                   Don't fill lines
                      April 4, 1984
.sp  3                                Skip three lines
Doug McCormick
Hayden Book Company
10 Mulholland Drive
Hasbrouck Heights, N. J.   07604
.sp  2                                Skip two more
Dear Doug:
.sp  2                                And two more
.fi                                   Now fill and adjust
Enclosed is the final installment of our book.
As soon as we receive the corrections from
your copy and production editors we will
incorporate them into the text and then
start work on the index.

Please call me if you have any questions.
.sp  3                                Skip three lines
Sincerely yours,
.sp  2                                Skip two lines
Steve Kochan
```

We entered "no-fill" mode at the start so that the address lines weren't filled by `nroff`. Later, when we were about to start the text of the letter, we turned fill mode back on. And since we never explicitly turned off adjust mode, all subsequent lines were filled *and* adjusted. (Remember, lines can only be adjusted if they're also filled. As long as adjust mode isn't turned off with a `.na` command, lines will always be adjusted whenever fill mode is enabled.)

Running this text through `nroff` produces the following result:

April 4, 1984

Doug McCormick
Hayden Book Company
10 Mulholland Drive
Hasbrouck Heights, N. J. 07604

Dear Doug:

Enclosed is the final installment of our
book. As soon as we receive the correc-
tions from your copy and production editors we will incorporate them into the
text and then start work on the index.

Please call me if you have any questions.

Sincerely yours,

Steve Kochan

Formatting Larger Documents

The last example shows how easy it is to format small documents with
nroff. Actually, it's just as easy to format larger documents, except
when dealing with such documents you'll need some features not provided by the commands we have presented. The most obvious feature is
page numbering; nroff does not number your pages for you. In fact,
it does nothing special at all at the start of a new page. This can be
annoying if you have to format multipage documents. Also, nroff
does nothing special at the bottom of a page. It will just keep on printing all the way to the bottom without leaving a margin.

In case you want to format multipage documents, you can insert
the following lines at the start of the document:

```
.lt  6.5i                    Change this to your line length
.de hd
.if  \\n%>1 \{\
'sp .5i
.tl ''-%-'' \}
'sp |1i
.ns
..
.de fo
'bp
..
.wh  0 hd
.wh  -1i fo
```

These nroff commands will cause each page after the first to be numbered using the format -n-, where n is the page number. This will
appear centered on the page, ½ inch down from the top. These commands will also cause 1 inch to be left at the bottom of each page.

nroff Add-On Packages

If you find that you still need more text-processing features, such as
automatic footnote processing, the ability to define a block of text that
can't be split across two pages, automatically numbered lists, and so on,
then you will have to use the special nroff add-on package known as
MM—which stands for Memorandum Macros. As the name implies, this
add-on package was developed for the express purpose of formatting
technical documents, in particular memoranda.[†] To find out how to use
the MM formatting package, consult the documents *MM—Memorandum
Macros*, by D. W. Smith and J. R. Mashey, Bell Laboratories, Inc. and *Typing Documents with MM* by D. W. Smith and E. M. Piskorik, Bell Laboratories, Inc.

There are also special packages designed to work with nroff to
format tables (like those used in this book) and mathematical equations.
The name of the former program is tbl and the latter neqn.

Typesetting Text: troff

This entire book was typeset by a program that is nearly identical to
nroff. This program is called troff and it differs from nroff primarily in that it produces its output for a phototypesetter. Since the
commands for nroff and troff are highly compatible, the former
can be used to debug text before it is sent off to the phototypesetter
machine for printing.

Available for use with troff is a program for drawing figures
called pic. Figures are described in a special language and then run
through the pic program. The output from pic is troff input.

---

† If the MM package is not available on your system then you may instead have an older add-on package called MS.

A program called `cip` allows you to interactively draw figures on a Teletype 5620 terminal. The output from `cip` is actually a `pic` description of the figure. All of the figures in this book were designed with `cip`, processed by `pic`, and then phototypeset by `troff`.

Initially, `troff` was designed with a specific phototypesetter in mind: the Wang Laboratories, Inc C/A/T phototypesetter. However, more recently `troff` has been made "device independent," i.e., it now can be used to produce high-quality output on a variety of devices provided they have the necessary hardware capabilities and support software.

The DOCUMENTER'S WORKBENCH System

As of System V, the programs related to formatting text have been grouped into a package known as the DOCUMENTER'S WORKBENCH system. These programs include `nroff`, `troff`, device-independent `troff`, `pic`, and `sroff` (a faster version of `nroff`). Also included is the `MM` memorandum macros package.

• The WRITER'S WORKBENCH System •

The WRITER'S WORKBENCH is a package of programs for analyzing documents. In this section we will give you an overview of this system. In Appendix C all of the functions available with the WRITER'S WORKBENCH system are listed. You may want to ask your system administrator whether this package is available on your system. (Or just type the command `wwb` and see what happens!)

To have a document processed by the WRITER'S WORKBENCH system, you simply type the command `wwb` followed by the name of the file that contains the document you want analyzed. You don't have to worry if this file is interspersed with `nroff` commands since `wwb` simply ignores them anyway.

After typing the `wwb` command, the specified document will be run through a battery of checks and an analysis report will be displayed at the terminal. The report is logically divided into two parts: the first part covers mistakes discovered by the proofreading system and identifies the following:

- spelling mistakes
- punctuation mistakes
- overused words
- wordy or misused phrases
- split infinitives

The second part of the report is an analysis of the writing style of the document. This includes commentary on the document's readability,

sentence variation and structure, and use of passives and nominalizations.

To demonstrate the analysis done by the WRITER'S WORKBENCH,
let's try it out on the following short document:

```
$ cat wwbtext
This is just a small sample of text to
see the type of report generated by
the ``Writer's Workbench''.  Since
wwb generates a large amount
of output, it's best to usually
redirect it to a file--or to
a paging program such as pg or
more which will display the output
one screenful at a time.

As the  report issued by wwb will
tell us, an analysis of the style of
a documnet of this size may be
misleading.  But who cares?  We only
want to see what the report looks
like anyway!
$
```

And now let's run it through wwb:

```
$ wwb wwbtext


    Apr  8 16:55 1984   PROOFR OUTPUT FOR wwbtext Page 1


*********************** SPELLING ***************************

Possible spelling errors in wwbtext are:

documnet                  pg                        wwb

If any of these words are spelled correctly, later type
                spelladd word1 word2 ... wordn
to have them added to your spelldict file.

*********************** PUNCTUATION ************************

The punctuation in wwbtext is first described.

0 double quotes and 0 single quotes
1 `` quotes and 1 '' quotes
2 apostrophes
0 left parentheses and 0 right ones

The program next prints any sentence that it thinks is
incorrectly punctuated and follows it by its correction.
```

```
line 3
OLD: the ``Writer's Workbench''.  Since
NEW: the ``Writer's Workbench.''  Since
```

For more information about punctuation rules, type:
                              punctrules

*********************** DOUBLE WORDS ***********************

For file wwbtext:

No double words found

*********************** WORD CHOICE ***********************

Sentences with possibly wordy or misused phrases are listed next,
followed by suggested revisions.

For file wwbtext

beginning line 3 wwbtext
Since wwb generates a large amount of output, it's best to usually
redirect it to a file--or to a paging program such as pg or more
[which] will display the output one screenful at a time.

Apr 8 16:55 1984 PROOFR OUTPUT FOR wwbtext Page 2

file wwbtext: number of lines 16 number of phrases found 1

Please wait for the substitution phrases

------------------ Table of Substitutions --------------------

PHRASE   SUBSTITUTION

which: use ""that" when clause is restrictive" for " which"
which: use "of which" for " of that"
which: use "when" for " at which time"

----

    * Not all the revisions will be appropriate for your document.

* When there is more than one suggestion for just one bracketed
  word, you will have to choose the case that fits your use.
* Capitalized words are instructions, not suggestions.
* To find out more about each phrase, type "worduse phrase."

NOTE: If you want this program to look for additional phrases
or to stop looking for some, for instance to stop
flagging "impact," type the command dictadd.

******************** SPLIT INFINITIVES ********************

For file wwbtext:

Possible split infinitives:

to usually redirect

For information on split infinitives type:

splitrules

Apr 8 16:55 1984 prose -mm -li -l -tm wwbtext Page 1

BECAUSE YOUR TEXT IS SHORT (< 2000 WORDS & < 100 SENTENCES),
THE FOLLOWING ANALYSIS MAY BE MISLEADING.

NOTE: Your document is being compared against standards
derived from 30 technical memoranda, classified as good
by managers in the research area of Bell Laboratories.

READABILITY

The Kincaid readability formula predicts that your text
can be read by someone with 7 or more years of schooling,
which is a low score for this type of document. If this is
an instructional text (in paragraph form), run prose -t for
a more appropriate review.

VARIATION

You have an appropriate distribution of sentence types.

SENTENCE STRUCTURE

Passives and Nominalizations

You have appropriately limited your use of passives and
nominalizations (nouns made from verbs, e.g. "description").

PROSE OUTPUTS

<u>Options</u>

You can request that your document be compared against different standards; typing -t with the prose command, e.g.,

                    prose -t filename

will compare your text against training documents.

A -s option will provide a very short version of the <u>prose</u> output.

                    prose -s filename

If you already have a style table in a file, you can save time by using it as the input to <u>prose</u> rather than the textfile. To do this, precede the style table filename with a -f, e.g.,

                  prose -f styletable-filename

All the options can be selected at the same time and listed in any order.

                  prose -f styletable-filename -s -t

<u>Statistics</u>

Apr 8 16:55 1984 prose -mm -li -1 -tm wwbtext Page 2

The table of statistics generated by the program <u>style</u> can be found in your file styl.tmp. If you want to look at it type:

                    cat styl.tmp

You can also use the <u>match</u> program, which provides a better format, type:

                    match styl.tmp

If you are not interested in the file, remove it by typing:

                    rm styl.tmp

ORGANIZATION

The <u>prose</u> program cannot check the content or organization of your text. One way to look at the overall structure of your text is to use <u>grep</u> to list all the headings that were specified for the <u>mm</u> formatter. To do this, type:

```
grep '^.H' filename
```

You can also use the organization program, org, to look at the structure of your text. Org will format your paper with all the headings and paragraph divisions intact, but will only print the first and last sentence of each paragraph in your text so you can check your flow of ideas.

```
org filename



$
```

As you can see, there's quite a bit of output produced by the program. This output can be reduced if desired by specifying the -s option to the wwb command.

The output produced by wwb is logically divided into two parts. The first part is produced by the proofreading program proofr. This program checks the document for spelling and punctuation mistakes, double words, possible wordy or misused phrases, and split infinitives.

The second half of the report is produced by the program prose. This program judges the readability level of the document, whether the use of the passive voice has been appropriately limited, and whether there is an appropriate distribution in the average sentence length.

If you're not interested in getting a full analysis of your document, you can execute individual programs from the WRITER'S WORK-BENCH. For example, to have just the proofreading program run on the file wwbtext, you can simply type:

```
proofr wwbtext
```

Most often, you'll probably want to use spellwwb to check your document for spelling mistakes:

```
$ spellwwb wwbtext
spellwwb -f /uxb3/steve/lib/wwb/spelldict wwbtext
Possible spelling errors in wwbtext are:

documnet                 pg                              wwb

If any of these words are spelled correctly, later type
                spelladd word1 word2 ... wordn
to have them added to your spelldict file.
$
```

If you don't have the WRITER'S WORKBENCH on your system, you can still check your document for spelling mistakes by using a program called spell.

```
$ spell wwbtext
documnet
pg
wwb
$
```

There are other WRITER'S WORKBENCH programs that are not executed when you run wwb. Consult Appendix C for a complete list of these programs.

Getting Help

There are three commands that you can use to get help in using the WRITER'S WORKBENCH.

The command wwbaid will give you a global overview of the WRITER'S WORKBENCH system.

The command wwbhelp will tell you all the commands that are available in the WRITER'S WORKBENCH that have to do with a specific topic area. For example, to find the name of all programs having to do with spelling, you type wwbhelp spelling.

The command wwbinfo will display a table of all WRITER'S WORKBENCH commands and functions. Try it at your terminal and see what happens.

As with most programs and packages, the best way to familiarize yourself with the WRITER'S WORKBENCH is to use it. Type in a small document and run the various commands that are available.

CHAPTER
9

PROGRAM DEVELOPMENT

We noted in the introduction to this book that the UNIX system was designed with ease of program development as a primary goal. The system provides a wide assortment of programming languages and development tools. The inherent power and flexibility of the UNIX system allows the programmer to use these tools easily and creatively. The net result is the development of programs in less time than would be required under other operating systems.

We don't have enough space here to go into detail about all of the development tools that are available. We hope, though, that we will be able to point you in the right direction. Table 9-1 shows the languages used most by UNIX programmers. It also gives a brief description of what they're used for. Each language has its own place in the sun. However, you will find that there are usually several choices of programming languages for solving a particular problem. Many times, a combination is the best choice. For example, it's not uncommon to see shell programs that execute programs developed in other languages (such as awk and C) to solve a part of the problem. The shell itself may simply control the execution of the other programs, or it may even do a lot of the processing itself.

Only experience will tell you which programming language is best suited for solving a particular problem. In many cases it may be a trade-off of development time versus execution speed. For example, for many applications you can usually develop a shell program in less time than an equivalent C program. However, the former usually takes *much* longer to execute than an equivalent program developed with the latter, largely due to the fact that the shell is an interpretive programming language.

TABLE 9-1. Programming languages

Program	Primarily used for
awk	String processing; file editing
C	General purpose and system programs; fast-executing programs
efl	Writing structured FORTRAN programs (see also f77 and ratfor)
f77 (Fortran 77)	Number-crunching; engineering, statistical and mathematical applications; fast-executing programs (see also efl and ratfor)
lex and yacc	Writing language processors (compilers)
ratfor	Writing structured (C-like) FORTRAN programs (*see also* efl and f77)
sh	General purpose programs; file manipulation; process control
sno (SNOBOL)	Pattern matching; string manipulation

In the next section of this chapter, we'll show you how to compile C programs under the UNIX system. Then, we'll introduce you to a program called make that allows for automatic program generation. This will be followed by a description of the *Source Code Control System* (SCCS) that enables you to automatically track and regenerate different versions of a program system.

• C Program Development •

C is the most popular programming language used under the UNIX system, and not without reason. As we mentioned, the operating system itself is primarily written in C with a just few assembly language routines added. The C programming language was developed with systems program development in mind. However, it has proven to be such a flexible and powerful programming language that it is now widely used for general purpose programming applications as well.

It is not our intention to teach you how to program in C here. Consult Appendix A for a list of books on the C programming language.

Compiling C Programs

A file that contains a program written in the C language must have .c
as the last two characters of its name in order for it to be compiled. So,
for example, monitor.c would be a valid name for a file that contained a C program.

The cc command is used to compile a C program, and its format
is rather straightforward:

cc *files*

where *files* is a list of files to be compiled. So the cc command

    cc monitor.c

would be used to compile the program contained in monitor.c. If
the compiler finds any errors in your program, it will proceed to list
them at the terminal, together with a number that locates the line in the
file that caused the error (to the best of the compiler's ability).

If no errors are discovered by the C compiler, then it will create
an object file with the same name as the source file, except the last two
characters will be .o instead of .c.

The final phase of compilation involves *linking* (or *loading*) the
object file to create an *executable object*. In this phase, the compiler tries to
resolve external references against the standard C library libc. This
library contains the *standard I/O library* routines such as printf and
fopen, as well as other functions such as strcat, malloc, and so
on.

If all external references are satisfied, then an executable object
file called a.out will be created. To execute that file, all you have to
do is type its name to the shell:

    $ a.out

If only one file is compiled with the cc command, then the .o
object file will be automatically removed by the compiler. However, if
you compile more than one file at once, these separate .o files will be
kept. This enables you to work efficiently with C programs that span
more than one source file. For example, suppose you have a C program
that is contained in four source files called main.c, init.c,
process.c, and cleanup.c. Well, you can proceed to compile all
four files at once by simply typing the cc command:

    cc main.c init.c process.c cleanup.c

The C compiler will then proceed to separately compile main.c,
init.c, process.c, and cleanup.c and to link them together if

no error is found in any source program.

　　If an error is found in one or more of the files, then the compiler will not attempt to link the program. It is now up to you to reedit the files that contained errors and then recompile them. This time, however, you have to recompile only the files that you made changes to.

　　Let's assume that after issuing the above cc command, the compiler came back and reported an error in init.c and cleanup.c. After making your changes to init.c and cleanup.c, you can again try to compile the program by typing the command:

```
cc main.o init.c process.o cleanup.c
```

This time you specify the files main.o and process.o instead of main.c and process.c, respectively, to tell the C compiler that these two files don't have to be recompiled. The compiler will use the object files it wrote the last time these files were compiled.

　　There are many options that can be specified to the C compiler. The -c option specifies that you don't want to have the program linked and forces creation of a .o file. For example,

```
cc -c main.c
```

causes main.c to be compiled but not linked. It also forces creation of the file main.o (even though only one file is being compiled).

　　The -O option causes a special optimization program to be run to try to improve the efficiency of your object code. So the command

```
cc -O main.c init.o process.o cleanup.o
```

causes the file main.c to be compiled and linked with init.o, process.o, and cleanup.o and also causes the special optimization program to be run.

　　The -o option enables you to designate a file name to place the final executable object code in, rather than a.out. So the command

```
cc main.c init.c process.c cleanup.c -o dact
```

will compile the four indicated .c files, placing the resulting executable program in the file dact. The contents of this file can subsequently be executed by simply typing the file name to the shell:

```
$ dact
```

　　The final option to be described here, -l, is particularly useful if you are using a function from a library other than the standard C library (see Section 3 of your *UNIX User's Manual*). For example, if you use a function from the UNIX math library, such as `sqrt`, then you must specify the `-lm` option to the C compiler when your program is linked:

```
cc stats.c -lm
```

You should note that the `-lm` must be placed *after* the names of the files that are being compiled/linked.

The letter `m` that immediately follows the `-l` indicates that you want to reference a function from the math library. Other libraries are available. As we mentioned earlier, the standard C library *libc* is automatically linked with your program by the C compiler.

For a description of all options that are available with the `cc` command, look up the `cc` and `ld` commands in Section 1 of your *UNIX User's Manual*.

C Programming Tools

There is a wide variety of tools that are available to help you develop and debug your C programs. These programs are summarized in Table 9-2. For more information about a specific tool, consult your manual.

TABLE 9-2. C programming tools

Tool	Used for
adb	Debugging C programs (better to use `sdb` or `ctrace` if available)
cb	Automatic formatting of C programs
cflow	Generating a flow graph of external references
ctrace	Tracing execution of a C program statement by statement
cxref	Generating a cross-reference listing of a C program
lint	Checking a C program (that may span many files) for bugs or nonportable uses of the language
make	Regenerating a program system by automatically tracking files that have changed since system was last made
prof	Obtaining performance data such as the number of times a function is called and the amount of time spent in each function
SCCS	Maintaining and updating source programs; automatic version tracking
sdb	Debugging C programs; symbolic debugger

• The make Program •

The UNIX system provides a very powerful program called make. This program is particularly useful for the development of program systems that comprise more than one file. make automatically keeps track of files that have changed and causes their recompilation when necessary. It also automatically relinks your program if required.

The make program takes a file, known as the *makefile*, as its input. This file describes the following to make:

- the names of the files that make up the program system
- their interdependencies
- how to regenerate the program system

This makefile is typically called makefile or Makefile by convention, although any file name will do. However, if you do use a different name, then you must supply the name as an argument whenever you execute the make command.

Once this information has been described to make, make takes over and does the rest. Simply typing the command make causes the program to examine your makefile and regenerate the system according to the *rules* you have laid out in the file. Typically, this will include recompiling any source program that you changed since the last time it was compiled and subsequently relinking the program system if no compilation errors are reported.

This automated method of program generation saves you from the bother of having to keep track of the files you change and also from recompiling each one yourself. Furthermore, it is not uncommon for several source files to depend on another source file (a .h header file in C is a prime example). If you change that file then you may need to recompile all of the files that depend on it. By specifying this dependency in the makefile, make will take care of recompiling the necessary files whenever that particular file is changed.

Let's take a simple example to see how make works. Here assume that you have a program called dact that is contained in four C source files called main.c, init.c, process.c, and cleanup.c. Also suppose that the file process.c needs a file of definitions called process.h. The file dependencies are depicted in Fig. 9-1.

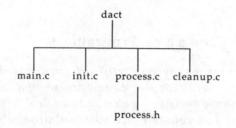

Fig. 9-1. File dependencies for dact program

Making a change to any source file (.c file) will necessitate recompiling that program and also relinking the dact program. Making a
change to process.h will require recompiling process.c and
relinking dact.

Suppose you have created the following Makefile to describe
your program system to make:

```
$ cat Makefile
#
#    Makefile to create the dact system
#

dact : main.o init.o process.o cleanup.o
        cc -o dact main.o init.o process.o cleanup.o

main.o : main.c

init.o : init.c

process.o : process.c process.h

cleanup.o : cleanup.c
$
```

The first three lines are merely comment lines that are ignored by
make. The next nonblank line tells the make program that the file
dact depends on the object files main.o, init.o, process.o, and
cleanup.o. That is, dact (the item on the left of the :) needs to be
remade if a change is made to any of the files to the right of the :. The
line that follows tells the make program how to remake dact. It will
automatically be executed any time a change is made to any of the four
.o files. This line executes the cc command to link together the four
indicated object files and place the resulting executable object in the file
dact. Note that this line must begin with a tab character. If more commands were needed to remake dact, then they would be included here

as well, each one preceded by a tab.

The next nonblank line

```
main.o : main.c
```

specifies that the file `main.o` needs to be remade if a change is made to the file `main.c`. Notice that there's no line that follows to tell `make` how to remake `main.o`. This is because `make` "knows" how to make a `.o` file from a `.c` file.

The line in the makefile that reads

```
process.o : process.c process.h
```

indicates that the file `process.o` must be remade if a change is made to either `process.c` or `process.h`.

Let's assume the current directory contains the `Makefile` shown previously as well as the source files previously mentioned:

```
$ ls
Makefile
cleanup.c
init.c
main.c
process.c
process.h
$
```

Now let's see what happens if you try to make the `dact` system. This is done by simply typing `make dact`:

```
$ make dact
        cc -O -c main.c
        cc -O -c init.c
"init.c", line 4: syntax error
*** Error code 1

Stop.
$
```

Typing in the command `make dact` initiates execution of the `make` program. The first thing `make` does is look for a file called either `Makefile` or `makefile` in your current directory. If either is found, then it is taken as the file that tells it what it's supposed to do. `make` then scans `Makefile`, looking for a line containing `dact` (the argument you gave to `make`) followed by a colon. When it finds the line

```
dact : main.o init.o process.o cleanup.o
```

it then looks to the right of the colon to see what files `dact` depends upon. Here, we specified that `dact` needs `main.o`, `init.o`, `process.o,` and `cleanup.o`. So `make` then starts with the first file in the list, `main.o`, and scans `Makefile` to see if a line containing `main.o` to the left of a colon exists in the file. The line

```
main.o : main.c
```

tells `make` that `main.o` depends on `main.c`. Since `main.c` does not appear to the left of a colon in the `Makefile`, `make` then proceeds to make `main.o`. But no commands immediately follow in the `Makefile` on how to make `main.o`. Luckily, `make` knows how to do this itself. So it issues the necessary C compiler command to compile the file `main.c` and place the output in the file `main.o`:

```
cc -O -c main.c
```

After `main.c` has been successfully compiled, `make` goes to the next file in the list, `init.o` and proceeds to make that file. Once again, the necessary C compiler command is issued to compile `init.c` and place the result of the compilation in `init.o`. As the output shown indicates, the C compiler found a syntax error at line 4 in `init.c`. Whenever an error occurs while making a file, `make` just quits right there. You've got to resolve the error in `init.c` before `make` will continue its work. Let's see what the file directory looks like now:

```
$ ls
Makefile
cleanup.c
init.c
main.c
main.o
process.c
```

Let's assume you edited `init.c` to correct the syntax error. Now you can reissue the `make` command:

```
$ make dact
        cc -O -c init.c
        cc -O -c process.c
        cc -O -c cleanup.c
        cc -o dact main.o init.o process.o cleanup.o
$
```

This time make picked up right where it left off. It didn't recompile main.c because that file was not changed since the last time main.o was created. So it proceeded to compile init.c, process.c, and then cleanup.c. After having satisfied all of dact's dependencies, it then proceeded to make dact by linking together the four .o files (recall that you specified in Makefile how to do this). Here's the files that you now have in your current directory:

```
$ ls
Makefile
cleanup.c
cleanup.o
dact
init.c
init.o
main.c
main.o
process.c
process.o
$
```

After using the dact program for a while, let's suppose you had to make a change to the file process.h. So assume you edited this file and made the necessary changes. Now all you have to do to generate a new version of dact is issue the same make command you've used all along:

```
$ make dact
        cc  -O -c process.c
        cc -o dact main.o init.o process.o cleanup.o
$
```

Isn't that nice? make recognized that dact depended upon the four .o files main.o, init.o, process.o, and cleanup.o, and that process.o in turn depended upon process.c and process.h. Realizing that process.h had been changed more recently than process.o, it automatically remade process.o. Then, it realized that process.o was changed more recently than dact, so it remade dact.

Don't worry if you run make without having made any changes to your files, as no harm will be done. make will simply tell you that your program is up to date and do nothing else:

```
$ make dact
`dact' is up to date.
$
```

You can use this feature to ensure that your program is in fact up to date. If not, then make will automatically remedy the situation.

We noted that make automatically knows how to make a .o file from a .c file. make also knows that a .o file depends upon a corresponding .c file. This makes specification of that dependency in you makefile unnecessary. So the makefile from the example we have shown can be more concisely specified as follows:

```
#
#    Makefile to create the dact system
#

dact : main.o init.o process.o cleanup.o
        cc -o dact main.o init.o process.o cleanup.o

process.o : process.c process.h
```

We hope this small example has shown how useful the make program can be. When developing large program systems that span many files, make is invaluable. Read the document *Make—A Program for Maintaining Computer Programs* by S. I. Feldman, Bell Laboratories, Inc., for a thorough description of all its features.

· SCCS ·

A package of programs called SCCS is available to help you manage the development and maintenance of your programs. SCCS stands for Source Code Control System and is of value mainly to developers and maintainers of large programs.

Suppose you are responsible for the support of a large programming system and that the current release version of this system is Version 3.5. Also suppose that you have customers out there who have earlier versions. Imagine now that a customer having Version 1.6 calls in with a problem. After diligently getting a detailed description of the problem you attempt to recreate it on your current version, Version 3.5. As you might expect, the problem does not appear in your version. What you really have to do is try to duplicate the problem on the same version the customer has, Version 1.6

If your programming system was developed using SCCS, then recreating Version 1.6 of your system is easy. You simply tell the SCCS system the version number you're interested in, and it does the rest.

The main purpose of the SCCS system is to automatically track changes between different versions of a program. The system automatically maintains a list of these changes and has the ability to quickly recreate a particular version on request.

SCCS only keeps track of the changes between versions and not the actual complete versions themselves. Thus, it does not waste much disk space.

A program system that has already been developed without using SCCS can easily be placed under the SCCS system. In this section we'll describe how to work with SCCS. This includes discussions on how to create files under SCCS and how to extract and update them.

Placing Your Program Under SCCS

To place a system of programs under the SCCS system you use the `admin` command. This command tells the SCCS system which files to keep track of for you. (It also serves another purpose that won't be described here.) The basic format of the `admin` command to perform this function is:

$$admin \quad -n \quad -i\textit{file} \; s.\textit{sccsname}$$

This command will have the effect of placing *file* under SCCS, giving it the name `s.`*sccsname*. *sccsname* and *file* are usually one and the same. Just note here that *all* SCCS files must begin with the characters `s.`.

The `admin` command must be run separately for each file you want to place under SCCS. As an example, the command

```
admin -n -imain.c s.main.c
```

would place the file `main.c` under SCCS, calling it `s.main.c`.

If you have many source files that you want to place under SCCS, then you can use a `for` statement as taught in Chapter 6:

```
for f in *.c
do
    admin -n -i$f s.$f
done
```

This would place all your `.c` files contained in the current directory under SCCS.

Every SCCS file has a number associated with it known as its *version number*. This number starts at 1.1, which means *release* 1, *level* 1. As you'll see, whenever a change is made to an SCCS file, 1 gets automatically added to its level number.

The help Command

If you run the `admin` command on some files in your directory, you may get some messages displayed at the terminal. Unless you did something wrong, it's probably just a warning message such as the one that follows. Anyway, a command called `help` is available in case you need more explanation about a particular message. It takes as its argument the message number that appears in parentheses at the end of the message. For example, this is the sort of result you might get when placing a file under SCCS:

```
$ admin -n -imain.c s.main.c
No id keywords (cm7)
$
```

The message number in parentheses is `cm7`. Let's get some help:

```
$ help cm7

cm7:
"No id keywords"
No SCCS identification keywords were substituted for.
You may not have any keywords in the file,
in which case you can ignore this warning.
If this message came from delta then you just made a
delta without any keywords.
If this message came from get then
the last time you made a delta you changed the lines
on which they appeared.
It's a little late to be
telling you that you messed up the last time you made
a delta, but this is the best we can do for now, and
it's better than nothing.

This isn't an error, only a warning.
$
```

Better than nothing? Well, we'll leave it for you to decide. Just know that this form of help is available when you need it.

Extracting Files from SCCS

Once you have placed your source files under SCCS, you should remove the original source files, leaving only the "s." versions. From that point on, any access to your source files must be done through the SCCS system. This includes displaying your files as well.

To retrieve an SCCS file, use the `get` command. This command takes several different options, but to just examine the file, use the `-p` option. So the command

```
get -p s.main.c
```

would write the latest version of the source file stored in `s.main.c` to your terminal. (It actually goes to standard output in case you want to redirect or pipe it somewhere.)

If you want to extract a copy of the file for editing, then use the `-e` option instead. The file that is extracted will have the same name as the SCCS file, except without the leading `s.` characters. So, for example, the command

```
get -e s.main.c
```

would extract the latest version from `s.main.c` and place it in the file `main.c`.

If you just want to extract a file and not edit it (perhaps you just want to compile it), then use the `get` command without any option:

```
get s.main.c
```

This works like the `-e` option, except you won't be given write permission on the file, meaning you won't be allowed to change it.

You can specify more than one file to `get`. For example, to extract the latest version from all your SCCS files, you could type

```
get s.*
```

You can also supply the name of a directory to `get`, and `get` will look in the directory and extract only the SCCS files (i.e., files beginning with `s.`) from the directory.

`get` takes other options that we won't describe here. One of these allows you to specify a specific version to extract. This is what makes it so easy to recreate an earlier version of a programming system. You simply use `get` to extract all of the files from the specific version; then you "remake" the program system.

Recording Your Editing Changes

Once you have finished making your editing changes to a file that you extracted from SCCS, you will want to put the new copy of the file back under SCCS. This is done with the `delta` command. This command takes as its argument the name of the SCCS file—that is, with the leading `s.`. The `delta` program will then look for the file of the same

name without the leading s. and will record the changes that you
made to that file. It will also automatically update the current level
number on the file. delta prompts you to enter an optional comment
to be recorded with this version of the file. After this has been done,
the delta program will remove the file you edited.

Here is an example of the use of the delta command.

```
$ delta s.main.c                Record changes
comments?fix timing bug         Comments are entered
No id keywords (cm7)
1.2
1 inserted                      New version number and summary of changes displayed
0 deleted
4 changed
$
```

Getting Information on SCCS Files

The prs command enables you to obtain information about your SCCS
files. Without any options other than an SCCS file name, a revision history is displayed.

```
$ prs s.main.c
s.main.c:

D 1.2 84/04/15 17:59:21 steve 2 100001/00000/00004
MRs:
COMMENTS:
fix timing bug

D 1.1 84/04/15 17:58:36 steve 1 000004/00000/00000
MRs:
COMMENTS:
date and time created 84/04/15 17:58:36 by steve

$
```

Here you see that this SCCS file was last updated on 4/15/84 at 5:59 P.M.
You also see the comment that you entered when you did the delta
on the file.

The four basic SCCS commands described in this section are summarized in the following table.

TABLE 9-3. Basic SCCS commands

Command	Used To
admin	create new SCCS files
delta	make a change to an SCCS file
get	extract SCCS files
prs	print information about an SCCS file

It is worth noting that SCCS and `make` work together quite well. If the `make` program doesn't find a particular file f, then it will automatically look for the file $s.f$. If it finds it, then it will assume it is an SCCS file and will issue the necessary `get` command to extract it. After `make` is finished with the extracted SCCS file, it will automatically remove it.

If you're interested in learning more about SCCS, then read the document *Source Code Control System User's Guide* by L. E. Bonanni and C. A. Salemi, Bell Laboratories, Inc.

C · H · A · P · T · E · R
10

SECURITY

In recent years, information and computer time have become valuable resources that require protection; security is now a very important part of multiuser systems. One need for security is to keep unauthorized people from gaining access to a computer system; another is to keep an authorized user from tampering with other users' (or the system's) files; still another is to allow some users certain privileges that others aren't allowed. Ideally, this should all be done with as little bother to the users as possible—security should be available when needed but unobtrusive when not.

Security on UNIX systems is made available through a few simple commands and features that form the basis for a complete security system that can be as lax or tight as desired. This chapter divides UNIX security into four major parts:

- Password security
- File security
- The su and newgrp commands
- File encryption

· Password Security ·

There's a file on UNIX systems called /etc/passwd that contains all the information the system needs to know about each user, *including the password*. Believe it or not, this file can be printed out by *anyone* on the system. Why is the system so trusting? Well, the passwords are *encrypted* (more on this later) using an encoding scheme that makes deciphering someone's password very difficult. A typical excerpt from /etc/passwd looks like this:

```
$ cat /etc/passwd
root:xyDfccTrt18Ox,M.y8:0:0:admin:/:/bin/sh
console:lo1ndT0ee0Mzp,M.y8:1:1:admin:/:/bin/sh
pat:XmotTvoyUmjlS:10:10:p wood:/usr/pat:/bin/sh
steve:J9exPd97Ftlbn,M.z8:15:10:s kochan:/usr/steve:/bin/sh
restrict:PomJk109JkY41,./:16:16::/usr/restrict:/bin/rsh
$
```

The user id is listed first, then a colon (:), then the encrypted password, then another colon, and then more information that is discussed in Chapter 12.

Whenever you log in, the password you type in at the terminal is encrypted and checked against the encrypted password for your id in /etc/passwd. If they match, you are allowed on the system; if they don't, you are given the message Login incorrect, and you must try again.

If you want to change your password, you can't modify /etc/passwd—that's not allowed on a UNIX system. If it were, sooner or later someone would go in and change all the passwords; then nobody would be able to log in. Instead, you use the passwd command. All you have to do is type in passwd and it prompts you for the rest:

```
$ passwd
Changing password for pat

Old password: wizzard1                    Not printed
New password: wom2bat                     Not printed

Re-enter new password: wom2bat            Not printed
$
```

Before allowing you to change a password, the passwd command requests that you type in the old password. This is just to make sure it's really you and not someone else using your terminal while you're away. If you make a mistake typing in the old password, the system responds with sorry, meaning that no change was made and that you should try again. If the old password is correct, the passwd command then asks you to enter the new password. Since the passwords are not printed, the command makes sure you don't unwittingly make a mistake by asking you to enter your new password a second time. If the two entries don't match, the passwd command will again ask you to enter the *new* password twice:

```
$ passwd
Old password: wom2bat                              Not printed
New password: wizzard1                             Not printed

Re-enter new password: wizrd1                      Not printed
They don't match; try again.
New password: wizzard1                             Not printed

Re-enter new password: wizzard1                    Not printed
$
```

The `passwd` command is like many other UNIX commands in that it prints nothing when your password has been successfully altered. It simply finishes and goes back to the shell.

Choosing Good Passwords

Although many UNIX systems don't put restrictions on passwords (some don't require them at all), if you want to keep your user id secure, you should use nonobvious passwords. First and last names, initials, birth dates, and the like are poor passwords. Even passwords from ordinary English words can be cracked given a weekend or two of computer time and an on-line dictionary. "Good" passwords are those that are at least six characters long, aren't based on personal information, and have some nonalphabetic characters in them: `4score`, `adv8ance`, `my_name`, `bon1jour`, and `a1b2c3` are unique enough to make discovery difficult, but not impossible.

Even better passwords are `dg71m33ex` and `z_1_y_2_x`. These are almost impossible to crack. Unfortunately, the former is almost impossible to remember. If a password is so weird that you have to write it down, it's not a good password—writing down passwords is not a good security procedure. Many computer systems require passwords like `dg71m33ex`. This just causes everyone to write down their passwords and tape them to their terminals!

You should change your password periodically, so that even if someone has discovered it, any unauthorized use would be cut off. The interval for changing a password depends on how secure an id has to be; however, you should change it at least every six months. Chapter 12 discusses how to have the UNIX system *require* users to change their passwords periodically.

The only times a password is typed in are when you log in and when you change your password. The password isn't printed at these times in order to keep prying eyes from seeing it. However, someone with sharp eyes and a good memory can get your password just by watching your fingers at the keyboard. When you type in your password, you should make sure no one is nearby.

· File Security ·

File security has to do with who can access a file, and what they can do with the file once they have accessed it. For example, you might want a file containing some sensitive information to be unreadable by other users (perhaps your secret recipe for baked basilisk). But you might want another file readable by everyone (your list of recipes and their prices). The UNIX system allows you to change the access *permissions* of a file to suit your needs. These permissions determine who can read a file, who can write to it, and who can execute it, if it happens to be a program.

File Attributes

If you use the `ls` command with the `-1` option, it prints out some cryptic information along with the size of the file, the last time it was modified, and the file name.

```
$ ls -l zombie
-rwxrwxrwx   1 pat    group1    70 Jul 28 21:12 zombie
$
```

Skipping the `-rwxrwxrwx` and the number following it for now, you can see there are two words listed before the file size (which is 70 bytes). These words tell the name of the *owner* and *group* associated with the file. Every file has an owner and group associated with it. The owner of a file is a user, usually the one who created the file; the group is a label for several users who have been logically *grouped* together and given a name. For example, several people working on the same project are usually put in one group so they can have free access to each other's files while restricting access to outsiders (i.e., users not in that group). Every user-id is in a group, even if it's the only one in it. It's also possible for you to belong to more than one group (for example, suppose you're simultaneously working on different projects).

In the previous example, `pat` is the owner of `zombie`, which is associated with `group1`.

Going back to the `-rwxrwxrwx`, you see the beginning `-`. This means that this is a regular file and not a directory (recall from Chapter 4 that a directory will have a `d` instead). After the `-` there is the `rwxrwxrwx`, which is called the *mode* or *permissions* of the file. It tells us who can do what with `zombie`. You'll notice that here the pattern `rwx` is repeated three times. Each of these three patterns tells us what a particular type of user can do with the file. The first `rwx` tells us that the owner of `zombie` (in this case the user `pat`) can read (`r`) from, write (`w`) to, and execute (`x`) the file. The second `rwx` tells us that any user who is a member of the group group1 can also do these things with the file. The third rwx says that *any* user can (Fig. 10-1).

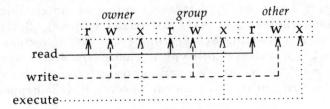

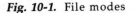

Fig. 10-1. File modes

If one of the permissions is denied, a - shows up in the place of the appropriate letter. For example, rw- means read and write, but no execute (good for plain text files that you have no need to execute as programs); r-x means read and execute, but no write (good for the permission of a program that you don't want someone to overwrite).

Changing File Permissions

So now you have a way to control the accessibility of your files for each of the three types of users: owner, group, and others. Let's say, for example, that you're pat, the owner of the file zombie, and you don't want any user other than pat to be able to write into (and thereby alter or destroy) zombie. On the other hand, since you feel zombie is a useful program, you want it to be available to all users to examine and execute. So you want the new mode of zombie to be rwxr-xr-x, thus allowing users in your group and others to read (or copy) and execute the file, but not to tamper with it.

To alter the mode of zombie, you must use the chmod command with the new mode and the file name as arguments. The new mode is not specified to chmod as rwxr-xr-x, but as a *three digit number* that is computed by adding together the numeric equivalents of the desired permissions (Fig. 10-2).

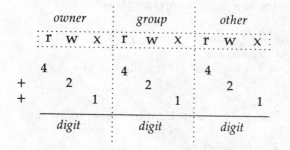

Fig. 10-2. Computing new permissions

In this case, the new mode is 755, where the 7 is rwx for the owner, the first 5 is r-x for the group, and the second 5 is r-x for others (Fig. 10-3).

	owner			group			other		
	r	w	x	r	w	x	r	w	x
	4			4			4		
+		2							
+			1			1			1
	7			5			5		

Fig. 10-3. Computing rwxr-xr-x

To change the mode of zombie to rwxr-xr-x, you use the chmod command (see Chapters 5 and 6) with the three digit number:

```
$ chmod 755 zombie
$
```

And if you look at the mode of zombie now, you can see it has indeed changed.

```
$ ls -l zombie
-rwxr-xr-x   1 pat    group1   70 Jul 28 21:12 zombie
$
```

Some other examples of chmod are shown here with the resultant modes. Note that only the owner or the system administrator can change the mode of a particular file; thus, if other users can't access the file, they cannot use chmod to gain access.

```
$ chmod 700 zombie
$ ls -l zombie
-rwx------    1 pat     group1    70 Jul 28 21:12 zombie
$
```

Now only pat is allowed any kind of access to zombie.

```
$ chmod 711 zombie
$ ls -l zombie
-rwx--x--x   1 pat     group1    70 Jul 28 21:12 zombie
$
```

Now group members and others are allowed to execute zombie, but not to examine or copy it.

```
$ chmod 771 zombie
$ ls -l zombie
-rwxrwx--x   1 pat     group1    70 Jul 28 21:12 zombie
$
```

Now users in group1 are allowed the same privileges as pat, but others can still only execute zombie.

The permissions can be used to prevent accidental overwriting or removal of an important file. All you have to do is change the mode to r-xr-xr-x and you can't change the file even though you are the owner. You have to change the mode to give yourself write permission before you can alter the file.

```
$ chmod 555 zombie
$ ls -l zombie
-r-xr-xr-x   1 pat     group1    70 Mar 18 16:57 zombie
$ echo hi there > zombie
sh: zombie: cannot create
$
```

Here the shell cannot redirect the output of the echo command into the file zombie because the write permission isn't set.

Even rm will not immediately remove the file; it will ask for confirmation first:

```
$ ls -l zombie
-r-xr-xr-x   1 pat     group1    70 Mar 18 16:57 zombie
$ rm zombie
zombie: 555 mode                  Do you really want to remove it?
```

If you type a y when rm asks for confirmation, the file will be removed, *regardless of the mode or owner*; any other input will cause rm to quit without removing the file.

```
$ rm zombie
zombie: 555 mode n            I don't want to remove it
$
```

Changing Group and Owner

As the owner of zombie, you can change the group associated with it with the chgrp command:

```
$ chgrp group2 zombie
$ ls -l zombie
-r-xr-xr-x   1 pat    group2    70 Jul 28 21:12 zombie
$
```

Now group2 has full read, write, and execute permission, and group1 no longer does. (Members of group1 now fall into the "others" category.)

You can even change the owner, although that is a little chancy, since once you change the owner, you cannot change it back—the new owner would have to do that. To change ownership of zombie, you use the chown command:

```
$ chown steve zombie
$ ls -l zombie
-r-xr-xr-x   1 steve group2    70 Jul 28 21:12 zombie
$
```

As you can see, steve is now the owner of zombie. To change the group, owner, or permissions, you would have to log in as steve.

For the commands chmod, chgrp, and chown, you can specify more than one file name, and appropriate file attributes of all of the files specified will be changed, provided you own the files to begin with:

```
$ chmod 666 *.c
$
```

This makes all C programs in this directory readable and writable by all users.

```
$ chmod 700 x y zzz
$
```

This denies access to files x, y, and zzz to all users but the owner, who can read, write, and execute the file.

```
$ chown steve *
$
```

This makes steve the owner of all the files in this directory.

Directory Permissions

Directories also have modes that work in ways similar to ordinary files. You need read (r) permission to use ls on a directory, you need write (w) permission to add or remove files from a directory, and you need execute (x) permission to cd into a directory or use it as part of a path. Note that to use any file, you must have the proper access permissions for the file *and all the directories* in the path to that file.

If you don't have execute permission in all directories along the path to a file, you cannot use the file, no matter what the file's permissions are. If you don't have read permission to a directory, an echo * will not work. You can still access a file in such a directory if the permission of the directory is set, but you must use its full name; file name expansion will not work. If you don't have write permission in a directory, you can't create files in that directory, nor can you move or remove them. The opposite is also true: If you do have write permission in a directory, you can remove a file, no matter what the file's permissions are or who the owner is.

Let's look at some possible directory modes:

```
$ ls -l
total 5
drwxrwxrwx   2 pat    group1    32 Aug   4 18:03 anyone
drwxrwxr-x   2 pat    group1    32 Aug   4 18:03 group
drwxr-xr-x   2 pat    group1    32 Aug   4 18:03 me
drwx------   2 pat    group1    32 Aug   4 18:03 just_me
d--x--x--x   2 pat    group1    32 Aug   4 18:03 nobody
$
```

The directory anyone is available to all users—anyone can create and remove files from this directory. The directory group is open to the owner and members of group1 for creating and removing; other users can list its contents and read from or write to *existing* files (if the permissions on those files allow access), but may not create new files. In the directory me, only the owner can create or remove files. The directory just_me is accessible only to the owner. No other user can access any of the files in it. The last directory nobody is only searchable; nobody can create or remove files, nor can anyone use ls on it; however, if you know the name of a file in nobody, you can access that file because you can search (execute) the directory.

Changing the access modes of a directory is the same as for a file. If you want to change the mode of nobody to rwx for all classes of users, you type in:

```
$ chmod 777 nobody
$ ls -ld nobody
drwxrwxrwx    2 pat      group1    32 Aug  4 18:03 nobody
$
```

As you can see, it's now open to all users. The -d option to ls tells ls that information about the *directory* should be listed, rather than information about its *contents*.

• The su and newgrp Commands •

The su command is helpful when you use more than one user id on a system and you want to do things with the files owned by a different id without logging off and logging in under that id. su changes the *effective* user-id to that of someone else's. For example, if you're logged on as pat and want to *become* for all intent and purposes the user steve, you would type in:

```
$ su steve
enter password: zaq123                    Not printed
$
```

If the password isn't the correct one for the user steve, your effective user-id isn't changed and the message sorry is displayed. If you do type in the right password, however, you'll be granted all the privileges associated with the user steve. In the meantime, you'll lose all privileges associated with the id pat. When you're finished being the other user and you want to go back to being yourself, you just press *CTRL-d*. This puts you back to the privileges you had before running su.

The su command has one other important feature. If used without a user-id, su attempts to change to the user root, which is an administrative id that has access to the entire system. root is often referred to as the "super-user" (su stands for "super-user"). root has access to all files and all devices on the system and can make any changes to the system. Needless to say, the password for root should be a well-kept secret, for use only by system administrators. Chapter 12 goes into greater detail about root.

Similar to the su command is the newgrp command. At any given time, you belong to only one group, so to change groups the newgrp command is used along with the new group name:

```
$ newgrp group2
$
```

This changes your current group to group2. Now you can access files as if you were in group2. As with su, you now have none of the privileges associated with group1.

Of course, having groups at all is rather silly without a mechanism for controlling which groups you can newgrp to. The file /etc/group contains a list of groups and eligible members.

```
$ cat /etc/group
root::0:root
console::1:root,console
bin::2:root,bin
sys::3:root,bin,sys
group1::10:pat,steve
group2::11:pat,steve
restrict::16:restrict
anyone:Juk1Ok08Kj11K:17:pat,steve
$
```

Like the /etc/passwd file, the information is separated by colons, with the group name first, an optional password next, a number that identifies the group next (this is described in Chapter 12), and a comma-separated list of the members of that group last.

You must be listed among the members of a group to change to it unless an encrypted password is associated with the group. If an encrypted password is given, then any user can newgrp to that group if he knows the password, and the members listed in the /etc/group file can newgrp to it without the password. As you can see, one group, anyone, has an encrypted password. In order to change to this group, newgrp will request any user except pat and steve to enter the correct password for the group.

```
$ newgrp anyone
enter password: a1b2c3                    Not printed
$
```

Of course, if the correct password isn't typed in, the change isn't allowed. Unlike su, you don't press CTRL-d when you want to get back to your previous group; `newgrp` without a group name changes you back to the default group.

• File Encryption •

As we said before, the passwords in `/etc/passwd` are *encrypted*—encoded in such a way so as to make reading them very difficult. An encryption program is available to users—the `crypt` command. `crypt` uses a key to scramble its standard input into an unreadable mess that is sent to standard output:

```
$ cat names
Pat
Tony
Ruth
Bill
$ crypt xyzzy < names
>.TCcb2@jedG0^K
$
```

As you can see, the encrypted form of a file is quite unreadable. In this example, `xyzzy` is the key used to encrypt the file.

The nice thing about `crypt` is that it also performs the decryption of text. In fact, the same key is used for both encryption and decryption. First you create an encrypted version of the file `names`:

```
$ crypt xyzzy < names > names.crypt
$ cat names.crypt
>.TCcb2@jedG0^K
$
```

Now you have a file called `names.crypt` that is the encrypted version of `names`. To reproduce the contents of `names`, you use the `crypt` command again, *specifying the same key that you used when encrypting the file.*

```
$ crypt xyzzy < names.crypt
Pat
Tony
Ruth
Bill
$
```

As you can see, the `crypt` command decrypted the file `names.crypt`.

If you don't give `crypt` a key as an argument, it will prompt you for one:

```
$ crypt < names
Enter key:xyzzy                        Not printed
>.TCcb2@jedG0^K
$
```

Normally, after you encrypt a file you should remove the original copy of the file, leaving yourself with only the encrypted version. In this way, the information in the file can be accessed only by someone who knows the key. What was said about good and bad passwords for logins applies here to keys, too. Simple keys allow a decrypter to try various possibilities until the correct one is found. Nontrivial keys make trial-and-error decryption almost impossible. Of course, you should use something you can remember; otherwise, you might have some trouble decrypting your own files!

File encryption is a helpful way of hiding information from other users, administrators, and casual intruders. The `crypt` command shouldn't be considered unbreakable, however, since the method it uses to encrypt text is not kept secret, and decryption methods are known. Anyone who is determined enough and has the time, patience, and computer facilities can crack the encrypted text.

11

COMMUNICATIONS

This chapter discusses how to communicate between UNIX systems, how to send mail and files to users on other UNIX systems, and how to use some of the communication equipment hooked up to your system.

· Telephone Communications ·

Some UNIX systems have communication equipment that allows them to be used *remotely*. Typically, this involves having a telephone line and a device called a *modem* hooked up to one of the ports that a terminal normally uses. The modem (short for *mo*dulator-*dem*odulator) is a converter that changes the binary codes that go between the computer and the terminal into sounds that can be transmitted over telephone lines.

By connecting a terminal to another modem, a user can then

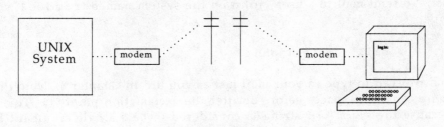

Fig. 11-1.

access a system from almost anywhere (Fig. 11-1). Most modems are fairly slow compared to directly connected lines. The most popular modems operate at 300 or 1200 bits per second (*baud*), which translates into about 30 or 120 characters per second, respectively. Directly connected lines run at up to 19,200 baud on some UNIX systems.

Your UNIX system may have *dial-out* capability—the ability to make calls as well as receive them. The modem, or a device attached to it, generates touch-tone® or rotary dial pulses under program control (referred to as *automatic calling*), thus allowing your system to call other systems and exchange data.

Inter System `mail`

One way for you to access this feature is with the `mail` command. In Chapter 8, the `mail` command was used to send mail from one user to another *on the same system*. You can also use it to send mail to a user *on another system*. First, you need to know what system the other user is on and what his user id is. Then you need to determine if your system can send mail to the other system. This can be done by typing in the `uuname` command, which prints out a list of systems known to your own:

```
$ uuname
remote1
remote2
vortex
$
```

If the system you want to send mail to is in the list, you're in business. If there are no systems printed out, or if a message such as `File "/usr/lib/uucp/L.sys "  is protected` is printed, then your system probably doesn't have dial-out capability. Even so, you should check with your system administrator just to be sure.

Let's say the system you want to send mail to is in the `uuname` list. To send mail to a user `john` on the system named `remote1`, you type

```
$ mail remote1!john
```

and proceed to type in your mail just as you did in Chapter 8. Note that there can be no spaces before or after the exclamation point (!). This is because the *system!user* string is considered to be a single argument by `mail`. In general, mail can be sent to any user on any system in the `uuname` list. Just remember, the user id must exist on the system you are mailing to; otherwise, the mail will be returned to you with a `User unknown` message.

Sending mail to a system that is not in your `uuname` list is a lot trickier. This can only be done if you know that one of the systems on the list communicates with the system you want to mail to. If so, you can use that system as a *link* between your system and the final destination. You simply mail to the known system followed by the final destination system:

```
$ mail known!final!user
```

Only the first system in the list must be known to your system; that system must then forward the mail to the final destination. Again, if the forwarding system doesn't know the final destination system, the mail will be returned.

As you might guess, you can have as many forwarding systems in the route as you want. You simply separate the system names with exclamation points:

```
$ mail system1!system2!...!system_last!user
```

Only system1 must be in your uuname list; each system along the line need only know about the next system in the list.

UUCP

Sending mail to remote systems is merely one function of a number of commands grouped under the label *UUCP* (UNIX-to-UNIX copy).

The UUCP commands, of which uuname is one, do the actual call-ups and file transfers between systems, maintain usage statistics, and ensure security. One of the UUCP commands is uucp. It is used to transfer files between two UNIX systems. uucp is similar in form to the cp command, only uucp allows you to copy files between systems. The general format of the command is:

uucp *source_file destination*

source_file is usually (but doesn't have to be) on your system, and *destination* is usually a file or directory on *another* system. *destination* is specified in the form *system ! filename* or *system ! directory*.

For example, use this to copy the file names to the directory /usr/tmp on system remote1:

```
$ uucp names remote1!/usr/tmp
$
```

This will copy names to /usr/tmp/names on remote1, as will the command:

```
$ uucp names remote1!/usr/tmp/names
$
```

Most of the time, you'll want to send a file to another system so that someone else can use it. In that case, you will want to copy the file directly into his directory structure. For example, suppose you want to send names to the user john on remote1. If he wanted it in his HOME directory, say /usr/john, you could type in

```
$ uucp names remote1!/usr/john/names
$
```

and have the file sent. You could also type in

```
$ uucp names remote1!~john/names
$
```

and get the same result. That's because ~john is replaced by uucp with john's HOME directory (in this case /usr/john). So to send a file to a user on another system, all you need is the user id. Then when you use ~*user id* in the filename, uucp will figure out the HOME directory for you.

We said before that the uucp system ensures security. It does this by giving system administrators the option to restrict incoming and outgoing uucp file transfers to a single directory structure headed by /usr/spool/uucppublic. Under this restriction, files can only be copied to a directory under /usr/spool/uucppublic. If you send a file to such a system, it must be directed to someplace in /usr/spool/uucppublic or you will get mail back saying remote access to path/file denied. uucp does give you some help with this: It allows you to use the construct ~/*user id*, which is replaced with /usr/spool/uucppublic/*user id*. For example,

```
$ uucp names remote1!~/john/names
$
```

is interpreted by uucp as

```
$ uucp names remote1!/usr/spool/uucppublic/john/names
$
```

~/ is simply a convenient shorthand for /usr/spool/uucppublic.

uccp can also be used to copy files *from* another system *to* your system. You simply specify the file you want (using the *system*!*file* notation) as the source file:

```
$ uucp remote1!/usr/john/file1 file1
$
```

This copies `/usr/john/file1` on `remote1` to the file `file1` in your current directory. If file transfers are restricted for either system, you won't get the file. The safest way to copy *to* your system is through the `uucppublic` directory on *both* systems:

```
$ uucp remote1!~/john/file1 ~/pat/file1
$
```

Of course, this requires that `file1` be in `/usr/spool/uucppublic/john` on `remote1`. You will probably need to coordinate any such copying with a user on the remote system.

After you run the `uucp` command to send a file to another system, you may have to wait several minutes for the file transfer to actually take place. When you get a `$` after running `uucp`, you are being informed that the file transfer has been *queued* or placed in line to be sent. (There may be other file transfers waiting to be performed before yours.) To find out whether the file has been sent, the command `uulog` can be used. The status of all `uucp` transfers for the user `pat` can be determined by using the `uulog` command with the `-u`*user id* option:

```
$ uulog -upat
remote1!pat (2/3-15:05:59) (U,405,0) QUE'D (C.remote1nA759)
$
```

The output of `uulog` tells you that the user `pat` has a file queued (`QUE'D`) to be sent to the system `remote1`. In this output, the *system* ! *user id* indicates the system the file is being *sent to* and the user id that is sending it.

```
$ uulog -usteve
remote1!steve (2/5-10:43:18) (U,355,0) QUE'D (C.vortexnA768)
remote1!steve (2/5-10:43:49) (C,358,0) REQUEST (S /tmp/names ~/john steve)
remote1!steve (12/5-10:43:53) (C,358,1) REQUESTED (CY)
$
```

Here we have a `uucp` request queued for the user `steve`. The second line says that the system has requested permission to start copying `/tmp/names` to `~/john`. The `REQUESTED (CY)` on the third line says that the send was successful. A `REQUESTED (CN)` message means the send wasn't successful.

You can also get information about the `uucp` activity between your system and another by using the `uulog` command with the `-s`*system* option. For example, to print out the `uucp` activity between your system and `vortex`, you can type in

```
$ uulog -svortex
vortex!steve (2/5-10:43:18) (U,355,0) QUE'D (C.vortexnA768)
vortex!uucp (2/5-10:43:29) (C,358,0) OK (DIAL cul0 P3060< 8)
vortex!uucp (2/5-10:43:35) (C,358,0) SUCCEEDED (call to vortex )
vortex!uucp (2/5-10:43:49) (C,358,0) OK (startup)
vortex!steve (2/5-10:43:49) (C,358,0) REQUEST (S /tmp/names ~/john steve)
vortex!steve (12/5-10:43:53) (C,358,1) REQUESTED (CY)
vortex!uucp (12/5-10:43:59) (C,358,2) OK (conversation complete  cul0 38)
$
```

Here you see all of the uucp transactions with the system vortex.
Included are the three lines seen in the last example (each beginning
with vortex!steve) and four lines detailing the dial-up of vortex
(DIAL), the success of the call (SUCCEEDED), the start of uucp processing between systems (startup), and the completion of the transaction
(conversation complete).

Chapter 12 contains information on installing and maintaining
the UUCP system.

cu

cu is a command that allows you to call another UNIX system, log in,
and use it *while you are still logged into your original system.* It works by using
your UNIX system's dial-out ability and connecting your terminal to the
outgoing modem; all you have to do is tell it what telephone number to
call:

```
$ cu 3865850
Connected
login:
```

At this point, you can log in and use the system that you called. Note
that you have not logged off of the system you were on before typing in
cu. Let's try logging into another system and doing some work:

```
$ cu 3865850                    Call up remote system
Connected
login: john                     Log in as john
Password:bye1bye
The Plant Dept. will be working on an air-
conditioning problem Sat. Dec. 3 and Sunday Dec. 4.

$ who am i                      Are we really john?
john        tty08        Dec  3 13:22
$ pwd                           Enter a few commands
/usr/john
```

```
$ ls
file1
names
uucpfiles
$ CTRL-d                              Log off
login:
```

After having done some work on the other system, you'll want to log off and continue working on your original system. Logging off is not enough, however, since the terminal is still hooked up to the outgoing modem, which is still dialed into the other system. You have to tell the cu command to *disconnect* you from the other system. This is done by typing in ~. at the beginning of a line, followed by a *RETURN*:

```
$ cu 3865850                         Call up remote system
Connected
login: john                          Log in as john
Password: bye1bye
The Plant Dept. will be working on an air-
conditioning problem Sat. Dec. 3 and Sunday Dec. 4.

$ ls
file1
names
uucpfiles
$ ~.                                 Disconnect
Disconnected
$
```

cu is useful if you regularly use more than one UNIX system since it lets you use another system without logging off the system you're using. cu is also useful when you want to transfer small *text* files between your UNIX system and another. It has some built-in commands that use the communications link established when you call another system to transfer the files. The commands are ~%take and ~%put, which take files from and put files onto the other system, respectively. To take a file (i.e., copy it) from the other system, you call it up, log in, and then type in

~%take *from to*

where *from* is the name of the file on the other system and *to* is the name you want for the file on your regular system. The *to* file name is optional; cu will use the *from* file name if it isn't given. For example, let's say you want to copy the file file1 from another system:

```
$ cu 3865850
Connected
login: john
Password: bye1bye
The Plant Dept. will be working on an air-
conditioning problem Sat. Dec. 3 and Sunday Dec. 4.

$ ~%take file1                          Copy file1 from other system
stty -echo;mesg n;echo '~>':file1;cat file1;echo '~>';
mesg y;stty echo
~>:file1
5 lines/63 characters
$ ~.
Disconnected
$ ls
abc
file1                                   It's been copied
test
$
```

The two lines following the ~%take are the control lines that go to the
other UNIX system to transfer file1. The last line is printed out when
the transfer is complete; it tells you the number of lines and characters
transferred.

Similarly, if you wanted to copy the file test to another system, you would use the ~%put command:

```
$ cu 3865850
Connected
login: john
Password: bye1bye
The Plant Dept. will be working on an air-
conditioning problem Sat. Dec. 3 and Sunday Dec. 4.

$ ~%put test                            Copy test to remote system
stty -echo; cat - > test; stty echo
5 lines/30 characters
$
```

This method of transferring files is really only useful for small
files since the terminal is locked during the transfer, and a 10,000-byte
file transferred at the rate of 30 characters per second takes around six
minutes to send across. Also, there is no checking performed for errors
in transmission, so there is a greater probability that large files may be
garbled.   uucp, however, has error checking and recovery built in,
making it more reliable for transferring large files.

▪ Networking ▪

We will mention networking only in passing since there are so many different types, each one with its own set of commands. A *network* is just a method of hooking two or more systems together to exchange information. The UUCP commands create what is known as the *dial-up UNIX network* (Fig. 11-2).

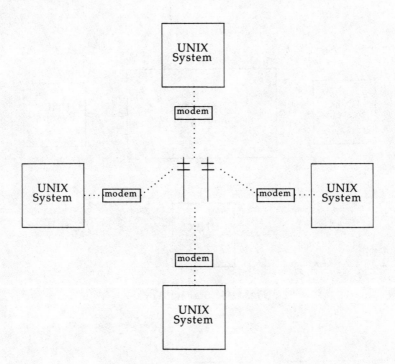

Fig. 11-2. UUCP dial-up network

This network is rather simple, due to the limited scope of the UUCP commands, and is used mainly for exchanging mail and news messages between member systems. The dial-up UNIX network currently consists of several hundred UNIX systems throughout the world.

Sometimes, other networking arrangements are used in large companies and universities that have UNIX systems. Usually, the number of file transmissions between systems is so great that the method of transfer that the UUCP network uses is not fast enough to keep up with the traffic. So the UNIX systems are hooked together in a network that allows faster (1000+ characters/second) data transmission.

The network may be as simple as a connection between the terminal ports on two UNIX systems, or as complex as several systems all tied into a large (and expensive) network manager that may handle millions of characters per second over specially designed communication links. Figs. 11-3 through 11-5 show some typical networking arrangements:

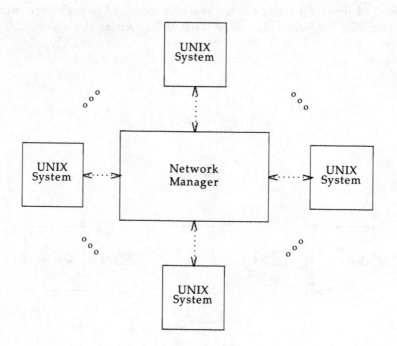

Fig. 11-3. Star network

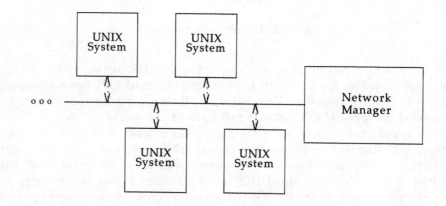

Fig. 11-4. Multidrop network

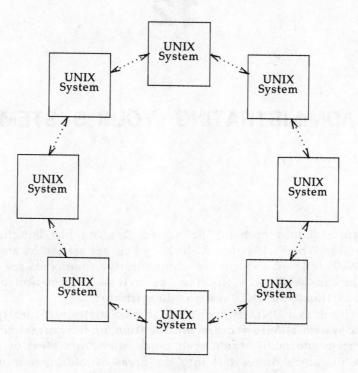

Fig. 11-5. Ring network

Quite often large networks are hybrids composed of several different types of smaller networks.

Commands to access a network can be as simple as uucp and cu (modified to run over the network hardware) or as complex as a whole new set of commands for file transfer, remote command execution, interdepartmental mail, etc.

You should ask your system administrator for information about networks that your UNIX system may be connected to.

ADMINISTRATING YOUR SYSTEM

This chapter should probably be named, "So You Just Bought a UNIX System—Now What?" It is meant to help you get started as an administrator. We'll tell you about what administrative commands are available and what can be done with them, as well as information about the overall functions of a UNIX system administrator.

Why does a UNIX system need an administrator? Ideally, a well-designed system should require no attention under normal conditions. UNIX systems normally don't need much attention. Most of the time, the administrator's duties fall into the areas of adding new users and removing old ones, backing up and restoring files, installing new software, and starting up and shutting down the system. These are things that can't be totally automated because of security reasons or because a human must be at the machine to mount disks or tapes and push buttons. All these functions are straightforward and require little to moderate effort. They occur so frequently that there are many administrative commands to perform them.

There are some administrative functions that come about due to abnormal conditions such as system crashes, faulty hardware, runaway user programs, and overloaded or faulty disk systems. In these cases, the administrator's duties are less clearly defined. Often the problem is obscure or the external manifestation of another, hidden problem. Some administrative commands are available to aid the administrator, but often fixing the problem requires a little floundering around at first.

This chapter is by no means complete, as it cannot cover problems that are specific to particular types of hardware. Instead we try to give you information about the various *functions* of an administrator and *solutions* to the more common problems you may encounter.

This chapter is divided into two parts; the first describes what every administrator should know, whether your system is a single-user home computer or a large multiuser commercial system. It is subdivided into the following sections:

- Getting to know your system
- UNIX system startup and shutdown
- The cron
- File systems
- Adding and removing users

The second half is devoted to topics that will interest only some administrators. It is broken down into the following sections:

- System security
- Accounting
- uucp

If you've just purchased a UNIX system, you may want to read the section on UNIX system startup and shutdown first. It describes some of the steps involved in getting your system running.

su

Some administrative commands can be run only by the *super-user*. The super-user is the user root. It has privileges other users don't have. It can read and write *any* file, regardless of permissions and can run *any* program. To become the super-user, you need to use the command su:

```
$ su
password: sys_1_yz
#
```

The # prompt tells you that you are the super-user. Be extremely careful when you're super-user (i.e., you have a # as your prompt) as it's very easy to remove important files. Use su only when necessary and do everything you can as a "normal" user.

We'll use # for all commands that *must* be run by the super-user and $ for all others. You'll see that you can read most of the system files we'll mention as a normal user, but you must be the super-user to change them.

• Getting to Know Your System •

All UNIX systems are equipped with a certain minimum amount of hardware. This usually includes a rigid disk of around 10 million (M) bytes of storage, a tape drive or floppy disk for backups, 256 thousand (K) bytes of memory, a terminal, and a printer. Additional equipment may include more terminals, communications equipment, such as modems or automatic call units (ACUs), and larger disks. As a system administrator, you should look at your UNIX system, see what is attached to it, and understand the functions of the various devices. The above devices have been described in previous chapters. This section shows you how to access them through the UNIX system.

Files, Files, and More Files

The first thing you should know about the way the UNIX operating system communicates with the various devices is that everything is treated as a file. As far as any program is concerned, disks are files, modems are files, even memory is a file. All the devices attached to your system have files in the directory /dev associated with them. When I/O is performed on these files, the actions are translated by the UNIX operating system into actions on the actual devices. For example, the file /dev/mem is the computer's memory. If you cat this file you will actually be displaying the system's memory at your terminal. For security reasons, this file is not readable by an ordinary user; however, as an administrator, you can look at it when you're the super-user.

These files (in /dev) are usually referred to as *device files*. To look at some of the devices on your system, change your directory to /dev and do an ls:

```
$ cd /dev          Change to device directory
$ ls               Look at device files
acu0               Automatic dialer for calling out
console            System console
dsk0        ⎫
dsk1        ⎬      Disks
dsk10       ⎬
dsk11       ⎭
lp                 Printer
mem                Memory
mt0                Tape
rdsk0       ⎫
rdsk1       ⎬      Same disks, different names
rdsk10      ⎬
rdsk11      ⎭
rmt0               Same tape, different name
swap               Swap disk
syscon             System console, different name
tty00       ⎫
tty01       ⎬      Terminal ports
tty02       ⎭
x25                Network
$
```

This example gives a partial list of the devices usually found in /dev. Your ls will give a different list of files, probably more than shown here, but the ones shown here will be found on most UNIX systems. These are the devices we'll be talking about throughout the chapter.

Starting at the top, the first file you see is acu0. Remember the automatic call units we talked about in the last chapter? Well, this is the file that the cu and uucp commands interact with to call other systems.

The console and syscon files are used to communicate with the console of your UNIX system. (They are one and the same.) If your system is a single-user system, then you're probably using the console when you use the system (surprise!).

The groups of files dsk0 through dsk11 and rdsk0 through rdsk11 correspond to disk drives.[†] Under the UNIX system, disk drives are logically divided into *sections* (see Fig. 12-1). The files dsk0 and dsk1 correspond to the first and second sections of disk number zero. The files dsk10 and dsk11 correspond to the first and second sections of disk number one.

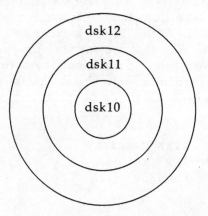

dsk12

dsk11

dsk10

Fig. 12-1. Three section disk drive

If there were more disks attached to this system, the sections would be numbered dsk*n*0, dsk*n*1, etc. for each disk *n*. The files beginning with rdsk are the same disk sections as the dsk files, but use a different method of I/O.

The lp file refers to a line printer and the mem file to memory. The file mt0 refers to a tape drive (magnetic tape), and rmt0 refers to the same tape but with a different form of I/O. The swap file refers to the area on the disk where processes are swapped. (Remember swapping from Chapter 2?)

---

† The disk and tape drive naming convention was changed as of UNIX System V, Release 2. All disks are in the directories /dev/dsk and /dev/rdsk, and all tape drives are in the directories /dev/mt and /dev/rmt.

The files tty*nn* are the ports for terminals (*nn* is the number of the port). For a multiuser UNIX system, there will be one tty*nn* file for each terminal or modem attached to the system. The last file, x25, is used to communicate with a network.

If you don't see all of these files in the /dev directory, don't panic. Not all UNIX systems have tape drives, terminal lines, networks, ACUs or line printers. Also, some UNIX systems have device files for devices that aren't there now but may be added later. So don't be concerned if you see an acu file but don't have an ACU attached to your system. Some UNIX systems have renamed some of the files to be more meaningful: tap or tp instead of mt, and so forth. The important thing is that you know that there are files in /dev corresponding to your disks, tapes, memory, and other devices. Usually a manual that comes with your system will describe the device associated with each file.

What's Going on Here?

The UNIX system provides all users with several commands that print information about the system. In previous chapters, we talked about one of them, the who command. Remember when we discussed processes in Chapter 2? Well, there's a command that will give you information about the ones that are running on your system. It is the ps (process status) command. ps without any options prints the status of all processes for a particular user. If you type in ps at your terminal, you'll get a few lines back describing the processes you have running:

```
$ ps
   PID   TTY   TIME  COMMAND
   195   01    0:21  sh              The shell
   253   01    0:00  ps              This ps command
$
```

The ps command prints out four columns of information: PID, the "process id," which is a unique number assigned to each process; TTY, the terminal number that the process was run from; TIME, the amount of computer time in minutes and seconds that process has used; and COMMAND, the name of the process. (The sh process in the above example is the shell that we got when we logged in, and it's used 21 seconds of computer time.) Almost every command you type in at your terminal creates a new process. Until the command is finished, it shows up in the output of the ps command as a running process. Process number 253 in the above example is the ps command that was typed in.

The ps command with the -e option lists information about *every* process running on the system:

```
$ ps -e
    PID  TTY  TIME COMMAND
      0    ?  0:08 swapper        Process swapper
      1    ?  7:19 init           UNIX state control
    129    ?  0:00 lpsched        Printer queue program
    181 sysc  0:28 cron           Alarm clock
     72   00  0:00 getty          Terminal program
    195   01  0:21 sh             Your shell
     51 sysc  1:33 sh             Console's shell
    197   02  0:00 getty          Terminal program
    302   08  0:00 ps             This ps
$
```

swapper performs a familiar operation: It's the swapping process that
swaps the programs from memory to /dev/swap and back again. It
has a ? in the TTY column because it was started automatically, not
from a terminal. (We'll see how that's done later.) The init and
getty processes we'll get to shortly. The lpsched process coordinates the printing of files on the printer /dev/lp. The cron process
is described in a separate section. sh showed up in the last ps; it's
the shell on this terminal. The second sh belongs to the system's console, indicated by the sysc in the TTY column, and ps is the command that produced the list.

When there are several users logged into a system, the output of
the ps -e command is much longer. There is usually a sh for each
user, as well as a line for each command they may happen to be running
at the time.

The getty Process

When you log in, several things take place. First you get a login:
prompt, and you type in your user id. You then get a Password:
prompt, and you type in your password. If the password is correct, messages are printed at your terminal, your .profile file is executed to
set up your shell environment, and finally you get a $ prompt from the
shell.

There's at lot of stuff going on behind the scenes here; let's see
what really happens when you log in. Each terminal port that *doesn't*
have someone logged in on it has a getty process associated with it.
The getty process does nothing until a terminal is connected to the
port or someone dials up the port. When you call up and are connected,
getty sends the string login: to the terminal. Then it waits for
your response. After you type in your user id, the getty process starts
up a new process called login, tells it what your user id is, and goes
away. The login process prompts you for your password, checks the

response, and either starts a shell for you if the password is correct or goes back to asking for your user id if it's not.

When your shell is started by the `login` process, it does two things before printing out your `$`. The first thing it does is run a shell program `/etc/profile`. `/etc/profile` is like your `.profile` but is for everyone on the system, not just you. It performs operations the administrator wants to be done when a user logs in. For example, `/etc/profile` prints out the file `/etc/motd`. This is the message of the day that we referred to at the beginning of Chapter 4. The `/etc/profile` may print out the time and date, system name, number of users, and other information of interest to users logging in. As an administrator, you can edit this file and put messages in it that you want everyone logging into your system to see. Also, `/etc/profile` might change the `PATH` shell variable to include a directory that contains commands local to your system. You should `cat` the `/etc/profile` file on your system and see what it contains.

After running the `/etc/profile` program, your shell process runs the `.profile` program in your `HOME` directory. After that your shell is ready for use, so it prints out your familiar `$`.

Here's a summary of the steps involved, from initiating the `getty` to obtaining the command prompt:

```
getty→login→sh→/etc/profile→$HOME/.profile→$
```

· System Startup and Shutdown ·

After hooking your system together and plugging it in, you must start it up. This involves something called *booting the system*. Put simply, this is the procedure of loading the UNIX kernel from disk into the system's memory. In the dark ages, this entailed a lot of switch setting, button pushing, typing, and praying. Newer UNIX systems *boot* automatically when turned on. Some systems may prompt you for some input; however, if you hit *RETURN*, this will usually load UNIX. Just to be sure, you should check the manuals that came with your system for a section entitled "Powering On," "Startup," "Booting Procedures," or some such nonsense. That section should tell you what you have to do to get your system started.

When a UNIX system is started, it runs in what's known as *single-user* mode. In this mode, there are no `gettys` running, no other users, and the only processes are `init`, `swapper`, and those run by the administrator from the console. UNIX systems start up in single-user mode to allow you to check the system's operation and make sure everything is OK before allowing other users onto the system. When the system is in single-user mode, the console runs as super-user, and `#` is the prompt. No passwords are requested; the system simply makes the console root and gives you a #. As we'll see later, some things having to do with file systems are best done in single-user mode.

The init Process

UNIX systems always run in one of several *modes* or *levels*. These levels are controlled by the init process. For example, when a UNIX system is started, it runs in single-user mode.

Of course, for other users to log in, the UNIX system must have at least one other level in which gettys run so that logins can occur. This level is called *multiuser* mode. The init process controls the level the system is in. It reads the file /etc/inittab that details which processes are to be run in which levels. When init *n* is typed in by root, the UNIX system goes into level *n*, and init reads /etc/inittab to decide what processes to kill and start up. For example, init 2 causes the system to enter multiuser mode. /etc/inittab has a list of gettys (one for each port) that init starts up when mode 2 is entered. Valid levels for init are numbers from 0 to 6 and the letter s.† s is single-user mode, and 2 is usually multiuser mode.

If you look at /etc/inittab, you'll see something like this:

```
$ cat /etc/inittab
is:s:initdefault:
sy:s:sysinit:/etc/brc </dev/console >/dev/console 2>&1
br:2:wait:/etc/bcheckrc </dev/console >/dev/console 2>&1
rc:2:wait:/etc/rc > /dev/console 2>&1
co:s0123456:respawn:/etc/getty console console
00:2:respawn:/etc/getty -t60 tty00 1200
01:2:respawn:/etc/getty -t60 tty01 1200
02:2:respawn:/etc/getty -t60 tty02 1200
$
```

The format of each line is

$$id:level:action:process$$

id is one or two characters that uniquely identify a line.

level is one or more numbers (0 through 6) or the letter s that determines what level(s) *action* is to take place in.

action can be one of the following:*

        initdefault—when init starts, it will enter *level*; the *process* field for this *action* has no meaning.

---

† Prior to System V, the levels range from 0 to 7, where 0 is single-user mode.
* Prior to System V, use c and k as *action* instead of respawn and off.

sysinit—run *process* before `init` sends anything to the system console.

respawn—if *process* doesn't exist, start it, wait for it to finish, and then start another, e.g.,

getty→login→sh→log off→respawn getty

wait—when going to *level*, start *process* and wait until it's finished (`init` doesn't wait by default).

off—when going to *level*, kill *process*.

process is any executable program, including shell programs.

When changing levels, `init` kills (forces finishing) all processes not specified for that level. The following example illustrates going to single-user mode:

```
# init s
INIT: New run level: S

INIT: SINGLE USER MODE
#
```

Going Multiuser

To go to multiuser mode, all you have to do is type `init 2`. This will initiate a series of events that ends with the `gettys` being started, allowing other users to log in. If you look at the `/etc/inittab` on your system, you'll see definitions for `gettys` under level 2, and at the very least, two shell programs `/etc/bcheckrc`, and `/etc/rc`.[†] These are run before the `gettys` are started.

    `/etc/bcheckrc` prompts you for the correct time and date (where do you think the `date` command gets the correct time—an hourglass?), and it asks you whether you want to check the file systems (usually a good idea before going multiuser). If you do, it will run the `fsck` command (see the section on file systems).

    `/etc/rc` is the file you can fiddle with and not feel guilty (and sorry) about later. It starts up the processes (except for `gettys`) that you want running in multiuser mode, such as the `cron` (next section), printer controllers, and network stuff. It mounts the file systems and may also start system accounting, error logging, and system activity logging.

---

† Prior to System V, only `/etc/rc` is used.

Let's take a look at a typical /etc/rc file:

```
$ cat /etc/rc

#       Prototype /etc/rc file:
#       Local modifications need to be made such as mounting
#       and unmounting file systems and startup commands for
#       various subsystems (uucp, error logging, etc.)

set `who -r`                    # get current level
clevel=$7

if [ "$clevel" = 2 ]            # init 2 was typed in
then
        /etc/mount /dev/dsk11 /usr
        /etc/mount /dev/dsk20 /tmp

        /usr/lib/lpsched        # for printer
        echo "printer spooler started"

        /usr/lib/errdemon       # for error logging
        echo "errdemon started"

        /etc/cron -1            # start cron
        echo "\nTHE CRON HAS BEEN STARTED"

        echo "\nTHE SYSTEM DATE IS: \c"
        date

        echo "\nTHE SYSTEM NAME IS: \c"
        uname                   # print system's name

        echo "MULTI-USER"
fi

echo "FILE SYSTEMS MOUNTED ARE:"
/etc/mount                      # print list of file systems
```

Shutdown

When you want to turn off your UNIX system, you shouldn't just unplug
it. First, if you have users logged in, they'll be just a little bit unhappy
with you (tar and feathers are not uncommon). Second, when you start
back up again, you may find that some of the files were scrambled at
random. To avoid all this, the UNIX system provides you with the

shutdown command. It performs all necessary actions before putting
the system in single-user mode. Let's take a look at a simple version of
shutdown:

```
$ cat shutdown

#       prototype shutdown command
#       local modifications should be made to unmount
#       and check file systems for integrity

echo "SHUTDOWN PROGRAM"
echo "SENDING THE 60 SECOND WARNING"
echo "The system will shutdown in 60 seconds" | wall
sleep 60                        # wait for 60 seconds

echo "DO YOU REALLY WANT TO SHUTDOWN? "
read yn                         # read reply
if [ "$yn" = "y" ]              # reply was affirmative
then
        echo "SENDING THE FINAL WARNING"
        echo "The system is shutting down now" | wall
        sleep 60                # final grace period

        echo "ALL USER PROCESSES WILL NOW BE KILLED"
        ps -ea
        killall                 # kill all user processes
        sync                    # finish pending disk I/O

        umount /dev/dsk1        # unmount file systems
        umount /dev/dsk10
        umount /dev/dsk11

        ps -ea                  # see what's running now
        init s                  # single-user mode
    fi
    $
```

Note the commands wall, sleep, and killall. These commands
are simple and straightforward. wall writes (Chapter 8) to all users,
sleep *n* suspends execution of the shell for *n* seconds, and killall
kills all processes not related to shutting down, logging off all users as a
result. umount and sync are file system related commands.

The shutdown shell sends a warning to the users to get off the
system, makes sure whoever is doing this is certain he wants to shutdown, and then goes about killing processes, unmounting the file systems and changing to single-user mode. Once in single-user mode, all

gettys are turned off, and no users can log in. At this point, you can turn off (power down) your system without fear. If you have disks in other cabinets, it's usually wise to turn them off first.

shutdown *must be run from the system console and you must be logged in as* root. You cannot use su and then run shutdown. If root is not logged into the system console, *you must log off the console and log in as* root.

The cron

The cron is a process that runs when the UNIX system is in multiuser mode. It runs commands on a regularly scheduled basis.[†] Once every minute it checks the file /usr/lib/crontab[*] to see if something is supposed to be run. If it finds something, it runs the command; otherwise, it sleeps for another minute.

```
$ cat /usr/lib/crontab
# sample crontab
# everything on a line is separated by blanks or tabs.
# min      hour     day      month    day-of-week  command
#(0-59)   (0-23)   (1-31)   (1-12)   (0-6
#                                     Sunday=0)
#-----------------------------------------------------------------
0         7        *        *        1-5          /morn/alarm
55        6        *        *        1-5          /morn/coffee
10        7        *        *        1-5          /morn/shower
15        7        *        *        1            /morn/leftovers
15        7        *        *        2,4          /morn/eggs
15        7        *        *        3            /morn/waffles
15        7        *        *        5            /morn/pancakes
45        7        *        *        1,3,5        /work/drive
45        7        *        *        2,4          /work/car_pool
0         10       *        *        0,6          /morn/alarm
1         10       *        *        0,6          /bin/sleep 600
0         13       *        5-9      6            /house/mow_lawn
0         12       15       4        *            /taxes/1040
$
```

An asterisk (*) means do it every time, a *number,number,number* means do it only when one of the *numbers* matches the appropriate time or date, and a *number—number* means do it when any number in that range matches the appropriate time or date.

[†] The at command can be used to run commands *once* at specified times and dates.
[*] On UNIX System V Release 2, the crontab is divided into a group of files in the directory /usr/spool/cron/crontabs. The file /usr/spool/cron/crontabs/root is equivalent to /usr/lib/crontab.

The first entry in the `crontab` is

```
0       7       *       *       1-5             /morn/alarm
```

This says that the program `/morn/alarm` is to be run at 7:00 A.M. every Monday through Friday (1-5). The next entry starts the coffee at 6:55 so it's ready when you wake up. At 7:15 you get breakfast. On Monday it's leftovers, Tuesday and Thursday it's eggs, Wednesdays it's waffles, and Friday it's pancakes. You car pool on Tuesday and Thursday, and you drive yourself on Monday, Wednesday, and Friday. On Saturday and Sunday the alarm goes off at 10:00 and at 10:01 you go back to sleep for 10 minutes (600 seconds). On Saturday at one o'clock in the afternoon, during the months from May to September, you mow the lawn. At noon on April 15, you fill out your 1040 form.

Of course, this is merely a sample `crontab`. You might want to replace the `/usr/lawn/mow` program with `/usr/pay/local_kid`.

On a real UNIX system, the `crontab` is used to run programs on a regular basis throughout the day and also to run programs at night that you don't want running during the day for fear of slowing down other users. Programs typically run via the `cron` are things like accounting and file saves. The `cron` is usually started from `/etc/rc` (above) when the system goes multiuser. It's stopped when `killall` is run by `shutdown`. In order to edit the `crontab`, you must be the super-user.

▪ File Systems ▪

The UNIX file system is one of the key parts of the UNIX system. It's what provides you with hierarchically-organized directories and files. The file system divides each disk drive into 1024—byte[†] portions called *blocks* numbered from zero to the number of blocks that can fit on that disk (Fig. 12-2).

---

† Prior to System V blocks were 512 bytes long.

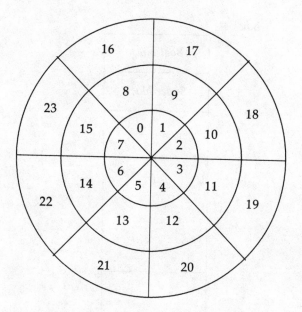

Fig. 12-2. Disk block numbering

For example, a 40 million (40M) byte disk will have blocks numbered from zero to around 39,000. The blocks are grouped into four sections: block zero is called the *boot block*. It is unused by the file system. Block one is called the *super block*. This block contains, among other things, the size of the disk and the sizes of the other two sections. Next comes the *i-list*. This is a variable number of blocks that contains *i-nodes*. We'll discuss i-nodes shortly. The rest of the disk is devoted to free storage (data) blocks that are available to store the contents of files (Fig. 12-3).

Block #

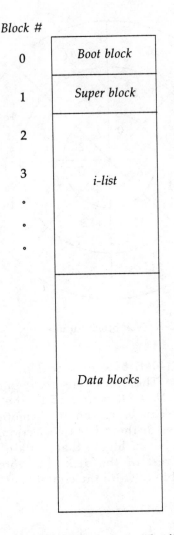

Fig. 12-3. Four sections of a file system

The *logical* representation of a file is very different from its *physical* representation. The logical representation is the file that you see when you type in `cat`. You get a stream of characters representing the contents of the file. The physical representation is how the file is actually organized on the disk. You think your file is one contiguous stream of characters, but in actuality it is probably not stored that way on the disk. A file that is longer than one block will usually have its contents scattered about the disk. When you access your file, however, the UNIX file system fetches the blocks in the proper order and gives you the logical representation of your file.

Of course, there must be a list somewhere in the UNIX system that tells the file system how to convert the physical representation to the logical. This is where the *i-node* comes in. An i-node is a 64-byte table that contains information about a file. Some of the things in an i-node are the file's size, its owner and permissions, and whether it's an ordinary file, a directory, or a special file. The most important item in the i-node is the *disk address list*. This is a list of 13 block numbers. The first ten block numbers are the first ten blocks of the file. So to give you the logical representation of a file up to ten blocks long, the file system will fetch the blocks in the order they appear in the disk address list.

What if you have a file larger than ten blocks? The eleventh block number in the disk address list gives the number of a block that contains up to 256 more block numbers. So for files of sizes up to 10+256 blocks (272,384 bytes) this method suffices. If your file is even larger than 266 blocks, the twelfth block number in the disk address list gives the number of a block that contains up to 256 more block numbers, and each of those blocks contains up to 256 block numbers that are used to fetch the file's contents. The thirteenth block number in the disk address list works similarly, only it goes one level further than the twelfth.

If you sat down and figured it out, you'd find that the maximum size of a file on a UNIX system is 16,842,762 blocks or 17,246,988,288 bytes! Fortunately, the UNIX file system imposes more practical limits on the maximum size of files (usually 1 to 2 million bytes) so that users can't inadvertently create a file that uses up all the blocks on an entire disk.

The way the file system translates file names to i-nodes is really quite simple. A directory is actually a file containing a table of information: for each file in the directory, there's an entry in the table that has the file's name and the i-node number associated with the file. When you type `cat` **xxx**, the file system looks for the entry named **xxx** in the current directory's table, gets the i-node number associated with it, and then starts fetching the blocks that contain the information in **xxx** (Fig. 12-4).

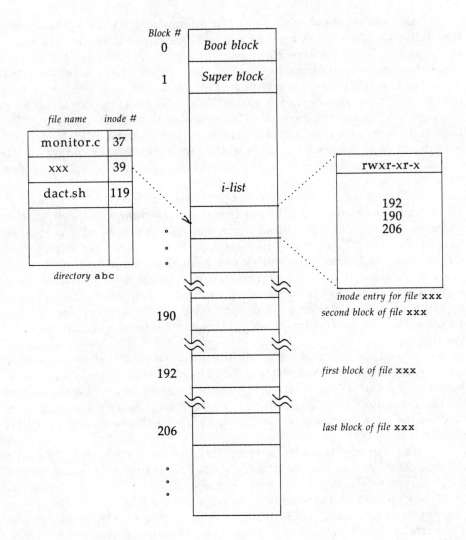

Fig. 12-4. Accessing the contents of **xxx**

Creating a File System

The administrator of a UNIX system can create a file system on a disk with the command /etc/mkfs (make file system).

```
# /etc/mkfs /dev/dsk10 10000        make a 10,000 block file system
#
```

The file /dev/dsk10, you'll remember, refers to the first section of the disk dsk1. The 10000 is the size of the file system in blocks.

Although you can use an entire disk for a single file system, the UNIX system allows you to create several *separate* file systems on one disk. Many UNIX systems run with one file system per disk. Many others run with several per disk. The reasons for this difference seem to be more philosophical than practical.

You can optionally give the second argument as *number:number*, where the first *number* is again the size in blocks, and the second *number* is the number of i-nodes (that is, the maximum number of files that can be stored in the file system). By default, the number of i-nodes is the number of blocks divided by four. The maximum number of i-nodes per file system is 65,500. If for some reason you need more than 65,500 i-nodes on a disk, you must create two or more file systems on that disk.

There are other values you can specify to /etc/mkfs, but the defaults are usually just fine. If you get instructions with your UNIX system that tell you to use /etc/mkfs in a particular way, then follow those instructions.

Mounting and Unmounting File Systems

A very nice feature of UNIX file systems is that they are *mountable*, meaning that each file system can be attached to the overall directory tree *at any point*. For example, the directory / is the *root* directory of the system. It is also the top of the root file system, which is always mounted. The directory /usr is in the directory /, but usually it's a separate file system from the root file system, with all the files in it residing on a separate portion of the disk or another disk entirely. The /usr file system is simply mounted onto the root file system at the point where the directory /usr exists in the overall hierarchy (Figs. 12-5 and 12-6).

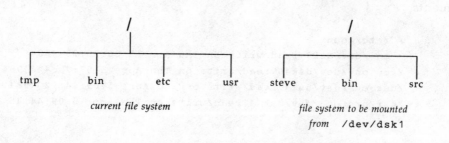

Fig. 12-5. File system before mounting /dev/dsk1

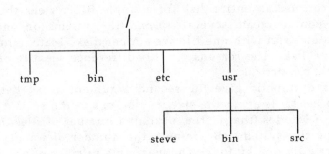

Fig. 12-6. File system after mounting /dev/dsk1 as /usr

To mount a file system, you use the /etc/mount command. This command lets you place a file system anywhere within the existing directory structure:

```
# /etc/mount /dev/dsk1 /usr          Mount /dev/dsk1 on /usr
# /etc/mount /dev/dsk11 /usr/src     Mount /dev/dsk11 on /usr/src
#
```

You can put a -r at the end of the /etc/mount command if the file system should be mounted read-only. Tape drives and disks that are *write-protected* must be mounted this way.

When you mount a file system, you should make sure the directory you're mounting it on is empty, as its contents are not accessible while the file system is mounted.

To get information about the file systems mounted on your UNIX system, you can use the /etc/mount command without any arguments.

```
# /etc/mount
/ on /dev/dsk0 read/write on Thu Apr  5 06:55:23 1984
/tmp on /dev/dsk10 read/write on Thu Apr  5 07:18:41 1984
/usr on /dev/dsk1 read/write on Thu Apr  5 09:44:22 1984
/usr/src on /dev/dsk11 read/write on Thu Apr  5 09:44:45 1984
#
```

The /etc/mount command has printed the directory where the file system is mounted (e.g., /usr), the device in /dev it's on, whether it's readable only or readable and writable, and the time and date it was mounted.

To unmount a file system, you use the /etc/umount command. This command is simply the reverse of the /etc/mount command. It removes a file system from the directory structure.

```
# sync                              Finish all pending I/O
# /etc/umount /dev/dsk10            Unmount /dev/dsk10
# /etc/mount                        List mounted file systems
/ on /dev/dsk0 read/write on Thu Apr  5 06:55:23 1984
/usr on /dev/dsk1 read/write on Thu Apr  5 07:18:42 1984
/usr/src on /dev/dsk11 read/write on Thu Apr  5 09:44:45 1984
#
```

The sync command should be used before unmounting a file system.
It makes sure all pending I/O is completed. You certainly don't want to
unmount a file system if there's still some I/O to be performed on it!
    You should note that the root file system cannot be unmounted.[†]
Also note that /etc/umount will not work if a user is using any file
in the file system you're trying to unmount. This includes being cded
to a directory in that file system. Unmounting file systems should be
done only after going to single-user mode (via /etc/shutdown).

File System Status Commands

There are many commands that give information about file systems. A
few of the more useful ones are given here.
    The df command prints out the number of free i-nodes and
blocks on the mounted file systems:

```
$ df
/usr          (/dev/dsk1 ):     138126 blocks     11675 i-nodes
/tmp          (/dev/dsk10):      19184 blocks      2437 i-nodes
/             (/dev/dsk0 ):       3066 blocks       670 i-nodes
$ df -t
/usr          (/dev/dsk1 ):     138126 blocks     11675 i-nodes
                    total:      209792 blocks     25216 i-nodes
/tmp          (/dev/dsk10):      19154 blocks      2436 i-nodes
                    total:       20000 blocks      2496 i-nodes
/             (/dev/dsk0 ):       3066 blocks       671 i-nodes
                    total:       23000 blocks      2864 i-nodes
$
```

df with the -t option prints the total number of i-nodes and blocks as
well. This command is used most often to see if a file system is getting
filled up. We'll talk later about what you can do if you run low on i-
nodes or blocks.
    du prints a list of each directory in a file system along with the
number of blocks used by the files in that directory and its subdirectories. The du command is not file system specific; it can be used on
any directory structure. It is useful when you want to find *how* the

---

† Some UNIX systems may allow you to unmount the root file system. Don't! Unpredictable things
  may happen.

space on a file system is being used:

```
$ du /usr                                  Print disk usage on /usr
1762   /usr/bin/graf
5622   /usr/bin
453    /usr/lib/acct
2325   /usr/lib/spell
797    /usr/lib/uucp
16583  /usr/lib
695    /usr/mail
334    /usr/man/a_man/man7
594    /usr/man/a_man/man1
204    /usr/man/a_man/man8
457    /usr/man/a_man/man0
1677   /usr/man/a_man
1713   /usr/man/u_man/man1
722    /usr/man/u_man/man3
366    /usr/man/u_man/man2
158    /usr/man/u_man/man5
237    /usr/man/u_man/man4
51     /usr/man/u_man/man6
426    /usr/man/u_man/man0
5153   /usr/man/u_man
9644   /usr/man
32     /usr/spool/lp
1      /usr/spool/uucppublic/oko
6      /usr/spool/uucppublic/weather
1      /usr/spool/uucppublic/tgd
10     /usr/spool/uucppublic
316    /usr/spool/uucp
455    /usr/spool
50794  /usr
$
```

du can point out where your file system is being used up by large files. The −a option to du causes it to print out the sizes of ordinary files as well as the totals for each directory.

Saving and Restoring File Systems

Due to the frailties of all things mechanical (and human), it's good to have backups of your files. That way if your disk decides to take a vacation, you have the information stored somewhere else. UNIX systems provide several mechanisms for backing up file systems, and for each, a corresponding method for restoring the saved files. As luck would have it, these methods vary from one UNIX version to the next and even from system to system within the same version. We will discuss `tar`, a method of file system backup that is available on most UNIX systems.

`tar`

`tar` stands for tape archiver. It takes as its arguments a command and a directory to be archived onto a tape or another disk. The commands used for saving a directory structure are `c` and `r`. The command `c` causes `tar` to create a new archive on the tape or disk. The command `r` causes `tar` to add a new archive to the end of one that's already there. There is also an optional number you can specify to tell it which tape drive to use (it's probably best to use the default).

```
# tar c /usr          Archive /usr to the default tape drive
# tar c2 /            Archive / to tape drive 2
# tar r2 /            Add new archive of / to existing archive on drive 2
#
```

If you want to archive to disk, you can do so by using the `f` option to `tar`. It tells `tar` that the next argument is the name of a file it should send its output to:

```
# tar cf /bck/1 /usr    Archive /usr to /bck/1
#
```

`tar` is also used to read an archive back in. You just use the `x` option, which causes files to be extracted from the archive:

```
# tar xf /bck/1          Extract files from /bck/1
# tar x                  Extract files from the default tape drive
#
```

`tar` places the extracted files and directories in the current directory.

If you just want to see what's in the archive, you can use the `t` command to get a table of contents:

```
# tar tf /bck/1          List the files in /bck/1
   . . .
# tar t                  List the files on the default tape drive
   . . .
#
```

Again, you can specify a number after the `x` or `t` command to tell it which tape drive to use.

What To Do When a File System Gets Full

Sooner or later, a file system will get filled up with too many files, causing you to run low on blocks, or i-nodes, or both. There are several
things you can do at this point. You can go through and remove old,
unnecessary files (perhaps saving them on tape or floppy disk first).
You can ask your users to get rid of their unnecessary files by putting a
message in /etc/motd. You can move some of the files to a different
file system; this usually entails moving users to another file system
along with their files. You can buy a new disk and move the old file
system (or parts of it) to a file system on the new disk.

To move a user to another file system, you have to do three
things (in single-user mode):

1.) move the user's files and directories to the other file system
2.) change the user's HOME in /etc/passwd to reflect the change
    (We'll discuss this in the section on adding and removing users.)
3.) send the user mail telling him you've moved him

tar is the easiest way to move a directory structure from one
file system to another. To move the entire structure in /usr/pat to
/usr1/pat, you would type in the following lines:

```
# mkdir /usr1/pat                          Make the new directory
# cd /usr/pat                              Change to the old directory
# tar cf - . ¦ (cd /usr1/pat; tar xf -)    Copy the structure
# rm -r /usr/pat                           Remove the old directory
#
```

The first tar runs in the directory /usr/pat and sends an archive of
this directory to its standard output. This is piped to another tar that
runs in /usr1/pat (cd /usr1/pat). That tar reads the first
tar's output and creates a new directory structure. The command rm
-r /usr/pat removes /usr/pat and all files and directories under
it. You also have to change the permissions as well as the owner and
group of the directory /usr1/pat so that it reflects the state of the
old one.

After you get a new disk and run mkfs on it, you can move
users from the old disk to the new using the previous method. If you
buy a larger disk than the old one, you can move the entire file system
using the same method. You simply run the previous tar sequence
once on the entire file system.

You might note that you can move a user's directory structure in
multiuser mode by telling the user to log off, disabling the user id by
changing the mode of the user's HOME to 000 or temporarily removing
his entry in /etc/passwd (see the next section), and then proceeding
to copy the user's files.

`/etc/fsck`

Before going to multiuser mode, it's best to check the file systems before mounting them. Also, if the system goes down without going through proper shutdown procedures (e.g., a power failure), the file systems should be checked. The UNIX system provides you with a tool to check file systems—`/etc/fsck`. `/etc/fsck` scans a file system and checks it for inconsistencies. To use it, all you have to do is type `/etc/fsck` and the file system in `/dev` that you want checked:

```
# /etc/fsck /dev/rdsk10

/dev/rdsk10
File System: usr Volume: pwb01

** Phase 1 - Check Blocks and Sizes
** Phase 2 - Check Pathnames
** Phase 3 - Check Connectivity
** Phase 4 - Check Reference Counts
** Phase 5 - Check Free List
2193 files 19572 blocks 3066 free
#
```

`/etc/fsck` normally goes through the five phases shown in the previous example. Phase 1 scans through the i-node list looking for inconsistencies in the block numbers and file sizes and i-node formats. Phase 2 removes files whose corresponding i-nodes were flagged in phase 1. Phase 3 checks directory connectivity by making sure all directories exist somewhere in the overall hierarchical structure. Phase 4 checks the number of *links* for all files and directories. The number of links for a file or directory is simply the number of times it is listed in a directory. This number is usually one, but can vary widely, particularly for directories. Phase 5 checks the *free-block list*, which is the list of empty blocks that are free to be used for new files or to grow old files. If an error in the free-block list is found in phase 5, phase 6 is performed. Phase 6 reconstructs the free-block list:

```
# /etc/fsck /dev/rdsk10

/dev/rdsk10
File System: usr Volume: pwb01

** Phase 1 - Check Blocks and Sizes
** Phase 2 - Check Pathnames
** Phase 3 - Check Connectivity
** Phase 4 - Check Reference Counts
** Phase 5 - Check Free List
1 DUP BLKS IN FREE LIST
BAD FREE LIST
SALVAGE? y

** Phase 6 - Salvage Free List
2193 files 19572 blocks 3066 free

***** FILE SYSTEM WAS MODIFIED *****
#
```

The SALVAGE? message is a request for you to input a y or n to determine whether the free-block list should be reconstructed. /etc/fsck will ask lots of questions like this when a file system has been corrupted. It's usually best to answer y to all questions, as /etc/fsck is fairly smart about repairing file systems. In fact, if you use the -y option with /etc/fsck, it will function as if you answered y to all questions. Note that most corrective actions will result in some loss of data.

The following is an example of /etc/fsck with a file system that has been corrupted by a power failure:

```
# /etc/fsck /dev/rdsk10

/dev/rdsk10
File System: usr Volume: pwb01

** Phase 1 - Check Blocks and Sizes
POSSIBLE FILE SIZE ERROR I=615
** Phase 2 - Check Pathnames
** Phase 3 - Check Connectivity
** Phase 4 - Check Reference Counts
UNREF FILE I=615  OWNER=uucp MODE=100400
SIZE=0 MTIME=Apr 10 16:23 1984
CLEAR? y
```

```
** Phase 5 - Check Free List
2193 files 19572 blocks 3066 free

***** FILE SYSTEM WAS MODIFIED *****
#
```

Here, /etc/fsck found an inconsistency in i-node number 615. It asked if it should clear the i-node and when it received a y, did so. After making any changes to the file system, /etc/fsck will print the message FILE SYSTEM WAS MODIFIED.

The different messages that can come from /etc/fsck are much too numerous to mention here; however, just remember that you can respond to any message that ends with a ? with a y with confidence. If you find that /etc/fsck has lost too much data when you mount the file system and look at it, you may have to restore the file system from a backup.

If /etc/fsck is typed in without a file system, it will use the file /etc/checklist as the list of file systems to check.

If you really want to go into a file system and repair it yourself, you should read more about the organization of UNIX file systems in "The UNIX Time-Sharing System," by D. M. Ritchie and K. Thompson, and "UNIX Implementation," by K. Thompson, in *The Bell System Technical Journal*, Vol. 57, No. 6, (July-August 1978). Then you should look under /etc/fsdb in your *UNIX System Administrator's Manual.*[†] /etc/fsdb is an interactive file system editor that allows you to patch up damaged file systems. Don't use it until you become very familiar with the UNIX file system structure.

Table 12-1 lists the file system commands covered in this section.

TABLE 12-1. File system commands

Command	Description
df	Print number of free i-nodes and Blocks for each file system
du	Print number of blocks for each Directory in a hierarchy
/etc/mkfs	Make a file system
/etc/mount	Mount a file system
/etc/umount	Unmount a file system
/etc/tar	Tape archiver
/etc/fsck	Check file system for inconsistencies
/etc/fsdb	Interactive file system editor

---

† Prior to System V, all administrative commands were included in the *UNIX User's Manual.*

· Adding and Removing Users ·

Even if you have a single-user UNIX system, you will want to know how to add and remove users. Single-user simply means that only one user can use the system at a time; there can be many user id's, but there is only one terminal for them to log into. Right now, you might be saying to yourself, "I'm the only one using this system, so I don't need more than one user id." That may be true now, but what happens when your kids decide they want to use the system for their homework, or you want to show off your new system to your friends? Do you want them logging into your HOME directory, where all your valuable files are? Probably not. What you'll have to do is add a new user id, say kids, and let them use that. This is a lot simpler than you might think. It requires two steps:

1.) enter a line for the user id in /etc/passwd
2.) create a HOME directory for that user id

To add a user to your system you will have to edit the /etc/passwd file and add a line for the new user id. Let's take a look at the /etc/passwd file and see what's in it now:

```
$ cat /etc/passwd
root:xyDfccTrt18Ox,M.y8:0:0:admin:/:/bin/sh
console:lo1ndT0ee0Mzp,M.y8:1:1:admin:/:/bin/sh
pat:XmotTvoyUmj1S:10:10:p wood:/usr/pat:/bin/sh
steve:J9exPd97Ft1bn,M.z8:15:10:s kochan:/usr/steve:/bin/sh
restrict:PomJk109JkY41,./:16:16::/usr/restrict:/bin/rsh
$
```

Before you can add a new user id to the file, you need to know what goes on the line. The general format of each line in the file is:

id:password:uid:gid:user info:home:shell

As you remember from Chapter 10, the first two items on each line are the user id and the encrypted password. The two numbers following are the *user id number (uid)* and the *group id number (gid)*. The uid is a unique number that is assigned to each user id. This is used by the system to distinguish one user from another. Every process has a uid associated with it; this determines what privileges and permissions that process has with respect to other processes and files (discussed in Chapter 10). The gid's purpose is to distinguish between the members of various groups.

The next item in `/etc/passwd` is any information about the user you want to put in, such as name or telephone number. The last two items on the line are two `PATH`s. The first is the `HOME` directory assigned to the user, and the second is the shell the user gets when he logs in (in most cases it is `/bin/sh`, `/bin/rsh`, or `/bin/csh`). If this field is blank, the user gets `/bin/sh` by default.

Now let's see what you have to do to add a new user to the `/etc/passwd` file. The user id is `kids`. You can ignore the password for now. The uid must be unique, so let's pick 17. The gid can be the same as one of the others, or it can be different; let's use a different one, 17. The `HOME` directory can be any name (remember, you're going to create it later), but it's a good idea to use the same name as the user id. So if users are put in the `/usr` file system (as they often are on most small UNIX systems), the `HOME` will be `/usr/kids`. If you use this method for all users, you can easily figure out any user's `HOME` directory. The shell can be the standard shell, `/bin/sh`. Now let's see what this line looks like:

```
kids::17:17:my kids:/usr/kids:/bin/sh
```

Now all you have to do is add this line to `/etc/passwd`:

```
# ed /etc/passwd              Note: running as root
270
$a                            Add kids at end of file
kids::17:17:my kids:/usr/kids:/bin/sh
.
w
308
q
# cat /etc/passwd
root:xyDfccTrt18Ox,M.y8:0:0:admin:/:/bin/sh
console:lo1ndT0ee0Mzp,M.y8:1:1:admin:/:/bin/sh
pat:XmotTvoyUmjlS:10:10:p wood:/usr/pat:/bin/sh
steve:J9exPd97Ftlbn,M.z8:15:10:s kochan:/usr/steve:/bin/sh
restrict:PomJkl09JkY4l,./:16:16::/usr/restrict:/bin/rsh
kids::17:17:my kids:/usr/kids:/bin/sh
#
```

The password is blank in the file above, so you should change it and tell the kids what the password for their user id is:

```
# passwd kids
New password:new_pwrd

Re-enter new password:new_pwrd          Make sure it's right
#
```

Note that if the password isn't set in /etc/passwd, a user logging in on the user id kids will not be required to enter a password.

After creating an entry in /etc/passwd for kids, you need to create the HOME directory for kids. This is simple; you've already created plenty of directories!

```
# mkdir /usr/kids                       Make /usr/kids
# chown kids /usr/kids                  Make kids the owner
# chgrp 17 /usr/kids                    Make 17 the group
#
```

Appendix F contains a shell program for adding new users.

Removing Users

Removing users is simply the opposite of adding them. First you delete the user's entry in /etc/passwd. Then you remove the user's HOME and all of his files:

```
# rm -r /usr/kids                       Remove entire directory tree
#
```

It might be a good idea to back up the user's files to tape before removing them, just in case the user decides he wants his files later on.

• System Security •

In Chapter 10 we talked about what users can do with UNIX security. Now we're going to say a few words about what a system administrator can do with the tools provided by UNIX. The first thing we'll look at is passwords. The format of the /etc/passwd file allows you to *require* users to change their passwords periodically. If you look at the /etc/passwd file again, you will see that some of the encrypted passwords have a comma (,) in them followed by a few more characters and a colon (:):

```
$ cat /etc/passwd
root:xyDfccTrt18Ox,M.y8:0:0:admin:/:/bin/sh
console:lo1ndT0ee0Mzp,M.y8:1:1:admin:/:/bin/sh
pat:XmotTvoyUmj1S:10:10:p wood:/usr/pat:/bin/sh
```

```
steve:J9exPd97Ftlbn,M.z8:15:10:s kochan:/usr/steve:/bin/sh
restrict:PomJk109JkY41,./:16:16::/usr/restrict:/bin/rsh
kids:fCqOCSNt8kFp2:17:17:my kids:/usr/kids:/bin/sh
$
```

The user ids `root`, `console`, and `steve` have four characters after the comma in the password, `restrict` has two, and `pat` and `kids` don't have commas at all.

The first character after the comma determines the *maximum* number of weeks the password is valid. The second character determines the *minimum* number of weeks that must transpire before the password may be changed again by the user. (This is to keep users from changing their passwords to a new one and immediately back to the old one.) The remaining characters tell when the password was most recently changed.

To read the information you must first know how to count in password-*ese*. The way you count is `.=0`, `/=1`, `0-9=2-11`, `A-Z=12-37`, and `a-z=38-63`. (Table 12-2 gives an interpretation of password-*ese*.)

TABLE 12-2. Counting in password-*ese*

Password-ese	Number it represents	Password-ese	Number it represents
.	0	B	13
/	1	C	14
0	2	D	15
1	3	E	16
2	4	. . .	. . .
3	5	Y	36
4	6	Z	37
5	7	a	38
6	8	b	39
7	9	c	40
8	10	. . .	. . .
9	11	y	62
A	12	z	63

Let's take a look at one of the user ids above. The user id `steve` has an `M` after the comma. This says that the password must be changed at least every 25 weeks. The period that follows the `M` says that the password may be changed as often as `steve` likes. Anything else would require some time to elapse before the password could be changed again. The `z8` tells the `passwd` command when the password was last changed. This field is also checked when the user logs in, and if the password has expired, the user is required to change it before he can log in.

You must put the first two characters in the /etc/passwd file (immediately after the encrypted password) in order to require periodic changing of passwords. The other two characters are put there by the passwd command when a user changes his password. Note that if you want to have a user change his password you can put two periods as the last time the password was changed (so the password entry looks something like *xxxxxxxxxx*,M...), and the user will be required to change his password the next time he logs in.

There are two special cases of this format that the system recognizes. The first is when the maximum number of weeks (first character) is less than the minimum (second character). In this case, the user is not allowed to change his password. Only the super-user can change this user's password. The user id restricted above is an example of this (.=0, /=1, first < second).

The second special case is when both the first and second character are periods (so the minimum and maximum are zero). In this case, the user is required to change his password the next time he logs in. After doing so, the periods are removed by the passwd command, and the user is never again required to change his password.

umask

The umask command can be used to set the default creation modes of users' files and directories. If you put umask in the /etc/profile, you can control the permissions of files that users create. The way it works is the opposite of the chmod command: the mode you give it tells the system which permissions should *not* be given when a file is created. For example, umask 002 means that files and directories will be created *without* write permission to others (recall that chmod 002 *gives* write permission to others), and umask 022 means that files and directories will be created without write permission to the group or others. Typical modes for umask are given in Table 12-3.

TABLE 12-3. Typical umask modes

Command	Description
umask 002	Create files without write permission for others
umask 022	Create files without write for group or others
umask 006	Create files without read or write for others
umask 026	Create files without read or write for others and without write for group
umask 007	Create files without read, write, or execute for others
umask 077	Create files without read, write, or execute for anyone but the owner

Putting umask in the /etc/profile will change only the *default* creation modes. It will not prevent users from changing the modes of their file (with chmod) to something of their own choosing, nor will it keep them from putting umask in their own .profile to override the one in /etc/profile.

The Restricted Shell (rsh)

You may have noticed something odd about the user-id restrict (besides the fact that he's not allowed to change his password). The shell for restrict isn't /bin/sh; it's /bin/rsh. This is the *restricted shell*. The restricted shell is almost the same as the regular shell, but it's designed to *restrict* a user's capabilities by disallowing certain actions that the standard shell (/bin/sh) allows. The list of actions disallowed is very short:

- cannot change directory (cd)
- cannot change PATH shell variable
- cannot use a command containing /
- cannot redirect output (> and >>)

These restrictions are enforced *after* the .profile is executed when logging in.

These simple restrictions allow the writer of a restricted user's .profile to have complete control over what commands that user can use. The example that follows shows a simple setup for a restricted environment.

```
$ cat .profile                    User restrict's .profile
PATH=/usr/rbin:$HOME/bin
export PATH
SHELL=/bin/rsh                    Some commands use SHELL variable
export SHELL
cd /usr/restrict/restdir          Don't leave user in HOME directory
$ ls -l .profile                  Restricted user shouldn't own his .profile
-rw-r--r--  1 pat    group1  179 Apr 14 17:50 .profile
$ ls /usr/rbin                    Directory of restricted commands
cat                               Harmless commands
echo
ls
mail                              Let them send us mail
red                               Restricted editor
write
$ ls /usr/restrict/bin            restrict's command directory
adventure                         Lots of games
backgammon
chess
hearts
poker
rogue
$
```

Here we have a restricted environment for the user restrict. When restrict logs in, his PATH is changed to search just the directories /usr/rbin and /usr/restrict/bin. The user restrict can run only the commands contained in these two directories. Any other command will get a *command*: not found response. The user is effectively bottled up in the directory /usr/restrict/restdir and cannot cd out of it. The .profile is owned by pat, not restrict, and the permissions are such that only pat can change the file. (Don't let a restricted user alter his .profile; that defeats the purpose of the restricted shell.)

One quick note about the commands in /usr/rbin: they were simply copied from the /bin and /usr/bin directories. You can put almost any command from /bin and /usr/bin in /usr/rbin; just use common sense in choosing the commands you allow restricted users to use. For example, don't give them access to the shell, a compiler, or chmod, as these may be used to bypass the restricted shell.

System Directories and Files

There are many files on a UNIX system that users should not be allowed to write. These include all commands in `/bin`, `/usr/bin`, `/usr/rbin`; files such as `/etc/passwd`, `/usr/lib/crontab`, `/unix`, `/etc/rc`, and `/etc/inittab`; and most system directories, particularly `/`, `/dev`, `/etc`, `/usr`, and `/usr/lib`.

Some files shouldn't even be *readable* by users. These include the disk-special files in `/dev`: `dsk0`, `dsk1`, etc. When a disk is readable, anyone can write a program that can read any file on the disk. Also, `mem` and `kmem` in the device directory shouldn't be user-readable. A talented programmer can pick out a lot of passwords by scanning memory.

It's probably easier to say what users *can* access than what they *can't*. Table 12-4 at the end of this chapter lists typical UNIX system directories and their usual modes.

• The UNIX Accounting System •

The UNIX accounting system is a sophisticated collection of programs that collects data on system usage by process and disk usage and connect time (the amount of time logged in) by user. Accounting can be used to charge various users for their use of the system, or it can be used to keep track of system usage and performance.

Whenever a process finishes, the accounting system stores information about it in the file `/usr/adm/pacct`. This information includes the command name of the process, the computer time used, the total elapsed time, the uid and gid of the user who ran the process, the amount of memory used, and the amount of I/O performed. When a user logs in or off, this action is recorded in the file `/etc/wtmp`. This information can later be processed to determine the amount of time the user was logged into the system.

When a UNIX system first starts up, accounting is not automatically started. The steps in starting up the accounting package are fairly simple, though.

Setting Up the Accounting System

First you must make sure there is a user id named `adm` on your system. It's uid must be 4, and its `HOME` directory must be `/usr/adm`. To do this, just put this line in your `/etc/passwd` file:

```
adm:np:4:4:Admin:/usr/adm:
```

Since all valid encrypted passwords are 13 characters long, the `np` in `adm`'s `/etc/passwd` entry means that no one can log in as or `su` to adm. Only the super-user can become adm by using su (the su command doesn't ask the super-user for a password).

The second thing you must do is create the following directory structure, making sure that all the files are owned by the user adm:

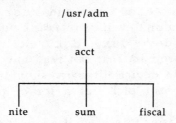

```
                          /usr/adm
                             |
                            acct
              ┌──────────────┼──────────────┐
            nite           sum           fiscal
```

The following commands will create this directory structure with the proper ownership and permissions:

```
# mkdir /usr/adm
# mkdir /usr/adm/acct
# mkdir /usr/adm/acct/nite
# mkdir /usr/adm/acct/sum
# mkdir /usr/adm/acct/fiscal
# chmod 755 /usr/adm /usr/adm/acct /usr/adm/acct/*
# chown adm /usr/adm /usr/adm/acct /usr/adm/acct/*
# chgrp 4 /usr/adm /usr/adm/acct /usr/adm/acct/*
#
```

The third thing you must do is put these lines in the .profile in /usr/adm:

```
PATH=/usr/lib/acct:$PATH
export PATH
```

Next you put this line in the multiuser section of the file /etc/rc:

```
/bin/su - adm -c /usr/lib/acct/startup
```

This starts up the accounting when the system goes into multiuser mode. You also need to put this line in the file /etc/shutdown so that accounting is turned off before the system is shut down:

```
/usr/lib/acct/shutacct
```

The last thing you need to do is add these lines to the file
/usr/lib/crontab:

```
 0   4   *   *   1-6     /bin/su - adm -c /usr/lib/acct/runacct
 0   2   *   *   4       /usr/lib/acct/dodisk
 5   *   *   *   *       /bin/su - adm -c /usr/lib/acct/ckpacct
15   5   1   *   *       /bin/su - adm -c /usr/lib/acct/monacct
```

runacct is the main daily accounting shell program. It produces daily
and cumulative summary files for printing with the prdaily command (more on that later). dodisk produces disk usage summary files
that are later merged with the cumulative summary files by runacct.
ckpacct checks on the file /usr/adm/pacct and makes sure is
doesn't grow too big. It also checks the size of the /usr file system
and turns off accounting if the number of free blocks falls below 500.
monacct produces monthly accounting summaries.

The Accounting Summary Files

Once the accounting system has run for a few days, your UNIX system
will have some files in the directory /usr/adm/acct/sum. The
accounting summary for a particular day is stored in the file
/usr/adm/acct/sum/rprt*mmdd* where *mmdd* is the month and day
of the report. The most recent report can be printed by typing in
/usr/lib/acct/prdaily:

$ /usr/lib/acct/prdaily

```
Apr 14 19:25 1984  DAILY REPORT FOR whuxb Page 1


from Thu Apr 12 07:31:25 1984
to   Fri Apr 13 07:30:25 1984
1         acctg off
1         run-level S
1         system boot
2         run-level 2
1         acctg on
1         runacct
1         acctcon1

TOTAL DURATION IS 1439 MINUTES
LINE      MINUTES PERCENT # SESS   # ON    # OFF
tty00     778     54      166      166     543
console   1404    98      3        3       4
tty02     0       0       0        0       3
tty01     705     49      1        1       6

TOTALS    2887    --      170      170     561
```

Apr 14 19:25 1984 DAILY USAGE REPORT FOR whuxb Page 1

UID	LOGIN NAME	CPU (MINS) PRIME	NPRIME	KCORE-MINS PRIME	NPRIME	CONNECT(MINS) PRIME	NPRIME	DISK BLOCKS	# OF PROCS	# OF SESS	# DISK SAMPLES	FEE
0	TOTAL	275	186	19008	11362	7022	4115	538687	59681	484	200	0
0	root	8	48	193	2907	114	96	2	3502	1	1	0
2	bin	0	0	0	0	0	0	3419	0	0	1	0
4	adm	1	15	24	877	23	0	8514	786	2	1	0
5	uucp	1	1	30	47	0	0	414	376	1	1	0
6	mail	0	0	0	0	0	0	780	0	0	1	0
71	lp	0	0	0	0	0	0	32	0	0	1	0
112	jeff	2	0	124	0	36	64	6276	149	1	1	0
115	ruth	18	0	700	0	42	48	4401	5685	1	1	0
124	blb	0	0	9	3	0	0	1141	103	0	1	0
125	ai	3	0	96	0	156	335	503	93	2	1	0
126	jdm	0	0	6	1	0	0	185	15	1	1	0
127	phw	41	5	5343	600	37	667	25071	1978	1	1	0
186	oko	0	0	0	0	0	0	3992	0	0	1	0
201	steve	84	6	6106	1342	530	174	26944	16552	1	1	0

Apr 13 07:48 1984 DAILY COMMAND SUMMARY Page 1

COMMAND NAME	NUMBER CMDS	TOTAL KCOREMIN	TOTAL CPU-MI	TOTAL REAL-MIN	MEAN SIZE-K	MEAN CPU-MIN	HOG FACTOR	CHARS TRNSFD	BLOCKS READ
TOTALS	59681	29913.50	461.02	8580.25	64.89	0.01	0.01	0510136	370551
gmacs	35	4746.65	15.43	356.40	307.63	0.44	0.04	1320157	7896
nroff	123	3155.54	42.12	204.19	74.91	0.34	0.21	2806115	18247
vi	116	936.57	8.98	672.87	104.31	0.08	0.01	0494244	6303
troff	8	735.98	7.73	11.82	95.25	0.97	0.65	7253768	1145
sh	6515	709.78	37.56	7408.12	18.90	0.01	0.00	7347979	22411
login	218	251.09	12.11	1625.50	20.73	0.06	0.01	2865961	1795
expr	5256	243.91	9.87	13.80	24.71	0.00	0.72	38847	830
echo	9345	232.67	11.73	24.83	19.84	0.00	0.47	236902	2763
ls	766	193.99	3.69	18.92	52.51	0.00	0.20	2725177	3994
cut	2784	191.87	5.56	7.96	34.51	0.00	0.70	562239	1194
cat	2580	183.54	7.49	161.62	24.51	0.00	0.05	4227017	4949
ed	200	142.06	4.00	1417.55	35.50	0.02	0.00	7945845	4532
mv	1848	137.90	4.41	9.39	31.26	0.00	0.47	10986	7171
sort	249	125.86	2.46	11.76	51.17	0.01	0.21	595024	1907
grep	1249	110.90	4.59	18.20	24.18	0.00	0.25	4111626	5871
paste	1502	101.25	2.78	3.59	36.47	0.00	0.77	479718	802
cu	47	97.24	4.00	683.70	24.31	0.09	0.01	334588	548
tbl	45	86.16	1.24	68.47	69.40	0.03	0.02	1494318	1417
mail	714	83.45	2.27	69.24	36.83	0.00	0.03	2658497	7367

Apr 13 07:48 1984 MONTHLY TOTAL COMMAND SUMMARY Page 1

COMMAND NAME	NUMBER CMDS	TOTAL KCOREMIN	TOTAL CPU-MIN	TOTAL REAL-MIN	MEAN SIZE-K	MEAN CPU-MIN	HOG FACTOR	CHARS TRNSFD	BLOCKS READ
TOTALS	337118	6961.97	941.45	78524.88	58.35	0.01	0.01	824898	16916
nroff	739	889.43	200.57	879.22	76.73	0.27	0.23	709995	6443
troff	69	847.30	70.40	172.92	94.42	1.02	0.41	680712	2413

```
vi         548  818.02   50.25  3392.06 108.82  0.09    0.01 426244   1278
gmacs       35  746.65   15.43   356.40 307.63  0.44    0.04 320157   7896
sh       35325  725.94  215.62 95660.02  19.60  0.01    0.00 659315  34164
awk       5475  692.86   45.92    81.60  80.43  0.01    0.56 352767   1733
sed      24034  581.22   81.51   294.60  43.93  0.00    0.28 973855   7747
echo     66200  527.91   78.61   192.18  23.25  0.00    0.41 935104   8738
login     1510  404.83   60.74 14883.27  23.13  0.04    0.00 615527   8947
ls        3606  127.26   19.99   155.39  56.40  0.01    0.13 871481   1499
cut      15464   93.57   29.68    54.17  36.85  0.00    0.55 097338   6183
cat      14795   90.38   33.56   654.41  26.74  0.00    0.05 580572   2713
ed        1335   70.31   24.49  7791.43  35.53  0.02    0.00 881767   1275
sort      1125   64.93   13.95    68.33  53.41  0.01    0.20 486651   9869
grep      7636   47.27   29.73   121.21  23.79  0.00    0.25 284834   3281
make       145   40.36    8.87   346.90  77.81  0.06    0.03 094541   4630
expr     18192   27.82   23.83    39.35  26.34  0.00    0.61 151231   4024
paste     8269   22.95   15.39    24.59  39.17  0.00    0.63 684675   5179
mail      4608   17.30   14.85   344.84  36.86  0.00    0.04 996289   9655
```

```
Apr 13 07:48 1984   LAST LOGIN Page 1


00-00-00   pds         84-01-17   jhp         84-04-10   gss
83-01-07   59311       84-02-20   uucp        84-04-11   oko
83-06-17   vac         84-03-06   monadm      84-04-12   blb
84-04-12   dewh        84-04-13   93111mf     84-04-13   jdm
84-04-12   kel         84-04-13   9311nsv     84-04-13   jeff
84-04-12   rcc         84-04-13   ai          84-04-13   mboot
84-04-12   wl          84-04-13   console     84-04-13   phw
84-04-13   3700jms     84-04-13   fls440      84-04-13   ruth
84-04-13   3722cal     84-04-13   gemadm      84-04-13   steve
```

The report is divided into five sections. The first prints out the accounting period (from/to) and lists statistics for each terminal port on the system. The second lists the daily usage of the system by each user. The third and fourth lists give summaries of the commands used during the accounting period and the current month. The last section prints the date each user id was last used.

To look at any other day's report, you just tell /usr/lib/acct/prdaily the month and day (*mmdd*) of the report you want printed:

$ **/usr/lib/acct/prdaily 0412**   *Print report for April 12*

   . . .

$ **/usr/lib/acct/prdaily 1127**   *Print report for November 27*

   . . .

If you want to look back at the monthly accounting summaries, you can simply cat the files /usr/adm/acct/fiscal/fiscrpt*n*, where *n* is a number from 1 to 12 corresponding to the report for that month.

The `acctcom` Command

One command that is available to all users for printing the *current* day's accounting is the `acctcom` command. To see what it does, just try typing it in:

```
$ acctcom
COMMAND                       START      END        REAL    CPU     MEAN
NAME      USER    TTYNAME     TIME       TIME      (SECS) (SECS) SIZE(K)
#accton   root    syscon      17:00:12 17:00:12    0.05    0.05   20.40
sh        root    syscon      17:00:00 17:00:12   12.97    0.08   13.50
sh        root    syscon      17:00:09 17:00:12    3.95    0.06   12.00
sync      root    syscon      17:00:13 17:00:13    0.32    0.21   10.95
sh        root    syscon      17:00:00 17:00:13   13.52    0.13   10.46
users     root    syscon      17:30:01 17:30:01    0.34    0.13   22.15
sh        root    syscon      17:30:02 17:30:04    2.73    0.05   13.60
sync      root    syscon      17:30:05 17:30:05    0.98    0.64   10.38
sh        root    syscon      17:30:00 17:30:06    6.41    0.05   14.00
cat       steve   tty00       17:30:06 17:30:06    0.39    0.11   35.64
ls        steve   tty00       17:30:09 17:30:09    0.15    0.13   45.38
cp        steve   tty00       17:30:42 17:30:42    0.44    0.15   33.47
help      steve   tty00       17:30:45 17:30:47    2.66    0.14   32.29
delta     steve   tty00       17:30:54 17:30:54    0.19    0.18   60.11
help      steve   tty00       17:30:59 17:30:59    0.99    0.14   33.86
ls        pat     tty01       17:31:02 17:31:02    0.60    0.38   59.53
nksh      pat     tty01       17:31:02 17:31:02    0.89    0.24   68.00
prs       steve   tty00       17:31:17 17:31:17    0.86    0.25   56.24
prs       steve   tty00       17:31:22 17:31:22    0.15    0.14   53.43
help      steve   tty00       17:33:05 17:33:05    0.87    0.16   32.13
ksh       steve   tty00       17:33:23 17:33:23    0.13    0.11   50.73
date      steve   tty00       17:33:26 17:33:26    0.10    0.10   36.00
ksh       steve   tty00       17:33:26 17:33:26    0.47    0.18   39.00
who       steve   tty00       17:33:29 17:33:29    0.33    0.33   34.18
ls        steve   tty00       17:33:31 17:33:31    0.18    0.13   46.46
ksh       steve   tty00       17:33:49 17:33:49    0.03    0.03   58.00
ksh       steve   tty00       16:29:44 17:33:54 3850.24   11.14   39.94
#ct       steve   ?           16:29:30 17:33:56 3866.24    0.32   29.81
#sh       steve   ?           16:29:29 17:33:56 3867.52    0.75   15.15
```

The output is fairly self-explanatory.

• Administrating the `uucp` System •

The `uucp` system is the most widely used networking facility for UNIX systems. There are two reasons for this. First, it's the only standard networking system available for any release of UNIX. `uucp` is part of the standard UNIX system distribution from AT&T Technologies and will run on any version of UNIX. Second, it's the cheapest network you can have; all you need is a cable between two UNIX systems, and you can set up `uucp`. Also, if you want to interact with UNIX systems that are hundreds or thousands of miles away, all you need is a modem that can automatically dial the numbers of the systems you want to communicate with. (There are 300 baud modems with auto-dial capability that cost less than $200.)

The uucp system is fairly simple to set up and maintain.

Setting Up uucp

The first thing you should do before trying to set up uucp is make sure
all of the programs uucp needs exist. You can do this by checking the
directory /usr/bin for the programs uucp, uux, uuname, and
uulog. You should also check the directory /usr/lib/uucp for the
programs uucico, uuclean, and uuxqt. If these programs or directories don't exist, you probably don't have the uucp software installed.
What you should do is check to see if you received the uucp software
with your UNIX system, and if you did whether it's on a tape or floppy
disk somewhere.

The next thing you need is a user id that other systems can use
to log into yours so they can send data. This user id is usually uucp.
For this you need a line in your /etc/passwd file like this:

```
uucp::5:5:UUCP:/usr/spool/uucp:/usr/lib/uucp/uucico
```

Then you should use the **passwd** command to change uucp's password.

If you look at the /etc/passwd line for uucp, you will notice
that it needs a HOME directory of /usr/spool/uucp. If this directory doesn't exist, create it and change the owner to uucp. Also note
that the shell for uucp is /usr/lib/uucp/uucico. This is the *copy
in—copy out* program that performs the transfer of data for uucp. Any
system calling yours expects this program to start up automatically
when it logs in.

Next you need a few command lines added to
/usr/lib/crontab. The uucico program needs to be in
/usr/lib/crontab to ensure that files that are queued are sent to
the other system. Also, the program uuclean should be entered in
/usr/lib/crontab. This cleans up files in the directory
/usr/spool/uucp that are older than 72 hours:

```
1    *    *    *    *       su - uucp -c /usr/lib/uucp/uucico -r1
1    *    *    *    *       su - uucp -c /usr/lib/uucp/uuclean -p
```

Some lines have to be added to the /etc/rc file, too. They also perform some cleanup of files in the /usr/spool/uucp directory. Some
of these files can get very large, as they have lines logged to them every
time uucp does something.

```
rm -f /usr/spool/uucp/LCK*
rm -f /usr/spool/uucp/LOGFILE
rm -f /usr/spool/uucp/SYSLOG
```

Finally you need to put this line in the file `/usr/lib/uucp/USERFILE`:

```
, /
```

Yes, that's a comma followed by a blank and a slash. This file tells uucp who should have access to what. Although various restrictions may be placed upon certain users, this line gives the broadest access to uucp. It says that any system may access any file, subject to the permissions of that file.

Now your uucp system is ready to run. The only problem is that other systems can log into yours, but yours may not be able to log into theirs. You need to hook a modem with automatic-dialing capability to one of your ports. After doing this you need to make sure that the getty for that port is turned off. You can do this by looking at your `/etc/inittab` for that port. If there is a line that looks like

`ttynum:2:respawn:getty ttyttynum ...`

you should replace it with the following:

`ttynum::off:getty ttyttynum !`

Now that port can be used only for dialing out. Nobody can log in on that port. If you have a special ACU port, you can connect your modem to it and ignore the `/etc/inittab` entry.

Well, you've got the modem hooked up; now you need to tell uucp about it. This is done via the `/usr/lib/uucp/L-devices` file. This file has one line for each dial-out port. The lines have the format

device line call-unit speed

device is the type of device on the port, such as DIR for a hard-wired connection or VEN for a Ven-Tel type automatic-dialing modem. *line* is the file (in `/dev`) for the port; *call-unit* is the automatic-dial unit associated with this port (zero for hard-wired connections, otherwise the same as *line*); and *speed* is the speed of the line (300 or 1200 for modems, up to 9600 for hard-wired connections). So typical entries in this file look like:

```
VEN      tty03 tty03 1200
DIR      tty04 0     9600
ACU      acu0  acu0  1200
```

The last step in setting up uucp is to tell it about the systems it's going to talk to. What you need to do is find out what UNIX systems you want to use uucp with, call the system administrators for those systems, and get the phone numbers, id's, and passwords for uucp. When you have gathered this information, put it in the file /usr/lib/uucp/L.sys. This file contains information about each remote system that your system can call and send data to. Each line looks something like this:

name time device speed phone login-sequence

name
The name of the remote system.

time
The days of the week and time when the remote system should be called (e.g., MoWeFr0800-1700 will allow calling on Monday, Wednesday, and Friday between 8 A.M. and 5 P.M.). The day portion may be a list containing Su Mo Tu We Th Fr Sa or Wk for any weekday or Any for any day. The time portion is a range of times (e.g., 0800-1230) in 24 hour format. If no time portion is specified, calls are allowed at any time.

device
This is either the device from the L-devices file or the hard-wired port to be used for the call.

speed
This is the speed of the connection to the remote system. It is usually 300, 1200, or 9600.

phone
This is the phone number to be used for calling the remote system.

login-sequence
The *login-sequence* is what uucp uses to establish a login on the remote system. It consists of pairs of words separated by blanks.

Each pair describes what prompt uucp expects from the remote system (e.g., login:) and the response it should make to that prompt (e.g., uucp). A typical *login-sequence* looks something like this:

login: uucp password: uucp123

You can also put a login:--login: in place of login:. This causes uucp to send a *RETURN* if it doesn't get a login: right away. This is good for systems that have only 300 baud modems for dialing out. Such a system, when calling a remote system with 1200 baud modems must send a *RETURN* to cause the 1200 baud modem to switch to 300 baud. You can also use portions of the words such as gin: and word: for login: and password:.

The /usr/lib/uucp/L.sys file will look something like this when you're done with it:

```
# cat /usr/lib/uucp/L.sys
remote1 Any ACU 1200 971-1770 gin:--gin: uucp word: UUCP
remote2 Any ACU 1200 971-1740 gin:--gin: uucp word: UUCP
un1 Any0000-0800 ACU 1200 317-325-5601 gin:--gin: uucp word: un1
local Any tty03 9600 tty03 gin:--gin: uucp word: uucp123
#
```

Here are four entries for remote systems. The first two are systems that can be called any time, any day. The system un1 can be called only between the hours of midnight and eight A.M. (probably to save on long-distance phone bills). The system local is hard-wired to the port tty03 at 9600 baud.

As an example of how this works, consider a user who sends mail to someone on un1 in the afternoon. mail starts uucp to send the mail, and uucp starts uucico to perform the actual call and data transfer. uucico looks at the entry for un1 and *doesn't* call un1 because the system can't be called until after midnight. Every hour, however, uucico is started by the cron. It looks around for data that hasn't been transferred. It sees the mail message for un1, and goes through the above process to decide if it's time to send it. The first time uucico is started after midnight, it will call un1 and send the mail. If un1 is down or all of its phone lines are busy, uucico will continue to try to send the mail every hour until after eight o'clock.

The following list summarizes the steps needed to set up uucp.

    1.) make sure uucp software is on your system.
    2.) add the user id uucp to /etc/passwd.
    3.) add lines that run uucico and uuclean to /usr/lib/
        crontab.
    4.) add lines that clean up uucp files to /etc/rc.
    5.) add access control line to /usr/lib/uucp/USERFILE.
    6.) turn off getty for ACU port in /etc/inittab.
    7.) add description of ACU port to /usr/lib/uucp/L-devices.
    8.) add remote system descriptions to /usr/lib/uucp/L.sys.

That's all you need to know to get uucp running. If you want more information about uucp, you should read "A Dial-up Network of UNIX Systems" and "UUCP Implementation Description," in *The UNIX Programmer's Manual, Volume II.*

A complete list of administrative commands, along with a short description of each command, is in Appendix D.

TABLE 12-4. Permissions of system files

Mode	File/ directory	Comments
rwxr-xr-x	/bin	System commands (owned by bin)
rwxrwxr-x	/dev	Device files (owned by root)
rwxrwxr-x	/etc	System files and administrative commands (owned by root)
rwxrwxr-x	/lib	System libraries (owned by bin)
rwxrwxr-x	/lost+found	Home for lost i-nodes (from fsck)
rwxrwxrwx	/tmp	Directory for temporary files
rwxrwxr-x	/unix	UNIX kernel
rwxrwxr-x	/usr	Multiuser files
rwxrwxrwx	/dev/acu0	Automatic call unit
rw--w--w-	/dev/console	
rw-------	/dev/dsk0	
rw-------	/dev/dsk1	
rw-------	/dev/dsk10	
rw-------	/dev/dsk11	
rw-------	/dev/dsk12	
r--r-----	/dev/error	Error logging device
rw-r-----	/dev/kmem	
-w-------	/dev/lp0	
rw-r-----	/dev/mem	
rw-rw-rw-	/dev/mt1	
rw-rw-rw-	/dev/null	System garbage can
rw-------	/dev/rdsk0	
rw-------	/dev/rdsk1	
rw-------	/dev/rdsk10	
rw-------	/dev/rdsk11	
rw-------	/dev/rdsk12	
rw-rw-rw-	/dev/rmt1	
rw-rw-rw-	/dev/rtp0	
rw-rw-rw-	/dev/rtp0n	
rw-r-----	/dev/swap	
rw--w--w-	/dev/syscon	Console
rw--w--w-	/dev/systty	Ditto
rw-rw-rw-	/dev/tp0	
rw-rw-rw-	/dev/tp0n	
rw-rw-rw-	/dev/tty	
rw--w--w-	/dev/tty00	
rw--w--w-	/dev/tty01	
rw--w--w-	/dev/tty02	
rw--w--w-	/dev/tty03	
rwxr--r--	/etc/bcheckrc	System startup files
rwxr--r--	/etc/brc	
r--r--r--	/etc/group	Group information
rw-rw-r--	/etc/inittab	Table for init
r--r--r--	/etc/passwd	Password information
rwxrwxr-x	/etc/profile	System profile
rwxr--r--	/etc/rc	

Mode	File/ directory	Comments
rwxr-xr-x	/usr/adm	Administrative programs that run in multiuser mode
rwxrwxr-x	/usr/adm/acct	
rw-rw-r--	/usr/adm/pacct	
rwxrwxrwx	/usr/adm/rje	Remote job entry directory
rwxrwxr-x	/usr/adm/sa	Code for sar
rwxrwxr-x	/usr/bin	Systems commands
rwxrwxr-x	/usr/games	Games
rwxrwxr-x	/usr/include	Files to be included in C programs
rwxrwxr-x	/usr/lib	Program libraries and multiuser system stuff (owned by bin)
rwxrwxr-x	/usr/lib/acct	Accounting programs
rwxr-xr-x	/usr/lib/uucp	uucp directory
rw-r--r--	/usr/lib/uucp/L-devices	
rw-r--r--	/usr/lib/uucp/L-dialcodes	
rw-------	/usr/lib/uucp/L.cmds	
rw-------	/usr/lib/uucp/L.sys	
rw-rw-rw-	/usr/lib/uucp/L_stat	
rw-r--r--	/usr/lib/uucp/L_sub	
rw-r--r--	/usr/lib/uucp/R_stat	
rw-r--r--	/usr/lib/uucp/R_sub	
rw-rw-rw-	/usr/lib/uucp/SEQF	
r--------	/usr/lib/uucp/USERFILE	
--s--x--x	/usr/lib/uucp/uucico	
--s--x--x	/usr/lib/uucp/uuclean	
--x------	/usr/lib/uucp/uusub	
--s--x--x	/usr/lib/uucp/uuxqt	
rwxrwxr-x	/usr/lost+found	
rwxrwxr-x	/usr/mail	Where mail is put before it's read
rwxrwxr-x	/usr/man	UNIX manual text
rwxrwxr-x	/usr/news	News items
rwxrwxr-x	/usr/nsc	NSC network software
rwxrwxrwx	/usr/spool	Spool directory for uucp and printer
rwxr-xr-x	/usr/spool/lp	Spooled files for printer
rwxrwxrwx	/usr/spool/uucp	Ditto for UUCP
rwxrwxrwx	/usr/spool/uucppublic	Incoming uucp files
rw-------	/usr/spool/uucp/AUDIT	UUCP log files
rw-r-----	/usr/spool/uucp/LOGDEL	
rw-rw-rw-	/usr/spool/uucp/LOGFILE	
rw-rw-rw-	/usr/spool/uucp/SYSLOG	
rwxrwxr-x	/usr/src	Directory of UNIX source code
rwxrwxr-x	/usr/src/cmd	Source for commands
rwxrwxr-x	/usr/src/games	Ditto for games
rwxr-xr-x	/usr/src/lib	Libraries
rw-r--r--	/usr/src/makefile	makefile for UNIX code
rwxrwxr-x	/usr/src/uts	Source for UNIX Time Sharing system
rwxrwxrwx	/usr/tmp	Another temporary directory

A

FOR MORE INFORMATION

There are many sources of information on the UNIX system; however, there is one reference that you cannot do without. This is the *UNIX User's Manual* for your particular version. It will give detailed descriptions of the syntax and various options for each of the commands.

Two issues of *The Bell System Technical Journal,* are devoted entirely to the UNIX system: Vol. 57, No. 6, Part 2 (July-August 1978), and Vol. 63, No. 8, Part 2 (October 1984). Reprints are available from AT&T Bell Laboratories.

The *UNIX Programmer's Manual, Volume II,* contains many documents on various tools available under the UNIX system. Some of these documents are listed below (marked with a [†]).

The following references are devoted to particular aspects of the UNIX system and are listed in case you want more detailed information on some of the UNIX subsystems described in this book:

ed

[†]"Advanced Editing on UNIX," B. W. Kernighan.

Covers advanced features of the editor ed.

The Shell

[†]"An Introduction to the UNIX Shell," S. R. Bourne.

A complete, albeit terse, description of the UNIX shell.

"Using a Command Language as the Primary Programming Tool," T. A. Dolotta and J. R. Mashey, *Command Language Directions* (Proceedings of the Second IFIP Working Conference on Command Languages), North Holland, Amsterdam, 1980, pp. 35-55.

A discussion on using the UNIX shell as a programming language.

†"SED—A Non-interactive Text Editor," L. E. McMahon.

A complete description of the sed editor.

"An Introduction to the C Shell," W. Joy, Computer Science Division, University of California, Berkeley.

An introduction to the C shell and many of its commonly used commands.

vi

"An Introduction to Display Editing with Vi," W. Joy, Computer Science Division, University of California, Berkeley.

An introductory guide to vi.

"Ex Reference Manual," W. Joy, Computer Science Division, University of California, Berkeley.

A complete description of the ex text editor, which underlies vi.

The C Language

Programming in C, S. G. Kochan, Hayden Book Company, Hasbrouck Heights, NJ, 1983.

A tutorial introduction to the C language; it contains many examples and teaches C in an organized fashion.

The C Programming Language, B. W. Kernighan and D. M. Ritchie, Prentice-Hall, Englewood Cliffs, NJ, 1978.

The standard reference book for the C language.

Program Development

The UNIX Programmer Reference Manual.
As of UNIX system V, Release 2, sections 2-5 of the *UNIX User's Manual* were put in this separate manual.

†"Make—A Program for Maintaining Computer Programs," S. I. Feldman.

"The Source Code Control System," M. J. Rochkind, *IEEE Transactions Software Engineering*, Vol. SE-1, No. 4, pp. 364-370, December 1975.

The motivation for and the underlying design of SCCS.

Calculators

†"DC—An Interactive Desk Calculator," R. H. Morris and L. L. Cherry.

An RPN calculator.

†"BC—An Arbitrary Precision Desk-Calculator Language," L. L. Cherry and R. H. Morris.

A desk calculator with a built-in programming language.

Text Processing

†"A TROFF Tutorial," B. W. Kernighan.

A quick introduction to the `troff` typesetting program.

†"NROFF/TROFF User's Manual," J. F. Ossanna.

A complete description of the `nroff` and `troff` programs.

†"TBL—A Program to Format Tables," M. E. Lesk.

†"A System for Typesetting Mathematics," B. W. Kernighan, L. L. Cherry.

A description of the `eqn` preprocessor for `troff`.

Security

†"On the Security of UNIX," D. M. Ritchie.

An overview of UNIX security.

†"Password Security: A Case History," R. H. Morris and K. Thompson.

Many reasons for choosing good passwords.

Administration

UNIX System Administrator's Manual.

As of UNIX System V, the administrative commands were put in this separate manual. Versions previous to System V will have the administrative commands in Sections 1 and 8 of the *UNIX User's Manual.*

†"Setting Up UNIX—Seventh Edition," C. B. Haley and D. M. Ritchie.

A lot of useful information on starting up a UNIX system. A copy of this (updated for new versions) is usually distributed with each release of UNIX.

"Administrative Advice for UNIX," R. C. Haight.

Hints for getting UNIX up, getting it going, and keeping it going. Because this document changes with each release of UNIX, it is distributed with each copy of the UNIX system itself.

†"UUCP Implementation Description," D. A. Nowitz.

A guide to setting up and maintaining the UUCP system.

APPENDIX

B

OVERVIEW OF COMMANDS

Often-used UNIX commands are listed here. All commands are fully described in the *UNIX User's Manual* and *UNIX System Administrator's Manual.*[†] Due to hardware constraints, not all the commands listed here will work on all the supported hardware configurations.

(Portions of this overview were adapted from the document "UNIX—Overview and Synopsis of Facilities," by T. A. Dolotta, R. C. Haight, and A. G. Petruccelli.)

▪ Basic Software ▪

Included are the operating system with utilities, an assembler, and a compiler for the programming language C—enough software to regenerate, maintain, and modify UNIX itself, and to write and run new applications.

Operating System

▪ UNIX   This is the basic resident code, also known as the kernel, on which everything else depends. It executes the system calls, maintains the file system, and manages the system's resources; it contains device drivers, I/O buffers, and other system information. A general description of UNIX design philosophy and system facilities appeared in an article in the *Communications of the ACM*. A more extensive survey is in *The Bell System Technical Journal* for July-August 1978. Further capabilities include:
                • Automatically-supported reentrant code.

---

† And the *UNIX Programmer Reference Manual* if you have UNIX System V, Release 2.

- Separation of instruction and data spaces (machine dependent).
- Timer-interrupt sampling and interprocess monitoring for debugging and measurement.

■ Devices   All I/O is logically synchronous. Normally, automatic buffering by the system makes the physical record structure invisible and exploits the hardware's ability to do overlapped I/O. Unbuffered physical record I/O is available for unusual applications. Software drivers are provided for many devices; others can be easily written.

User Access Control

■ login   Signs on a new user:
- Adapts to characteristics of terminal.
- Verifies password and establishes user's individual and group (project) identity.
- Establishes working directory.
- Publishes message of the day.
- Announces presence of mail.
- Lists unseen news items.
- Executes an optional user-specified profile.
- Starts command interpreter (shell) or other user-specified program.

■ passwd   Changes a password:
- User can change own password.
- Passwords are kept encrypted for security.

■ su   Allows a user to assume the permissions and privileges of another user or root (super-user) provided that the proper password is supplied.

■ newgrp   Changes working group (project id). This provides access with protection for groups of related users.

■ stty   Sets up options for control of a terminal:
- Erase and line kill characters.
- Speed.
- Parity.
- Mapping of upper-case characters to lower case.
- Carriage-return plus line-feed versus newline.

- Interpretation of tab characters.
- Delays for tab, newline, and carriage-return characters.
- Raw versus edited input.

■ tabs Sets terminal's tab stops. Knows several "standard" formats.

Manipulation of Files and Directories

■ ed Interactive line-oriented context editor. Random access to all lines of a file. It can:
- Find lines by number or pattern (regular expressions). Patterns can include: specified characters, "don't care" characters, choices among characters, (specified numbers of) repetitions of these constructs, beginning of line, end of line.
- Add, delete, change, copy, or move lines.
- Permute contents of a line.
- Replace one or more instances of a pattern within a line.
- Combine or split lines.
- Combine or split files.
- Do any of above operations on every line (in a given range) that matches a pattern.
- Escape to the shell (UNIX command language) during editing.

■ vi Screen-oriented display editor for video terminals. When using vi, changes made to the file are reflected by what is displayed on the terminal screen. Note: this command is available in System V Release 2 and later releases of UNIX.

■ sed A stream (one-pass) editor with facilities similar to those of ed.

■ cat Concatenates one or more files onto standard output. Mostly used for unadorned printing, for inserting data into a "pipe," and for buffering output that comes in dribs and drabs.

■ pg Prints files one screenful at a time. Note: this command is available in System V Release 2 and later releases of UNIX.

■ pr   Prints files with title, date, and page number on every
              page:
              • Multicolumn output.
              • Parallel column merge of several files.

■ split   Splits a large file into more manageable pieces.

■ csplit   Like split, with the splitting controlled by context.

■ sum   Computes the check sum of a file.

■ dd   Physical file format translator, for exchanging data
              with non-UNIX systems, especially OS/360, VS1, MVS,
              etc.

■ cp   Copies one file to another or many files to a directory.
              Works on any file regardless of its contents.

■ ln   Links another name (alias) to an existing file.

■ mv   Moves one or more files. Usually used for renaming
              files or directories.

■ rm   Removes one or more files. If any names are linked to
              the file, only the name being removed goes away.

■ chmod   Changes access permissions on a file(s). Executable by
              the owner of the file(s) or by the super-user.

■ chown   Changes owner of a file(s).

■ mkdir   Makes one or more new directories.

■ rmdir   Removes one or more (empty) directories.

■ cd   Changes working (i.e., current) directory.

■ find   Searches the directory hierarchy for, and performs
              specified commands on, every file that meets given
              criteria:
              • File name matches a given pattern.
              • Modified date in given range.
              • Date of last use in given range.
              • Given permissions.
              • Given owner.

- Given special file characteristics.
- Any logical combination of the above.
- Any directory can be the starting "node."

■ tar   Tape file archiver: tar saves and restores files and directory structures on magnetic tape.

■ cpio   Copies a subtree of the file system (directories, links, and all) to another place in the file system. Can also copy a subtree onto a tape and later recreate it from tape. Often used with the find command.

■ SCCS   SCCS (Source Code Control System) is a collection of UNIX commands (some interactive) for controlling changes to files of text (typically the source code of programs or the text of documents). It provides facilities for:
- Storing, updating, and retrieving any version of any source or text file.
- Controlling updating privileges.
- Identifying both source and object (or load) modules by version number.
- Recording who made each change, when it was made, and why.

Execution of Programs

■ sh   The shell, or command language interpreter, understands a set of constructs that constitute a full programming language; it allows a user or a command procedure to:
- Supply arguments to and run any executable program.
- Redirect standard input, standard output, and standard error files.
- Pipes: simultaneous execution with output of one process connected to the input of another.
- Compose compound commands using:
  if ... then ... else
  case switches
  while loops
  for loops over lists
  break, continue, and *exit*
  parentheses for grouping.
- Initiate background processes.

- Perform shell procedures (i.e., command scripts with substitutable arguments).
- Construct argument lists from all file names matching specified patterns.
- Take user-specified action on traps and interrupts.
- Specify a search path for finding commands.
- Upon login, automatically create a user-specifiable environment.
- Optionally announce presence of mail as it arrives.
- Provide variables and parameters with default settings.

■ rsh   Restricted shell; restricts a user to a subset of UNIX commands. The system administrator may construct different levels of restriction.

■ shl   Shell layer manager: shl allows a user to interact with more than one shell from a single terminal. Note: this command is available in System V Release 2 and later releases of UNIX.

■ test   Tests argument values in shell conditional constructs:
- String comparison.
- File nature and accessibility.
- Boolean combinations of the above.

■ expr   String computations for calculating command arguments:
- Integer arithmetic
- Pattern matching
- Like test above, expr can be used for conditional side-effect.

■ echo   Prints its arguments on the standard output. Useful for diagnostics or prompts in shell procedures or for inserting data into a "pipe."

■ sleep   Suspends execution for a specified time.

■ wait   Waits for termination of a specific or all processes that are running in the background.

■ nohup   Runs a command immune to interruption from "hanging up" the terminal.

■ nice   Runs a command at low (or high) priority.

- **kill**   Terminates named process(es).

- **at**   Runs commands at specified times.

- **batch**   Queues commands to be run when system load level permits.

- **cron**   Runs commands on a regularly scheduled basis.
  - Actions are arbitrary shell procedures or executable programs.
  - Times are conjunctions of month, day of month, day of week, hour, and minute. Ranges are specifiable for each.

- **crontab**   Command to allow user access to the cron. Note: this command is available in System V Release 2 and later releases of UNIX.

- **tee**   Passes data between processes (like a "pipe"), but also diverts copies into one or more files.

- **help**   Explains error messages from certain other programs.

Information Commands

- **man**   Prints UNIX manual entries at the terminal.

- **ls**   Lists the names of one, several, or all files in one or more directories:
  - Alphabetic or chronological sorting, up or down.
  - Optional information: size, owner, group, date last modified, date last accessed, permissions.

- **file**   Tries to determine what kind of information is in a file by consulting the file system index and by reading the file itself.

- **date**   Print current date and time. Has considerable knowledge of calendrical and horologic peculiarities; can be used to set UNIX's idea of date and time. (As yet, cannot cope with Daylight Saving Time in the Southern Hemisphere.)

- **df**   Reports amount of free space in file system.

■ du   Prints a summary of total space occupied by all files in a hierarchy.

■ tty   Prints the "name" of your terminal (i.e., the name of the port to which your terminal is connected).

■ who   Tells who is logged onto the system:
- Lists logged-in users, their ports, and time they logged in.
- Optional history of all logins and logouts.
- Tells you who you are logged in as.

■ ps   Reports on active processes:
- Lists your own or everybody's processes.
- Tells what commands are being executed at the moment.
- Optional status information: state and scheduling information, priority, attached terminal, what the process is waiting for, its size, etc.

■ acctcom   Reports a chronological history of all processes that have terminated. Information includes:
- User and system times and sizes.
- Start and end real times.
- Owner and terminal line associated with process.
- System exit status.

■ pwd   Prints name of your working (i.e., current) directory.

■ rjestat   Reports on the status of the Remote Job Entry (RJE) interface(s) to an IBM host.

■ what   Prints informational lines found in files usually inserted by SCCS.

Interuser Communication

■ mail   Mails a message to one or more users. Also used to read and dispose of incoming mail. The presence of mail is announced by login.

■ news   Prints out current general information and announcement files.

■ **calendar**   An automatic reminder service.

■ **write**   Establishes direct, interactive terminal-to-terminal communication with another user.

■ **wall**   Broadcasts a message to all users who are logged in.

■ **mesg**   Inhibits or permits receipt of messages from **write** and **wall**.

Intermachine Communication

■ **uucp**   Sends files back and forth between UNIX machines.

■ **send**   Collects files together to be sent as a "job" to an IBM host.

■ **cu**   Dials a phone number and attempts to make an interactive connection with another machine.

■ **ct**   Dials the phone number of a modem that is attached to a terminal and spawns a **login** process to that terminal.

■ **VPM**   A software package for implementing communications protocols. It consists of a protocol script interpreter that runs in a front-end microprocessor, allowing a variety of different protocols to be implemented with the same hardware.

■ **BX.25**   A superset of the international X.25 communications protocol; it is implemented using VPM.

Program Development Package

A kit of fundamental programming tools. Some of these are used as integral parts of the higher-level languages described in the next section.

■ **ar**   Maintains library archives, especially useful with **ld**. Combines several files into one for housekeeping efficiency:
- • Creates new archive.
- • Updates archive by date.
- • Replaces or deletes files.

- Prints table of contents.
- Retrieves from archive.

■ Libraries   Basic run-time libraries. They are used freely by all
               system software:
- Number conversions.
- Time conversions.
- Mathematical functions: *sin, cos, log, exp, atan, sqrt, gamma.*
- Buffered character-by-character I/O.
- Random number generator.
- An elaborate library for formatted I/O.
- Password encryption.

■ sdb   Symbolic debugger for C and FORTRAN 77 programs:
- Interactive debugging of C code.
- Knows about structures and arrays.
- Postmortem dumping.
- Examination of arbitrary files, with no limit on size.
- Interactive breakpoint debugging; the debugger is a separate process.
- Symbolic reference to local and global variables.
- Stack trace for C programs.
- Output formats:
     1-, 2-, or 4-byte integers in octal, decimal, or hex
     single and double floating point
     character and string
     disassembled machine instructions
- Patching.
- Searching for integer, character, or floating patterns.

■ adb   Absolute debugger.

■ ctrace   C program debugger. ctrace prints a statement by
               statement trace of the execution of a C program. Note:
               this program is available with System V Release 2 and
               later releases of UNIX.

■ od   Dumps any file:
- Output options include: octal or decimal by words, octal by bytes, ASCII, operation codes, hexadecimal, or any combination thereof.
- Range of dumping is controllable.

■ ld
Linkage editor. Combines relocatable object files. Inserts required routines from specified libraries; resulting code:
- Can be made sharable.
- Can be made to have separate instruction and data spaces.

■ nm
Prints the *namelist* (symbol table) of an object program. Provides control over the style and order of names that are printed.

■ size
Reports the main memory requirements of one or more object files.

■ strip
Removes the relocation and symbol table information from an object file to save file space.

■ prof
Constructs a profile of time spent in each routine from data gathered by time-sampling the execution of a program; gives subroutine call frequencies and average times for C programs.

■ make
Controls creation of large programs. Uses a control file specifying source file dependencies to make new version; uses time last changed to deduce minimum amount of work necessary. Knows about SCCS, cc, yacc, lex, etc.

Utilities

■ cxref
Makes cross-reference listings of a set of C source files. The listing contains all symbols in each file separately or, optionally, in combination. An asterisk appears before a symbol's declaration.

■ sort
Merges and/or sorts ASCII files line-by-line:
- In ascending or descending order.
- Lexicographically or on numeric key.
- On multiple keys located by delimiters or by position.
- Can fold upper-case characters together with lower-case into dictionary order.

■ uniq
Deletes successive duplicate lines in a file:
- Prints lines that were originally unique, duplicated, or both.

- Can give redundancy count for each line.

■ tr   Does character translation according to an arbitrary code:
- Can "squeeze out" repetitions of selected characters.
- Can delete selected characters.

■ diff   Reports line changes, additions, and deletions necessary to bring two files into agreement; can produce an editor script to convert one file into another.

■ comm   Identifies common lines in two sorted files. Output in up to three columns shows lines present in first file only, present in second file only, and/or present in both.

■ cmp   Compares two files and reports disagreeing bytes.

■ grep   Prints all lines in one or more files that match a pattern of the kind used by ed (the editor):
- Can print all lines that fail to match.
- Can print count of "hits."

■ wc   Counts lines and "words" (strings separated by blanks or tab characters) in a file.

■ time   Runs a command and reports timing information about it.

• Programming Languages •

The Programming Language C

■ cc   Compiles and/or link-edits programs in the C language. The UNIX operating system, almost all of its subsystems, and C itself are written in C:
- General-purpose language designed for structured programming.
- Data types:
        character
        short
        integer

> long integer
> floating point
> double
> pointers to all types
> functions returning all types
> arrays of any type
> structures containing various types

- Provides machine-independent control of all machine facilities, including to-memory operations and pointer arithmetic.
- Macro-preprocessor for parameterized code and for the inclusion of other files.
- All procedures recursive, with parameters passed by value.
- Run-time library gives access to all system facilities.

■ pcc   Portable version of cc for a variety of computers.

■ cb   C beautifier: gives a C program that well-groomed, structured, indented look.

FORTRAN

■ f77   A full compiler for ANSI Standard FORTRAN 77:
- Compatible with C and supporting tools at object level.
- Optional source compatibility with FORTRAN 66.
- Free format source.
- Optional subscript-range checking, detection of uninitialized variables.
- All widths of arithmetic: 2- and 4-byte integer; 4- and 8-byte real; 8- and 16-byte complex.

■ ratfor   Ratfor adds rational control structure a la C to FORTRAN:
- Compound statements.
- *If-else, do, for, while, repeat-until, break, next* statements.
- Symbolic constants.
- File insertion.
- Free format source.
- Translation of relationals like >, >=, etc.
- Produces genuine FORTRAN to carry away.
- May be used with f77.

■ efl   Compiles a program written in the EFL Language into
                 clean FORTRAN on the standard output. It provides
                 the C-like control constructs of RATFOR.

Other Algorithmic Languages

■ awk   Pattern scanning and processing language. Searches
                 input for patterns and performs actions on each line
                 of input that satisfies the pattern:
                 • Patterns include regular expressions, arithmetic
                   and lexicographic conditions, Boolean combina-
                   tions, and ranges of these.
                 • Data treated as string or numeric as appropriate.
                 • Can break input into fields; fields are variables.
                 • Variables and arrays (with nonnumeric subscripts).
                 • Full set of arithmetic operators and control flow.
                 • Multiple output streams to files and pipes.
                 • Output can be formatted as desired.
                 • Multiline capabilities.

■ bs   An interactive interpreter, containing features of both
                 BASIC and SNOBOL4:
                 • Statements include:
                       for/while ... next
                       goto
                       if ... else ... fi
                       trace
                       symbolic dump
                 • All numeric calculations in double precision.
                 • Recursive function defining and calling.
                 • Built-in functions include *log, exp, sin, cos, atan, ceil,
                   floor, sqrt, abs, rand.*
                 • String operations include regular expression pat-
                   tern matching.
                 • Very general I/O (including pipes to commands) is
                   provided.

■ dc   Interactive programmable desk calculator. Has named
                 storage locations, as well as conventional stack for
                 holding integers and programs:
                 • Arbitrary-precision decimal arithmetic.
                 • Appropriate treatment of decimal fractions.
                 • Arbitrary input and output radices, in particular
                   binary, octal, decimal, and hexadecimal.

- Postfix ("Reverse Polish") operators:
  +, −, *, /, remainder, power, square root load, store, duplicate, clear print, enter program text, execute

■ bc

A C-like interactive interface to the desk calculator dc:
- All the capabilities of dc with a high-level syntax.
- Arrays and recursive functions.
- Immediate evaluation of expressions and evaluation of functions upon call.
- Arbitrary-precision elementary functions: *exp, sin, cos, atan.*

■ sno

An interpreter very similar to SNOBOL 3; its limitations are:
- Function definitions are static.
- Pattern matches are always anchored.
- No built-in functions.

Macro-Processors and Compiler-Compilers

■ m4

A general-purpose macro-processor:
- Stream-oriented, recognizes macros anywhere in text.
- Integer arithmetic.
- String and substring capabilities.
- Condition testing, file manipulation, arguments.

■ cpp

The C language preprocessor. cpp has the same features as the m4 macro-processor above.

■ yacc

An LALR(1)-based compiler-writing system. During execution of resulting parsers, arbitrary C functions can be called to do code generation or take semantic actions:
- BNF syntax specifications.
- Precedence relations.
- Accepts formally ambiguous grammars with non-BNF resolution rules.

■ lex

lex helps write programs whose control flow is directed by instances of regular expressions in the input stream. It is well suited for editor-script type transformations and for segmenting input in preparation for a parsing routine.

• Text Processing •

DOCUMENTER'S WORKBENCH

Note: as of UNIX System V Release 2, the programs described in this section are not supplied with the standard distribution of the UNIX system; they are now available in a separate software package known as the DOCUMENTER'S WORKBENCH.

High-level formatting macros have been developed to ease the preparation of documents with `nroff` and `troff`, as well as to exploit their more complex formatting capabilities.

■ `nroff`　　　　Advanced formatter for terminals. Capable of many elaborate feats:
- Justification of either or both margins.
- Automatic hyphenation.
- Generalized page headers and footers, automatic page numbering, with even-odd page differentiation capability, etc.
- Hanging indents and one-line indents.
- Absolute and relative parameter settings.
- Optional legal-style numbering of output lines.
- Nested or chained input files.
- Complete page format control, keyed to dynamically-planted "traps" at specified lines.
- Several separately-definable formatting environments (e.g., one for regular text, one for footnotes, and one for "floating" tables and displays).
- Macros with substitutable arguments.
- Conditional execution of macros.
- Conditional insertion or deletion of text.
- String variables that can be invoked in midline.
- Computation and printing of numerical quantities.
- String-width computations for unusually-difficult layout problems.
- Positions and distances expressible in inches, centimeters, ems, ens, line spaces, points, picas, machine units, and arithmetic combinations thereof.
- Dynamic (relative or absolute) positioning.
- Horizontal and vertical line drawing.

- Multicolumn output on terminals capable of reverse line-feed or through the postprocessor `col`.

■ `troff` This formatter generates output for a phototypesetter or other suitable graphics device. Its output is independent of the final printing device. Postprocessors are available to translate the `troff` output into a stream of device-specific codes that produce the correct representation. Devices presently supported by postprocessors are the Autologic APS-5 phototypesetter (`daps`), the Imagen Imprint-10 laser printer (`di10`), the Xerox 9700 laser printer (`dx9700`), and the Tektronix 4014 graphics terminal (`tc`). The old version of `troff`, renamed `otroff`, produces output for the Wang CAT phototypesetter.

`troff` provides facilities that are upward-compatible with `nroff`, but with the following additions:
- Vocabulary of thirty 102-character fonts (any four simultaneously) in 29 different point sizes.
- Character-width and string-width computations for unusually difficult layout problems.
- Overstrikes and built-up brackets.
- Dynamic (relative or absolute) point size selection, globally or at the character level.
- Terminal output for rough sampling of the product.

This entire book was typeset by `troff`, *assisted by* `cip`, `pic`, `tbl`, *and* `eqn`.

■ `sroff` Fast formatter similar to `nroff` but with fewer capabilities.

■ `pic` A `troff` preprocessor for drawing pictures. Translates in-line pictures from a simple language into phototypesetter commands. The basic objects are box, line, arrow, circle, ellipse, arc, spline and text. For example:

```
.PS
circle "book"
arrow
box "pic"
arrow
box "troff"
arrow
```

```
ellipse "typesetter"
.PE
```

produces

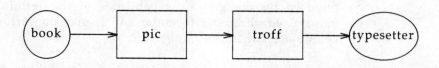

- **cip**   An interactive drawing system for the TELETYPE® 5620 Dot-Mapped Display (DMD) terminal. The output of `cip` is compatible with the input to `pic`, allowing pictures to be created by `cip` and later incorporated into documents processed by `troff`. *All figures in this book were created using* `cip`. Note: `cip` is *not* part of the DOCUMENTER'S WORKBENCH; it is part of a software package distributed by AT&T Technologies for the TELETYPE 5620 DMD terminal,

- **eqn**   A mathematical preprocessor for `troff`. Translates in-line or displayed formulae from a very easy-to-type form into detailed typesetting instructions. For example:

```
.EQ
sigma sup 2 = 1 over N sum from j=1 to N ( x sub j - x bar ) sup 2
.EN
```

produces:

$$\sigma^2 = \frac{1}{N} \sum_{j=1}^{N} (x_j - \bar{x})^2$$

- Automatic calculation of point size changes for subscripts, superscripts, sub-subscripts, etc.
- Full vocabulary of Greek letters, such as γ, Π, Γ, α.
- Automatic calculation of the size of large brackets.
- Vertical "piling" of formulae for matrices, conditional alternatives, etc.
- Integrals, sums, etc., with arbitrarily complex limits.
- Diacriticals: dots, double dots, hats, bars, etc.
- Easily learned by nonprogrammers and mathematical typists.

Formulae can appear within tables to be formatted by
`tbl` (see below).

■ `neqn`
A mathematical preprocessor for `nroff` with the
same facilities as `eqn`, except for the limitations
imposed by the graphic capabilities of the terminal
being used. Prepares formulae for display on various
Diablo-mechanism terminals, etc.

■ `MM`
A standardized manuscript layout macro package for
use with `nroff` and `troff`. Provides a flexible,
user-oriented interface to these two formatters;
designed to be:
- Robust in face of user errors.
- Adaptable to a wide range of output styles.
- Can be extended by users familiar with the for-
  matter.
- Compatible with both `nroff` and `troff`.

Some of its features are:
- Page numbers and draft dates.
- Cover sheets and title pages.
- Automatically-numbered or "lettered" headings.
- Automatically-numbered or "lettered" lists.
- Automatically-numbered figure and table captions.
- Automatically-numbered and positioned footnotes.
- Single- or double-column text.
- Paragraphing, displays, and indentation.
- Automatic table of contents.

■ `MV`
A `troff` macro package that makes it easy to typeset
professional-looking projection foils and slides.

■ `tbl`
A preprocessor for `nroff` and `troff` that translates
simple descriptions of table layouts and contents into
detailed formatting instructions:
- Computes appropriate column widths.
- Handles left- and right-justified columns, centered
  columns, and decimal-point aligned columns.
- Places column titles; spans these titles, as
  appropriate.

For example:

```
.TS
center doublebox;
cfB s s s.
Composition of Foods
```

```
.T&
cfI ¦¦ cfI s s
c  ¦¦  c s s
c  ¦¦  c ¦ c ¦ c.
Food  Percent by Weight
      ‾
      Protein   Fat  Carbo-
                     hydrate
=
.T&
l ¦¦ n ¦ n ¦ n.
Apples      .4    .5    13.0
Halibut   18.4   5.2    ...
Lima beans 7.5    .8    22.0
Milk 3.3   4.0    5.0
Mushrooms 3.5     .4    6.0
Rye bread 9.0     .6    52.7
.TE
```

produces:

Composition of Foods		
	Percent by Weight		
Food	Protein	Fat	Carbo-hydrate
Apples	.4	.5	13.0
Halibut	18.4	5.2	...
Lima beans	7.5	.8	22.0
Milk	3.3	4.0	5.0
Mushrooms	3.5	.4	6.0
Rye bread	9.0	.6	52.7

■ ocw   A preprocessor for troff that prepares text to be displayed in a special "constant-width" typeface; this typeface is very useful for printing examples of computer output in, e.g., programming manuals. Note: this command is obsolescent and may not be supported in further releases of the UNIX system.

Other Text—Processing Tools

■ wwb   The WRITER'S WORKBENCH: wwb performs a battery of checks and analyses on a document. It prints a

report covering
- Spelling mistakes.
- Punctuation mistakes.
- Overused words.
- Wordy or misused phrases.
- Split infinitives.
- Readability.
- Sentence variation and structure.
- Use of passives and nominalizations.

Note: The WRITER'S WORKBENCH system is not distributed with the standard release of the UNIX system. It is available as an add-on software package from AT&T Technologies.

■ spell   Finds spelling errors by looking up all words from a document in a large spelling list. Knows about prefixes and suffixes and can cope with such rotten spellings as "roted."

■ ptx   Generates a permuted index, like the one in the *UNIX User's Manual*.

■ graph   Given the coordinates of the points to be plotted, draws the corresponding graph; has many options for scaling, axes, grids, labeling, etc.

■ tplot   Makes the output of graph suitable for plotting on a Diablo-mechanism terminal.

■ 300, 450   Exploits the hardware facilities of GSI 300, DASI 450, and other Diablo-mechanism terminals:
- Implements reverse line-feeds and forward and reverse fractional-line motions.
- Allows any combination of 10- or 12-pitch printing with 6 or 8 lines/inch spacing.
- Approximates Greek letters and other special characters by overstriking in plot mode.

■ hp   Like 300, but for the Hewlett-Packard 2640 family of terminals.

■ col   Reformats files with reverse line-feeds so that they can be correctly printed on terminals that cannot reverse line-feed.

■ Graphics

Graphics is the name of a collection of commands for manipulating and plotting statistical and graphical data on a Tektronix series 4010 terminal or a Hewlett-Packard 7221A Graphics Plotter. Its facilities include:
- A sophisticated graphical editor.
- Pie and bar chart generators.
- Built-in mathematical functions such as powers, roots, logarithms, and slope and intercept generation.
- Histograms.
- Additive sequence, prime number, and random sequence generators.
- Table of contents generators.

• System Administration •

Normal Day-to-Day Administration and Maintenance

■ mount

Attaches a device containing a file system to the tree of directories. Protects against nonsense arrangements.

■ umount

Removes the file system contained on a device from the tree of directories. Protects against removing a busy device.

■ mkfs

Makes a new file system on a device.

■ mknod

Makes a file system entry for a special file. Special files are physical devices, virtual devices, physical memory, etc.

■ volcopy

File system backup/recovery system for disk/disk or disk/tape. Protective labeling of disks and tapes is included.

■ fsck

Used to check the consistency of file systems and directories and make interactive repairs:
- Print statistics: number of files, space used, free space.
- Report duplicate use of space.
- Retrieve lost space.

- Report inaccessible files.
- Check consistency of directories.
- Reorganize free disk space for maximum operating efficiency.

■ sync   Forces all outstanding I/O on the system to completion. Used to shut down the system gracefully.

■ config   Tailors device-dependent system code to a specific hardware configuration. As distributed, UNIX can be brought up directly on any supported computer equipped with an acceptable tape drive and disk, sufficient amount of main memory, a console terminal, and a clock.

■ crash   Prints out tables and structures in the operating system. May be used on a running system, but more useful for examining operating system core dumps after a "crash."

System Monitoring Facilities

■ Accounting   The process accounting package covers connect time accounting, command usage, command frequency, disk utilization, and line usage. All of these are summarized by user and by command on a daily, monthly, and fiscal basis. The system lends itself to local needs and modification.

■ Error Logging

The UNIX operating system incorporates continuous hardware error detection and reporting.

■ Equipment Test Package

The Equipment Test Package (ETP—available on a separate tape) is a useful addition to a hardware supplier's diagnostic software. It is essentially a UNIX-based hardware exerciser and verifier.

■ System Activity Report

The System Activity Report (SAR) package is a body of programs for sampling the behavior of the operating system. The sampling consists of several time counters, I/O activity counters, context-switching counters, system-call counters, and file-access counters. Reports can be generated on a daily basis or as desired.

- **Profiler**   The Profiler is another group of commands for study-
                        ing the activity of the operating system. It reports the
                        percentage of time that the operating system spends
                        on user tasks, on system functions, and in being idle.

Installation, Administration, and Operation

- **Installation**   The document *Setting up UNIX* contains the procedures
                        and advice for the first-time installation and for the
                        periodic upgrading of the operating system.

- **Administration**

                        The document *Administrative Advice for UNIX* describes
                        various problems that can occasionally arise during
                        normal operation and suggests possible solutions.
                        Included are tips on data-set options, specifications for
                        phototypesetter fonts and chemicals, for system tun-
                        ing, security, troubleshooting, as well as other useful
                        information.

- **Operation**   The *UNIX Operations Manual* contains a description of
                        console operations, step-by-step operator functions,
                        and operating system error messages and their mean-
                        ings.

• Demonstration Programs (Games) •

Unless otherwise indicated, source code for the following interactive
programs is *not* included:

- **arithmetic**   Provides a drill in number facts.

- **quiz**   Tests your knowledge of Shakespeare, presidents, cap-
                   itals, etc. Source code included.

- **bj**   A blackjack dealer.

- **moo**   A fascinating number-guessing game, rather like
                   Mastermind®.

- **jotto**   A Word-guessing game, like Mastermind®.

■ cal   Prints a calendar of specified month or year between A.D. 1 and 9999. Source code included.

■ chess   Class D chess program. Note: this program only runs on PDP-11 machines and is not supported in UNIX System V.

■ craps   The game of craps.

■ maze   Generates a maze.

■ sky   Predicts the locations of the Sun, Moon, the planets out to Saturn, and other celestial objects. Note: this program only runs on PDP-11 machines and is not supported in UNIX System V.

■ reversi   Board game (Othello). Note: this program only runs on PDP-11 machines and is not supported in UNIX System V.

■ units   Converts quantities between different scales of measurement. Knows hundreds of units; for example, how many kilometers/second (or furlongs/fortnight) is a parsec/megayear? Source code included.

■ ttt   A traditional 3×3 tic-tac-toe program that learns. It never makes the same mistake twice, unless you make it forget what it has learned.

■ back   The game of backgammon.

■ hangman   Children's "guess the word" game.

■ wump   Thrilling hunt for the mighty wumpus in a dangerous cave.

C

COMPLETE COMMAND SUMMARY

All of the following commands are available on UNIX System V and System V Release 2, except as noted: all commands marked with a † are new to System V Release 2. All commands in the WRITER'S WORKBENCH section are not distributed with either release; the command marked with IWB is part of the INSTRUCTIONAL WORKBENCH and is not distributed with either release; all commands marked with DWB are part of the DOCUMENTER'S WORKBENCH and are not distributed with either release (although old versions of these commands are distributed with UNIX System V); All WORKBENCHes are available from AT&T Technologies for UNIX System V and UNIX System V Release 2. All commands in the last section of this appendix (Berkeley UNIX Commands) are distributed by the University of California, Berkeley, and are available only to holders of source licenses of UNIX.

Commands marked with OBS are obsolescent and may be phased out in future releases of the UNIX system.

· Directory Commands ·

cd	change working directory
chgrp	change group of a file or directory
chmod	change mode of a file or directory
chown	change owner of a file or directory
cpio	copy directory structures in and out
dircmp	compare directory contents
du	summarize disk usage
find	walk a directory tree
ls	list contents of directories
mkdir	make directory
pwd	working directory name
rm	remove files
rmdir	remove directory

tar   tape archiver for directory structures

· File Commands ·

cat   concatenate and print files
chgrp   change group of a file or directory
chmod   change mode of a file or directory
chown   change owner of a file or directory
cp   copy files
csplit   context split
cut   cut out selected columns from each line of a file
dd   convert and copy a file between ASCII and EBCDIC
egrep   search a file for a pattern (variant of grep)
fgrep   search a file for a pattern (variant of grep)
file   determine file type
find   walk a directory tree
fsplit   split f77, ratfor, or efl files
gath   gather files interpreting keywords
grep   search a file for a pattern
hpio   HP 2645A terminal tape file archiver
join   relational database operator
ln   link files
ls   list contents of directories
mv   move files
newform   change the format of a text file
nl   line numbering filter
od   dump file in octal, decimal, or hexadecimal
pack   compress files
paste   merge same lines of several files or subsequent
                         lines of one file
pcat   print files compressed with pack
pg[†]   file scanning program for screen terminals
pr   format files for line printer listings
rm   remove files
split   split a file into pieces
sum   print checksum and block count of a file
tail   print the last part of a file
touch   update access and modification times of a file
tr   translate characters
umask   set file-creation permissions mask
uniq   report repeated lines in a file
unpack   expand file compressed with pack
vc   version control

• Editors •

bfs	big file scanner
ed	text editor
edit[†]	Berkeley text editor for casual users
ex[†]	Berkeley text editor (superset of ed)
red	restricted version of ed
se	screen editor for video terminals
sed	noninteractive stream editor
vi[†]	Berkeley screen editor

• File Comparison •

bdiff	diff for big files
cmp	compare two files
comm	select or reject lines common to two sorted files
dd	convert and copy a file between ASCII and EBCDIC
diff	print differences between files
diff3	three file diff
diffmk	diff preprocessor for nroff/troff
dircmp	compare directory contents
sccsdiff	compare two versions of an SCCS file
sdiff	side-by-side diff
uniq	report repeated lines in a file

• Information, Please •

acctcom	search and print process accounting file(s)
date	print or set the date
du	summarize disk usage
id	print user and group id's and names
logname	print login name
ls	list contents of directories
man	print entries in the *UNIX User's Manual* (DWB)
mesg	permit or deny writes to your terminal
news	print news items
ps	report process status
pwd	working directory name
sag	system activity graph
sar	system activity reporter
stty	set the options for a terminal port
time	time execution of a command
timex	better version of time
tty	get the terminal's name in /dev

uname	print UNIX system name
uulog	print log of uucp actions
uuname	print names of remote systems known to uucp
uustat	uucp status inquiry and job control
who	print who is on the system

· Shell Programming ·

basename	extract file name from path
cut	cut out selected columns from each line of a file
dirname	extract directory name path
echo	print arguments
egrep	search a file for a pattern (variant of grep)
env	set environment for command execution
expr	evaluate arguments as an expression
false	provide false value
fgrep	search a file for a pattern (variant of grep)
getopt	parse command options
grep	search a file for a pattern
line	read one line
logname	print login name
paste	merge same lines of several files or subsequent lines of one file
rsh	restricted shell
sed	noninteractive stream editor
sh	shell, the standard command interpreter
shl†	shell layer manager (not on PDP-11)
sleep	suspend execution for an interval
sort	sort and/or merge files
tail	print the last part of a file
tee	send intermediate pipeline output to file
test	condition evaluation for shell programs
tr	translate characters
true	provide truth value
wait	await completion of process
wc	character, word, and line count
xargs	construct argument list(s) and execute command

· Office Automation ·

bc	arbitrary-precision arithmetic language
cal	print calendar
calendar	reminder service
date	print or set the date

dc	desk calculator
mail	send mail to users or read mail
mailx†	Berkeley version of mail
mesg	permit or deny writes to your terminal
rmail	restricted version of mail
sort	sort and/or merge files
spell	find spelling errors
units	conversion program for weights and measures
write	write to another user

WRITER'S WORKBENCH System

abst	evaluate text abstractness
acro	find acronyms
dictadd	add phrases to ddict, spelldict, sexdict dictionary
diction	find awkward phrases and suggests changes
double	detect repeated typings of words
findbe	identifie difficult syntax
match	collate statistics from different texts
mkstand	build standards for prose from user documents
org	show text structure
parts	assign grammatical parts of speech
proofr	give proofreading comments
prose	give extended editorial comments
prosestand	print standards used by prose to evaluate documents
punct	check punctuation
punctrules	explain punctuation rules
sexist	find sexist phrases and suggests changes
spelladd	add words to spelldict dictionary
spelltell	print commonly misspelled words containing a pattern
spellwwb	check spelling, using spelldict
splitrules	find split infinitives
style	summarize stylistic features
syl	print number of syllables
topic	provide clue to topic, keywords
worduse	explain frequently misused or confused words
wwb	run proofreading and stylistic analysis
wwbaid	describe programs and explains how to use them
wwbhelp	give information about commands and functions
wwbinfo	print a copy of this table

Text Processing

checkcw	check input to ocw (DWB OBS)
checkeq	check eqn input (DWB)

checkmm	checks documents for proper use of MM macros (DWB)
daps	postprocessor for Autologic APS-5 phototypesetter (DWB)
deroff	remove `nroff`/`troff`, `tbl`, and `eqn` constructs (DWB)
di10	postprocessor for Imagen Imprint-10 laser printer (DWB)
dx9700	postprocessor for Xerox 9700 laser printer (DWB)
eqn	format mathematical text for `troff` (DWB)
greek	terminal filter for `nroff`
hp	handle special `nroff` functions for Hewlett-Packard terminals
hyphen	find hyphenated words (DWB)
macref	print cross-reference listing of macro files (DWB)
man	print entries in the *UNIX User's Manual*
mm	print/check documents formatted with the MM macros (DWB)
mmlint	`nroff`/`sroff` document compatibility checker (DWB)
mmt	typeset documents (DWB)
mvt	typeset view graphs and slides (DWB)
neqn	format mathematical text for `nroff` (DWB)
nroff	text formatter (DWB)
ocw	prepare constant-width text for `otroff` (DWB OBS)
osdd	same as `mm -mosd` (DWB)
otc	`otroff` terminal filter for Tektronix 4014 terminal (DWB OBS)
pic	figure drawing preprocessor for `troff` (DWB)
ptx	permuted index generator for `nroff`/`troff`
sroff	fast version of `nroff` (DWB)
tbl	format tables for `nroff`/`troff` (DWB)
tc	`troff` terminal filter for Tektronix 4014 terminal (DWB)
troff	text formatting for phototypesetters (DWB)
x9700	`nroff` filter for Xerox 9700 laser printer (DWB)

▪ Program Development ▪

Programming Languages

/lib/cpp	the C language preprocessor
as	assembler

awk	pattern scanning and processing language
bc	arbitrary-precision arithmetic language
bs	a compiler/interpreter for modest-sized programs
cc	C compiler
efl	Extended FORTRAN Language
f77	FORTRAN 77 compiler
lex	generate programs for simple lexical tasks
m4	macro processor
pcc	portable C compiler (PDP-11 only)
ratfor	rational FORTRAN preprocessor
scc	C compiler for stand-alone programs (DEC only)
sno	SNOBOL interpreter
yacc	yet another compiler-compiler

Program Development Tools

machid*	provide truth value about your processor type
adb	absolute debugger (OBS)
ar	archive and library maintainer for portable archives
arcv	convert archive files from PDP-11 to common archive format (PDP-11 only)
cb	C program beautifier
cflow[†]	generate C flow graph
convert	convert object and archive files to common formats (not on PDP-11)
cprs[†]	compress an IS25 object file (3B only)
ctrace[†]	C program debugger
cxref	generate C program cross-reference
dis	disassembler (3B only)
dump	dump selected parts of an object file (not on PDP-11)
fsplit	split f77, ratfor, or efl files
ld	link editor
lint	a C program checker
list	produce C source listing from object file (3B only)
lorder	print ordering relation for an object library
make	maintain, update, and regenerate groups of programs
nm	print name list
prof	display profile data for C programs
regcmp	regular expression compile
sdb	symbolic debugger (not on PDP-11)
size	print sizes of object files
strip	strip symbol table and relocation bits from object

---

* The commands distributed with the standard AT&T release of the UNIX system are pdp11, u3b, u3b5, and vax. They provide true or false values depending upon which machine you're using. If you're using a machine other than the four above, your system may provide a similar command (e.g., onyx or Z8000).

module

tsort   topological sort for use with `lorder` in creating object libraries

SCCS

admin	create and administer SCCS files
cdc	change the delta commentary of an SCCS delta
comb	combine SCCS deltas
dd	convert and copy a file between ASCII and EBCDIC
delta	make a delta (change) to an SCCS file
get	get a version of an SCCS file
help	ask for help
prs	print an SCCS file
rmdel	remove a delta from an SCCS file
sact	print current SCCS file editing activity
sccsdiff	compare two versions of an SCCS file
unget	undo a previous get of an SCCS file
val	validate SCCS file
what	identify SCCS files

• Security •

chgrp	change group of a file or directory
chmod	change mode of a file or directory
chown	change owner of a file or directory
crypt	encrypt/decrypt files
id	print user and group id's and names
makekey	generate encryption key
newgrp	change to a new group
passwd	change password
red	restricted version of `ed`
rsh	restricted shell
su	become super-user or another user
umask	set file-creation permissions mask

• Communications •

ct	spawn getty to a remote terminal
cu	call another UNIX system
net	execute a command on the PCL network (DEC only)
nscstat	query the operation status of the NSC network
nsctorje	reroute jobs from the NSC network to RJE

nusend	send files to another UNIX on the NSC network
rjestat	report RJE status
send	gath files and submit as an RJE job
uucp	UNIX-to-UNIX copy
uulog	print log of uucp actions
uuname	print names of remote systems known to uucp
uupick	get files from /usr/spool/uucppublic
uustat	uucp status inquiry and job control
uuto	public UNIX-to-UNIX file copy
uux	UNIX-to-UNIX remote command execution

• Process Control •

at	execute commands at a later time
batch	execute commands when system load is low
crontab†	user access to cron
kill	terminate a process
nice	run a command at low priority
nohup	run a command immune to hangups and quits
ps	report process status

• Instructional •

| arithmetic | provide drill in number facts |
| teach | computer aided instruction system (IWB) |

• Graphics •

gdev*	graphical device routines and filters
gutil*	graphical utilities
stat*	statistical commands useful with graphical commands
toc*	graphical table of contents routines
ged	graphical editor for TEKTRONIX 401X series terminals
graph	draw a graph
graphics	access graphical and numerical commands
spline	interpolate smooth curve
tplot	graphics filters for printing terminals
vpr	Versatec printer spooler (DEC only)

---

* These graphical commands are too numerous to mention. Refer to the *UNIX User's Manual* for more information.

• Line Printer Commands •

asa	interpret ASA carriage control characters
cancel	cancel request to an LP line printer
disable	disable LP printers
enable	enable LP printers
lp[†]	send request to an LP line printer
lpr	line printer spooler (OBS)
lpstat	print LP status information
nl	line numbering filter
pr	format files for line printer listings
x9700	nroff filter for Xerox 9700 laser printer (DWB)

• Terminal Commands •

300	handle special functions of DASI 300 terminal
300s	handle special functions of DASI 300s terminal
4014	paginator for the Tektronix 4014 terminal
450	handle special functions of the DASI 450 terminal
col	filter reverse line-feeds
ged	graphical editor for Tektronix 401X series terminals
greek	terminal filter for nroff
hp	handle special nroff functions for Hewlett-Packard terminals
hpio	HP 2645A terminal tape file archiver
otc	otroff terminal filter for Tektronix 4014 terminal (DWB OBS)
pg[†]	file scanning program for screen terminals
stty	set the options for a terminal port
tabs	set tabs on a terminal
tc	troff terminal filter for Tektronix 4014 terminal (DWB)
tplot	graphics filters for printing terminals
tput[†]	shell program access to terminfo database
tty	get the terminal's name in /dev

Synchronous Terminals

scat	concatenate and print files on synchronous printer
stlogin	login for synchronous terminals
ststat	report synchronous terminal facilities status

• Games •

`arithmetic`	provide drill in number facts
`back`	the game of backgammon
`bj`	the game of blackjack
`chess`	the game of chess
`craps`	the game of craps
`hangman`	guess the word
`jotto`	secret word game
`maze`	generate a maze
`moo`	number guessing game
`quiz`	test your knowledge
`reversi`	a game of dramatic reversals (Othello)
`sky`	obtain ephemerides
`ttt`	tic-tac-toe
`wump`	the game of hunt-the-wumpus

• Miscellaneous •

`banner`	make posters
`factor`	factor a number
`ipcrm`	remove a message queue, semaphore set, or shared memory id
`ipcs`	report interprocess communication facilities status
`join`	relational database operator
`login`	sign on
`prime`	print prime numbers (OBS)
`trenter`[†]	enter a trouble report
`units`	conversion program for weights and measures

• Berkeley UNIX Commands •

`clear`	clear terminal screen
`csh`	C shell
`head`	print first lines of a file (opposite of `tail`)
`lf`	horizontal `ls`
`more`	print files one screen at a time
`see`	list file showing nonprinting characters
`vi*`	Berkeley screen editor

---

* Also included in UNIX System V Release 2.

D

ADMINISTRATIVE COMMANDS

All of the following commands are available on UNIX System V and System V Release 2, except as noted: all commands marked with a [†] are new to System V Release 2.

Commands marked with OBS are obsolescent and may be phased out in future releases of the UNIX system.

· Information, Please ·

/etc/bdblk[†]	print/change bad disk block information
/etc/ff	list file names and statistics for a file system (not on PDP-11)
/etc/fuser	identify processes using a file or file structure
/etc/whodo	see who is doing what
df	report number of free disk blocks and i-nodes
du	summarize disk usage
lpstat	print LP status information
nscstat	query the operation status of the NSC network
ps	report process status
rjestat	report RJE status
sar	system activity reporter
time	time execution of a command
timex	better version of time
uulog	print log of uucp actions
uustat	uucp status inquiry and job control
who	print who is on the system

· Startup/Shutdown ·

/etc/bcheckrc	system initialization shell script
/etc/brc	system initialization shell script

`/etc/config`	configure a UNIX system
`/etc/init`	process control initialization
`/etc/killall`	kill all active processes
`/etc/mount`	mount file system
`/etc/powerfail`	power failure shell script
`/etc/rc`	system initialization shell script
`/etc/setmnt`	establish mount table
`/etc/shutdown`	shutdown system
`/etc/telinit`	process control initialization
`/etc/umount`	unmount file system
`/etc/wall`	write to all users
`date`	print or set the date

▪ File Systems ▪

`/etc/bcopy`	interactive block copy (OBS)
`/etc/bdblk`[†]	print/change bad disk block information
`/etc/checkall`	fast file system checking procedure
`/etc/chroot`	change root directory for a command
`/etc/clri`	clear i-node
`/etc/dcopy`	copy file systems for optimal access time
`/etc/devnm`	print file system device associated with a file
`/etc/ff`	list file names and statistics for a file system (not on PDP-11)
`/etc/filesave`	daily/weekly disk-to-disk UNIX file system backup
`/etc/finc`	fast incremental backup (not on PDP-11)
`/etc/frec`	recover files from a backup tape (not on PDP-11)
`/etc/fsck`	file system consistency check
`/etc/fscv`	convert files between PDP-11 and VAX-11/780 systems (DEC only)
`/etc/fsdb`	file system debugger
`/etc/fuser`	identify processes using a file or file structure
`/etc/labelit`	label file system
`/etc/link`	exercise link system calls
`/etc/mkfs`	construct a file system
`/etc/mknod`	build special file
`/etc/mount`	mount file system
`/etc/mvdir`	move a directory
`/etc/ncheck`	generate path names from i-numbers
`/etc/setmnt`	establish mount table
`/etc/tapesave`	daily/weekly disk-to-tape UNIX file system backup
`/etc/umount`	unmount file system

/etc/unlink	exercise unlink system calls
/etc/volcopy	copy file systems with label checking
df	report number of free disk blocks and i-nodes
diskusg[†]	same as acctdusg
du	summarize disk usage
sadp[†]	disk access profiler
sync	complete pending I/O on file systems
tar	tape archiver for directory structures

• Security •

/etc/grpck	/etc/group file consistency checker
/etc/pwck	/etc/passwd file consistency checker
chgrp	change group of a file or directory
chmod	change mode of a file or directory
chown	change owner of a file or directory
passwd	change password
su	become super-user or another user
umask	set file-creation permissions mask

• Accounting •

/usr/lib/acct/acctcms	summarize per-process accounting records
/usr/lib/acct/acctcon1	connect-time accounting (pass 1)
/usr/lib/acct/acctcon2	connect-time accounting (pass 2)
/usr/lib/acct/acctdisk	merge disk usage report with other accounting information
/usr/lib/acct/acctdusg	report disk usage by userid
/usr/lib/acct/acctmerg	merge accounting files
/usr/lib/acct/accton	turn per-process accounting on or off
/usr/lib/acct/acctprc1	process accounting (pass 1)
/usr/lib/acct/acctprc2	process accounting (pass 2)
/usr/lib/acct/acctwtmp	put comments into /etc/wtmp
/usr/lib/acct/chargefee	charge user for something
/usr/lib/acct/ckpacct	make sure /usr/adm/pacct doesn't get too big
/usr/lib/acct/dodisk	performs disk accounting functions
/usr/lib/acct/fwtmp	format and print connect accounting records
/usr/lib/acct/lastlogin	update log of last time each user logged in
/usr/lib/acct/monacct	run monthly accounting summary

	programs
`/usr/lib/acct/nulladm`	create accounting file with correct permissions
`/usr/lib/acct/prctmp`	format and print `/usr/adm/acct/nite/ctmp` created by `acctcon1`
`/usr/lib/acct/prdaily`	format and print daily accounting reports
`/usr/lib/acct/prtacct`	format and print an accounting file in `tacct` format (produced by `acctcon2`, `acctprc2`, and `acctmerg`) AD,AC
`/usr/lib/acct/runacct`	run daily accounting summary programs
`/usr/lib/acct/shutacct`	turn accounting off
`/usr/lib/acct/startup`	turn accounting on
`/usr/lib/acct/turnacct`	smart interface to `accton`
`/usr/lib/acct/wtmpfix`	check consistency of and fix connect accounting records
`acctcom`	search and print process accounting file(s)

· Line Printer (LP) ·

`/etc/stprint`	synchronous terminal control for printers
`/usr/lib/accept`	allow LP requests
`/usr/lib/lpadmin`	configure the LP spooling system
`/usr/lib/lpmove`	move LP requests
`/usr/lib/lpsched`	LP scheduler
`/usr/lib/lpshut`	stop the LP request scheduler
`/usr/lib/reject`	prevent LP requests
`disable`	disable LP printers
`enable`	enable LP printers
`lpstat`	print LP status information

· Networking ·

`/etc/nscmon`	control the NSC local network
`/etc/x25lnk`	attach, detach, activate, deactivate, or get status for a BX.25 link
`/etc/x25pvc`	install, remove, or get status for a BX.25 link
`/usr/lib/pcldaemon`	PCL link monitor (DEC only)

`/usr/lib/uucp/uuclean`	uucp spool directory cleanup
`/usr/lib/uucp/uusub`	monitor uucp network
`/usr/nsc/nscloop`	perform the NSC local network loopback functions
`nscstat`	query the operation status of the NSC network
`nsctorje`	reroute jobs from the NSC network to RJE
`rjestat`	report RJE status
`uulog`	print log of uucp actions
`uustat`	uucp status inquiry and job control

▪ Input/Output ▪

`/etc/getty`	set up line discipline for logging in
`/etc/stcntrl`	activate/deactivate synchronous terminal
`/etc/stgetty`	getty for synchronous terminal
`/etc/stload`	load synchronous terminal in virtual protocol machine (VPM)
`/etc/stprint`	synchronous terminal control for printers
`/etc/vpmfmt`	print VPM event traces
`/etc/vpmsave`	save VPM event traces
`/etc/vpmset`	connect VPM drivers and programmable communication devices
`/etc/vpmstart`	load VPM drivers and programmable communication devices
`kasb`	assembler for the KMC11B microprocessor (DEC only)
`kunb`	disassembler for the KMC11B microprocessor (DEC only)
`vpmc`	compiler for the VPM

▪ Operating System ▪

`/etc/config`	configure a UNIX system
`/etc/crash`	examine system core images
`/etc/errdead`	extract error records from system dump
`/etc/errstop`	terminate the errdemon
`/etc/mkboot`	convert a.out file to boot image (3B20S only)
`/etc/prfdc`	collect data from operating system profiler
`/etc/prfpr`	format data from prffdc and prfsnap
`/etc/prfld`	initialize operating system profiler
`/etc/prfsnap`	give snapshot of operating system profiler

/etc/prfstat	enable/disable operating system profiler
/etc/sysdef	extract system definition information from operating system file
/etc/sysfix	convert a.out file to boot image (PDP-11 only)
/usr/lib/errdemon	error-logging program
/usr/lib/sa/sa1	variant of sadc for automatic data collection
/usr/lib/sa/sa2	variant of sar for automatic reporting of output from sa1
/usr/lib/sa/sadc	system activity data collection program
errpt	process a report of logged errors
sag	system activity graph
sar	system activity reporter

• Command Installation •

/etc/install	install commands
cpset[†]	install object files in bin directories

• Miscellaneous •

/etc/cron	clock daemon
/etc/wall	write to all users
/usr/adm/qasurvey[†]	quality assurance survey
/usr/src/cmd/text/macros.d/non-bt1.sh[†]	
	reinstall MM macros without AT&T Bell Laboratories specific features
tic[†]	terminfo compiler

E

COMPARISON OF SH AND CSH

This appendix gives a side-by-side comparison of the standard UNIX shell `sh` and the Berkeley UNIX shell `csh`. The tables list the similarities and differences between `csh` and what you learned about `sh` in Chapter 6. The shells vary mainly in their control commands (e.g., `if`, `while`, and `for`) and the way variables are set. Most command line operations, such as I/O redirection and file name substitution are the same in both shells.

sh	csh
I/O redirection	
`<   >   >>   ¦`	same
File name substitution	
`?   *   [ ]`	same
Shell variables	
`HOME`	`home`
`PATH`	`path`
`CDPATH`	`cdpath`
`MAIL`	`mail`
`TERM`	`term`
File used when logging in	
`.profile`	`.login`
Variable operations	
var=value	`set` *var=value*
var=`command`	`set` *var=`command`*
var=`*`expr $var + 1`	`@` *var=$var + 1*
Default prompt	
`$`	`%`
Comments	
`#` *comment*	`#` *comment*

sh	csh

```if [test expr]```
```then```
  `...`
```fi```
	```if (C expr) then```
	
	  `...`
	```endif```

```if [test expr]```
```then```
  `...`
```else```
  `...`
```fi```
	```if (C expr) then```
	
	  `...`
	```else```
	  `...`
	```endif```

```if [test expr]```
```then```
  `...`
```elif [test expr]```
```then```
  `...`
```else```
  `...`
```fi```
	```if (C expr) then```
	
	  `...`
	```else if (C expr) then```
	
	  `...`
	```else```
	  `...`
	```endif```

```for var in words```
```do```
  `...`
```done```
	```foreach var (words)```
	
	  `...`
	```end```

```while [test expr]```
```do```
  `...`
```done```
	```while (C expr)```
	
	  `...`
	```end```

```case var in```
   `pattern1)`
     `... ;;`
 	
   `pattern2)`
     `... ;;`
 	
   `*)`
     `... ;;`
```esac```
	```switch (string)```
	   `case pattern1:`
	     `...`
	     ```breaksw```
	   `case pattern2:`
	     `...`
	     ```breaksw```
	   ```default:```
	     `...`
	     ```breaksw```
	```endsw```

Expressions used in if and while statements	
sh	csh
-f *file*	-f *file*
-d *file*	-d *file*
-s *file*	! -z *file*
-z *string*	*string* == " "
-n *string*	*string* != " "
string1 = *string2*	*string1* == *string2*
string1 != *string2*	*string1* != *string2*
num1 -eq *num2*	*num1* == *num2*
num1 -ne *num2*	*num1* != *num2*
num1 -lt *num2*	*num1* < *num2*
num1 -le *num2*	*num1* <= *num2*
num1 -gt *num2*	*num1* > *num2*
num1 -ge *num2*	*num1* >= *num2*
expr1 -a *expr2*	*expr1* && *expr2*
expr1 -o *expr2*	*expr1* ¦¦ *expr2*

F

ADDING NEW USERS

The following shell program prompts the administrator for information about a new user (user id, HOME, etc.) and creates a new entry for that user in /etc/passwd.

```
# check to make sure user can write /etc/passwd
if [ ! -w /etc/passwd ]
then
    echo "** you must be super-user to add news users **"
    echo "** abort **"
    exit 1
fi

echo "** creating a new user id **"
echo "** to abort at any time press DEL or RUBOUT **"
echo "enter new user id: \c"
read userid

# check to see if this user already exists
if grep "^$userid:" /etc/passwd > /dev/null
then
    echo "** $userid already exists **"
    echo "** abort **"
    exit 2
fi

# create a unique uid for new user
uid=`cut -f3 -d: /etc/passwd|sort -n|tail -1`
uid=`expr $uid + 1`

# get group info for new user
echo "enter group name or RETURN for unique group: \c"
```

```
read gname

# check to see if this group exists
# if so, get that group's gid
if grep "^$gname:" /etc/group > /dev/null
then
    gid=`grep "^$gname:" /etc/group|cut -f3 -d:|tail -1`

#if not, gid=uid
else
    gid=$uid
    gname=$userid
fi

# get the rest of the /etc/passwd entry
echo "enter user info (e.g., name, phone number, room, etc)"
echo "user info: \c"
read uinfo
echo "enter HOME directory (default /usr/$userid): \c"
read home

# /usr/$userid is the default HOME
if [ -z "$home" ]
then
    home=/usr/$userid
fi

# check to be sure the HOME directory isn't a regular file
if [ -f "$home" ]
then
    echo "** $home already exists and is a regular file **"
    echo "** abort **"
    exit 3
fi

echo "enter login shell (default /bin/sh): \c"
read shell
if [ -z "$shell" ]
then
    shell=/bin/sh
fi

# default shell is /bin/sh.
# if the shell entered doesn't exist, use /bin/sh.
if [ ! -x $shell ]
then
```

```
    echo "** $shell doesn't exist or isn't executable **"
    echo "** using /bin/sh **"
    shell=/bin/sh
fi

echo "********************************************"
echo "new user id will be created:"
echo "/etc/passwd entry is"
echo "$userid::$uid:$gid:$uinfo:$home:$shell"
echo
echo "/etc/group entry is"
echo "$gname::$gid:$userid"
echo
echo "is this OK? (y/n) \c"
read yn
if [ "$yn" != "y" ]
then
    echo "** $userid not created **"
    echo "** abort **"
    exit 4
else
    echo entering user $userid in /etc/passwd and /etc/group
    echo "$userid::$uid:$gid:$uinfo:$home:$shell" >> /etc/passwd
    echo $gname::$gid:$userid >> /etc/group
    echo "$userid currently has no password."
    echo "would you like to create a password for $userid? (y/n) \c"
    read yn
    if [ "$yn" = "y" ]
    then
        passwd $userid
    fi
    if [ ! -d "$home" ]
    then
        mkdir $home
        chmod 775 $home
        chown $userid $home
        chgrp $gname $home
    fi
    echo "** $userid created `date` **"
fi
```

INDEX

HAYDEN BOOKS

UNIX®

System Library

UNIX SHELL PROGRAMMING

By STEPHEN G. KOCHAN and PATRICK H. WOOD. A complete, easy-to-understand introduction to UNIX shell programming that covers the standard shell, C shell, restricted shell, and the newer Korn shell. It also shows how to tailor the UNIX environment to individual requirements, and how to customize UNIX commands.

No. 46309, $24.95

UNIX SYSTEM SECURITY

By PATRICK H. WOOD and STEPHEN G. KOCHAN. This practical guide to UNIX system security describes available programs for administering passwords, security auditing, checking file permissions, securing terminals, DES data encryption, and setting up a restricted environment. Includes sources for the programs described.

No. 46267, $34.95 cloth

UNIX SYSTEM AMINISTRATION

By DAVID FIEDLER and BRUCE H. HUNTER. An easy-to-read complete reference for anyone who owns or operates a UNIX system. Using step-by-step guidelines, this is an essential guide to system configuration, making back-ups, writing shell programs, communications, security, connecting a printer, terminal and other devices, and much more.

No. 46289, $24.95

EXPLORING THE UNIX SYSTEM

By STEPHEN G. KOCHAN and PATRICK H. WOOD. An indispensable hands-on guide produced with AT&T Bell Laboratories' support, this complete introduction to the UNIX environment covers the file system, shell programming, program development, screen editing, and system administration.

No. 46268, $22.95

UNIX® TEXT PROCESSING

This practical, in-depth reference presents a range of useful UNIX tools that facilitate such word processing functions as format design, printing, and editing. It introduces the tools and illustrates how they can work together to create large writing projects such as technical manuals, reports, and proposals.

No. 46291, $26.95